Anyang

UNIVERSITY OF
WASHINGTON PRESS
Seattle

Anyang

by Li Chi

LIBRARY OF CONGRESS CATALOGING IN PUBLICATION DATA
Li, Chi, 1896–
    Anyang.
    Bibliography: p.
    Includes index.
    1. An-yang, China—Antiquities.   2. Excavations
(Archaeology)—China—An-yang.   I. Title.
DS796.A55L5   951'.18   75-40873
ISBN 0-295490-5

Foreword

THE ANYANG EXCAVATION was, from its inception, directed toward the recovery of the early written history of China. It was never conceived as a search for works of art or buried treasure. Hence the story of Anyang properly begins with the discovery that "dragon bones" were inscribed with archaic Chinese characters. Dr. Li Chi therefore describes the various accounts of how this discovery was made and introduces us to the principal characters of the drama. Once it was recognized that the so-called "dragon bones" were the shells of tortoises, or occasionally the scapulae of cattle, on which diviners had written questions directed to the gods, these precious objects became known as "oracle bones" and there was a great rush to find more inscribed specimens and translate their inscriptions into modern Chinese.

For centuries Chinese scholarship had concentrated on subtle analysis of ancient texts; thus a number of specialists were eager to learn the questions asked on the oracle bones so that they could speculate about the possible answers. Proper interpretation of these inscriptions required that the bones be discovered in association with the total archaeological record of ancient sites by qualified scholars. This raised a serious problem because the Chinese scholar's proper domain was his study and to engage in manual labor was considered an activity unworthy of his learning. The social and physical adjustments necessary to make the Anyang expedition a possibility demanded a revolution in Chinese society as well as in scholarship. Fortunately China was ready for such a revolution for there was a new atmosphere of social and intellectual change without which the investigation at Anyang would not have been possible. Thus the Anyang project was born of social revolution and was to its very end dependent on the ever-changing political situation.

Dr. Li, the key figure throughout the Anyang adventure, was well prepared for this heroic task. Having acquired a classical Chinese education, Dr. Li went to Harvard where he earned his Ph.D. in archaeology. Meanwhile, foreign archaeologists had been very active in China but their energies were directed mainly toward the discovery of early man and the study of Chinese culture from the paleolithic through the neolithic periods. On returning to China, Dr. Li became acquainted with these eminent foreign scholars who were already busily at work unraveling the record of China's past. Although Dr. Li's earliest field work was also in search of neolithic materials, he soon became involved in the activities of the Academia Sinica's Institute of History and Philology which took a characteristically Chinese approach, that is, the search for, and the decipherment of, the early written records of China.

From the beginning the task of the Institute of History and Philology was the blending of Chinese literary scholarship with the careful field methods of archaeology. The institute chose wisely when they selected Dr. Li to lead the Anyang excavation, for he was trained in both techniques. This was the proper combination to investigate the still-legendary early Bronze Age of China and place it in its proper perspective within the realm of Chinese written history. Today Dr. Li is the person best qualified to record the events that led up to the Anyang excavation, describe the work at Anyang, and finally summarize the knowledge obtained by a team of scholars from the wealth of material recovered from the "Waste of Yin," in the general area of Anyang.

In the first two chapters, Dr. Li sets the stage by introducing us to the principle characters involved in the first part of this modern archaeological drama, explaining in considerable detail the role of each from the first recognition that "dragon bones" used in Chinese medicine were actually documents that would illuminate the early Bronze Age and bring the Shang dynasty into the realm of written history.

In the third and fourth chapters Dr. Li explains the situation in Chinese archaeology during the early years of the twentieth century and describes the contributions of the prominent foreigners. This leads into the planning of the Anyang expedition, the troubles of financing the work, the early association with the Freer Gallery, and the ultimate divergence between the gallery and the institute.

With the fifth chapter he begins the narrative of the excavations and describes the principal finds. The work at Anyang is traced year by year until all work in the field was brought to a halt in 1937 by the Japanese invasion. The succeeding chapters deal with the flight of the Institute of History and Philology before the advancing armies of the Japanese. They made the long, difficult trip to west China with their precious excavated material and such parts of their library and technical apparatus as could be moved at that time. Even in west China they were not able to establish a permanent base, for they had to move again with the tide of war. These seemingly insurmountable difficulties did not dampen the general enthusiasm for research because, as soon as the institute set up a temporary base, they resumed their analysis of the material and even succeeded in publishing some preliminary results. With the end of World War II the institute returned to its original quarters in east China, but, while the end of World War II brought peace to much of the world, it did not bring peace to China. The revolution, intellectual and physical, that had made Anyang possible continued to escalate, and so the institute was soon forced into exile in Taiwan where a new base was set up, new recruits were gathered, and work was resumed.

The final chapters present a summary of the findings of the Anyang expedition with a description of some of the major publications that have come out of this monumental project. From the very beginning the Anyang project, like all archaeology in China, was closely related to politics and the political situation. It is very much to the credit of Dr. Li that he has never permitted political considerations either to permanently halt the project, or to color his findings as a scholar. As the pioneer Bronze Age excavation in China, Anyang has served as a model and inspiration to those who have continued Chinese archaeological exploration.

MILLARD B. ROGERS
School of Art
University of Washington

Preface

THE ARCHAEOLOGICAL MATERIALS recovered from the Anyang excavations by the Institute of History and Philology, Academia Sinica, in the period between 1928 and 1937, published in several series of Archaeologia Sinica since wartime, have laid a new foundation for the study of ancient China. They are important for a number of reasons; the following three may be considered primary.

In the first place, when oracle bone inscriptions became known to the antiquarians at the end of last century, they were considered as mere curiosities and left in the hands of peddlers and curio-dealers. The learned world at large was more or less skeptical about the academic value of these written inscriptions. In fact one of the leading paleographers in the early Republican era openly charged that these new curiosities were mere forgeries, in spite of the publication of many scholarly investigations and inquiries about the nature and contents of the inscriptions by a few serious students. When the

Archaeological Section of the Institute of History and Philology started digging at Hsiao-t'un (known as the Waste of Yin, or Yin-hsü) in Anyang in 1928, and found the inscribed oracle bones through scientific excavation, the fact that oracle bone inscriptions actually existed in the Yin-Shang time was settled beyond dispute. From then on, Chinese paleography advanced on a new basis. Hsü Sheng, the compiler of the *Shuo-wen* dictionary during the Eastern Han dynasty, was no longer considered as the final authority in the definition of all Chinese written characters as he had been for almost two millennia.

Second, what was totally new to historians of the old school was the discovery of many prehistoric sites through modern archaeology. Field archaeologists digging the Hsiao-t'un site systematically recorded, season after season, all the artifacts whether associated with the inscribed oracle bones or not, including of course all the potteries and the pot-sherds. From a total of nearly a quarter million sherds, nearly fifteen hundred complete specimens could be restored. From this group of ceramic materials the author has been able to compile a corpus of the Yin-hsü pottery on the basis of their shapes and stratified typology. And this pottery corpus, completed during wartime and published in Archaeologia Sinica in 1954, has provided the most substantial link of the earliest written history with newly discovered prehistoric cultures—both the Lungshan and the Yangshao type. The turning point occurred in the course of the Anyang excavations, when the field archaeologists working on the site of Hsiao-t'un discovered that beneath the main cultural stratum of Yin-Shang period, as dated by inscribed oracle bones, there is another cultural deposit of prehistorical remains, similar in contents to the prehistoric Lungshan culture widely distributed in Shangtung and the eastern seacoast.

Equally significant is the fact that the pottery corpus has provided important background material for the study of ritual bronzes in many burials at Hsiao-t'un and the royal tombs of Hou-chia-chuang. Two characteristics of the ritual bronzes from the various tombs deserve special notice. On the one hand, most of these ritual vessels are obviously the forerunners of what were used in the early Chou dynasty, such as the *ting, li, ku, chia, chüeh, yü, p'an*, and so on. The other aspect is perhaps even more interesting, namely, most of the shapes of these ritual bronzes find their prototypes in the pottery either contemporary with the bronzes or in the prehistorical deposit underneath. So these metallic finds from the burials in these two localities actually have provided definite ancestral types of the better-known *chou* vessels; and in addition the establishment of a strong linkage with possible prehistorical utensils for ritual purposes may be clearly shown in the external forms of the neolithic pottery which the Anyang ritual bronzes closely followed.

The Anyang discoveries are important in many other respects, cultural and social as well as geographical. This book covers the contents of these discoveries only in a general way. In preparing the text of this book, the author has been assisted by many friends. He must mention first and foremost the debt he owes to his colleagues and fellow workers of the institute; all of them have assisted him in one way or another, in checking source materials, re-examining the archaeological finds, and tracing bibliographical sources. Among his American friends, Mrs. Wilma Fairbank, who has for more than ten years read all his English texts published in the new series of Archaeologia Sinica, has once more given her time to read the manuscripts of this book with many valuable suggestions for making the language more readable. Professor Millard Rogers, an old friend of the author, has not only improved the text but has also contributed a Foreword which the author deeply appreciates.

Miss Shih-heng Chia has assisted the author in more than one way; from the beginning she helped him gather the source materials, compile the bibliography, type the notes and the text, and finally read with care all the galley proofs; to her patient and skillful assistance, he is particularly grateful. The author's thanks are also due to Mr. Y. N. Kung who helped to secure all the photographical works. The author is also grateful to the authority of the Institute of History and Philology for giving him special permission to make use of a number of unpublished photographs.

Li Chi

Contents

Illustrations

General reference map xx

FIGURES

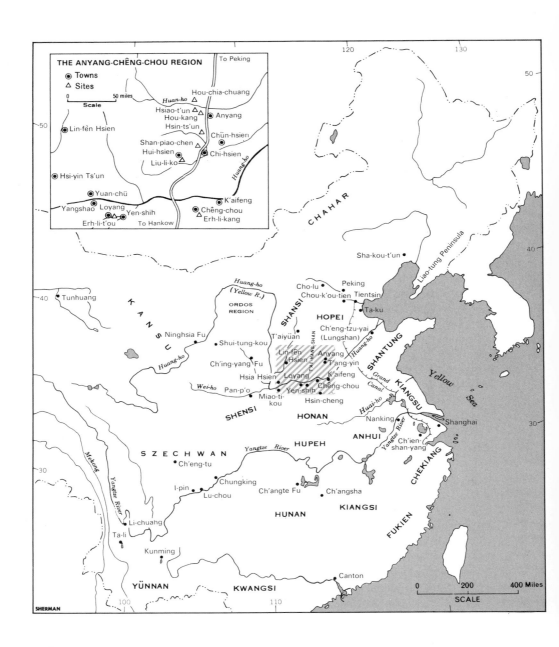

THE ANYANG-CHÊNG-CHOU REGION

⊙ Towns
△ Sites

0   Scale   50 miles

To Peking

Huan-ho

Hou-chia-chuang △
Hsiao-t'un △△ ⊙ Anyang
Hou-kang
Hsin-ts'un
⊙ Lin-fèn Hsien
Chün-hsien ⊙
Shan-piao-chen △
Hui-hsien ⊙ △ ⊙ Chi-hsien
Liu-li-ko △
Huang-ho
⊙ Hsi-yin Ts'un
Yuan-chü ⊙
Yangshao ⊙ Loyang △ ⊙ K'aifeng
⊙ Yen-shih
Erh-li-t'ou ⊙ ⊙ Chêng-chou
To Hankow △ Erh-li-kang

120
130
50

CHAHAR

Sha-kou-t'un •
Liao-tung Peninsula
40

Tunhuang •
K A N S U
Huang-ho (Yellow R.)
ORDOS REGION
Cho-lu • Peking •
Chou-k'ou-tien • Tientsin •
HOPEI
Ta-ku •
SHANSI
Ch'eng-tzu-yai (Lungshan) •
Ninghsia Fu •
Shui-tung-kou •
T'aiyüan •
Lin-fen Hsien
Anyang •
SHANTUNG
Yellow Sea
Ch'ing-yang Fu •
Hsia Hsien •
Loyang •
Yen-shih •
Hsin-cheng •
Wei-ho
Pan-p'o •
Miao-ti-kou •
T'ang-yin •
K'aifeng •
Chêng-chou •
Grand Canal
KIANGSU
40
30
Huang-ho
TAI-HANG-SHAN
HONAN
SHENSI
Huai-ho
Nanking •
ANHUI
Ch'ien-shan-yang •
Shanghai •
CHEKIANG
30
SZECHWAN
Ch'eng-tu •
HUPEH
Yangtze River
Mekong
Yangtze River
I-pin • Chungking •
Lu-chou •
Ch'angte Fu •
Ch'angsha •
KIANGSI
Li-chuang •
HUNAN
FUKIEN
Ta-li •
Kunming •
YÜNNAN
KWANGSI
Canton •
0   200   400 Miles
SCALE
100
110
SHERMAN

Anyang

1 *Oracle Bone Inscriptions*

Their First Appearance and
Initial Reception in the Learned World

THE ORACLE BONE inscriptions of the Shang dynasty were known to learned circles in China and to a few European and American scholars for almost thirty years before scientific digging was started at Anyang by the Institute of History and Philology of the Academia Sinica in 1927. How did it happen that the learned world in old China came to recognize the importance of this new discovery, which revolutionized Chinese paleography and paved the way to the development of archaeological science in the land of Cathay?

It is definitely known to field archaeologists that the "Waste of Yin" was used as a graveyard at least as early as the Sui dynasty,[1] if not earlier. There is evidence indicating that when the Sui people dug holes in this place for burying their dead, they frequently found inscribed oracle bones hidden underneath. If at that time some scholars, as cultivated as the paleographers of the nineteenth century, had come upon this hidden treasure, oracle bone inscriptions might have become known to Chinese scholars thirteen centuries earlier! This assumption is based on the fact that modern excavations of Sui tombs have uncovered more than once, in the stratum overlying these tombs, many fragments of inscribed oracle bones. I mention this interesting underground stratification to show only one fundamental point: that is, in intellectual development there are definite stages which follow each other in a certain order. That the oracle bone inscriptions were recognized at the end of the nineteenth century as a significant discovery which academicians continue to cultivate was not merely accidental. There was a long intellectual history preparatory for what took place in 1899 (1898?). It is important to take into consideration the intellectual history of the Manchu (Ch'ing) dynasty, which provided and nourished scholars to a mature stage ready to appreciate and acknowledge the importance of oracle bone inscriptions.

Two branches of classical learning cultivated in the Manchu dynasty are closely related to the maturity of this intellectual stage. I should first like to mention the intense cultivation of textual criticism. Its origin can be traced back to a period as early as the Northern Sung dynasty, but its full development did not take place until the beginning of the seventeenth century. Ku Yen-wu (1613–82) was the first master of this particular branch of learning. He was followed in the early period of the Manchu dynasty by a school of other eminent scholars who developed the spirit of pursuing knowledge for its own sake—a spirit that Liang Ch'i-ch'ao, one of the leaders of the Kuang Hsü Reform Movement and a pioneer in the literary revolution of modern China, succinctly summarized by saying, "The current motifs and chief elements of learning of the Ch'ing dynasty in the main are similar to the Renaissance Movement in Europe during the fourteenth-sixteenth centuries." [2] Besides Ku Yen-wu, Liang also mentioned as the co-founder of this movement Yen Jo-chü (1636–1704), the man who successfully proved that a large portion of the *Shu-ching* (Book of Documents), which had been regarded for more than a thousand years as sacred as the Old Testament in the West, is a forgery fabricated by later pretentious classicists. The success of Yen Jo-chü helped to promote *k'ao chü hsüeh* (or classic textual criticism) as the main stem of classical scholarship. Subsequently we find Tai Chen (1723–77) as the leader of this school; he was followed by a long list of illustrious scholars such as Tuan Yü-ts'ai (1735–1815), Wang Nien-sun (1744–1832), Wang Yin-chih (1766–1834), and Wu Ta-ch'eng (1835–

1902). The trend of this new movement was directed in the main to the re-examination of all the other classics. Gradually this scholastic initiative was extended to all the important ancient texts, reaching its climax in the Ch'ien Lung to the Tao Kuang eras.

An accompanying development in this period took place in antiquarianism or the science of paleography (*chin shih hsüeh*) which, as everybody knows, was in China initiated as early as the Northern Sung dynasty. Although it was almost completely neglected during the following dynasties, Yüan and Ming, toward the beginning of the seventeenth century, in China's Renaissance movement, this branch of learning was also reborn. The study of ancient bronze and stone inscriptions constituted a necessary discipline in the training of *chiao k'an hsüeh* (a more advanced branch of textual criticism) that required not only a close familiarity with all ancient classical texts, but also a profound knowledge of the history of all the ancient Chinese characters. Liang Ch'i-ch'ao, in the monograph cited above, said regarding the significance of the paleographers' study of ancient bronze and stone inscriptions: "What they achieved represents the opinion of collective scholastic efforts. . . . These achievements started a revolution in the ancient learning of Chinese paleography." Previously, Liang said in addition, Chinese paleography started and ended with Hsü Shen's *Shuo-wen* dictionary, which, like the ancient classics, had been taken by all educated men as the only authoritative interpretation of the origins and meanings of Chinese written words. With the beginning investigations of ancient bronze inscriptions, paleographers started to cast doubt on *Shuo-wen*'s authority. And many antiquarians discovered that *chin shih hsüeh* could provide a more correct interpretation of many ancient texts.

According to Yung Keng, the catalogue of studies of inscriptions that Yeh Ming compiled in 1910 listed 492 titles.[3] Although the catalogue is considered to be full of mistakes, nevertheless it indicates the enormous amount of intellectual effort that scholars of the Ch'ing dynasty applied to this particular field of learning. As to what these scholars have contributed to the advancement of paleography, one example may be sufficient to illustrate their distinguished service.

The name of Wu Ta-ch'eng is well known as his antiquarian investigations attracted the attention of Western sinologues very early. Among his numerous contributions, his studies of antique jades are especially famous. When Berthold Laufer, one of the pioneers devoted to the pursuit of Chinese learning in North America, published his well-known monograph on jade in 1912, he said in the introductory chapter: "I was forced to reproduce the material of Wu almost in its entirety, owing to its great archaeological importance." Laufer continued: "Wu Ta-ch'eng is not bound by the fetters of the past and not hampered by the accepted school traditions. With fair and open mind, he criticized the errors of the commentators to the *Chou-li*, the *Ku-yü t'u-p'u*, and many others, and his common sense leads him to new and remarkable results not anticipated by any of his predecessors. . . ." [4]

Wu Ta-ch'eng's *Ku-yü t'u-k'ao* (Studies of Ancient Jade) was first published in 1889. Five years earlier Wu published an even more important work, *Shuo-wen ku-chou pu* (Supplements to the Ancient Seal Characters of the *Shuo-wen* Dictionary), which may be said to be the first systematic effort made by a Chinese classical scholar of the Ch'ing dynasty to point out, on the bases of his study of ancient bronze and stone inscriptions, the errors of Hsü Shen's dictionary. An appendix volume, *Tzǔ-shuo* (Ancient Chinese Characters), published together with *Shuo-wen ku-chou pu*, studies about three dozen written characters, found mainly in the bronze inscriptions, which the author shows to be definitely different from, and even contradictory to, the definitions and interpretations of the *Shuo-wen* dictionary. These differences were mainly attributed to erroneous interpretations or wrong identifications of pre-Ch'in scripts. In other words, the evidence provided by bronze inscriptions proved definitely that Hsü Shen's *Shuo-wen* dictionary was by no means a faultless authority. Detailed instances seem unnecessary here; those who are interested may consult Wu's original work. What I wish to note here is the general tendency of scholarly work in academic circles toward the end of the nineteenth century. At this time, on the basis of the accumulated achievements of textual criticism and the study of stone and bronze inscriptions, cultivated in general among the intellectuals and the literati and encouraged by imperial sanctions of the Ch'ien Lung and Chia Ch'ing eras (1736–1820), Chinese epigraphy had already advanced to a stage ready for new source materials and new ideas which were eagerly looked for and studied. The fetters and shackles on Chinese literati set by the *Shuo-wen* dictionary for more than a millennium were at this moment completely loosened and even shattered.

So, when the oracle bone inscriptions were accidentally noticed by scholars nourished in this tradition, such as Wang I-yung (Fig. 1), the Dean of Hanlin College, whose attention was at once attracted, steps were immediately taken to collect the strange, previously unknown inscriptions. The exact circumstances in which Wang I-yung, an eminent scholar and statesman, discovered inscribed oracle bones still remain obscure. Even the exact year of his discovery cannot be stated definitely.[5] What is not disputed is that he started his collection of inscriptions before the climax of the Boxer Movement, which took place in 1900. A widely circulated story concerning Wang I-yung's epoch-making discovery begins with a case of malaria which occurred among his family. The medical prescription of the attending physician included an ingredient of "decayed tortoise shell." The master of the family was evidently also a medical connoisseur, so, when the medicines were brought back from the store, he examined all the ingredients personally. To his great astonishment, he found on the decayed tortoise shells ancient Chinese characters, which, although unknown to him, he found fascinating. He immediately ordered his servant to purchase all the decayed tortoise shells in the store where the original dosage had been purchased.

To what extent this story is true nobody has so far been able to confirm. What is generally known is that Wang I-yung was the first scholar to collect inscribed oracle bones.

Our main source of information concerning the earliest discoveries of oracle bones is Tung Tso-pin, whose subsequent role in the Anyang excavations will be narrated in the following chapters. In 1928 when Tung was sent to the Hsiao-t'un area to investigate Anyang as a possible archaeological site, he took extensive notes, based primarily upon conversations with Hsiao-t'un villagers, concerning the early history of the oracle bone discoveries. From his report to the sponsoring Institute of History and Philology, he extracted a condensed chronological account, listing events concerning the discovery, collection, and study of oracle bone inscriptions, which was published in 1930 as *Chia-ku nien-piao* (Oracle Bone Chronicles). In the course of the ensuing excavations, Tung continued his investigations of the previous history of oracle bone discoveries, studying written accounts and interviewing early participants. In his revised edition of *Chia-ku nien-piao*, published in 1937, Tung included these new data, even though diverse in origin and sometimes contradictory.[6] As the earliest entries listed in

Tung's Chronicles have implications for subsequent events in oracle bone scholarship, and for the relationships (often obscure) among the various participants, I would like here to translate or summarize, and briefly comment upon, Tung's five entries for the first year, 1899. The following account is based upon the 1937 edition of Tung's Chronicles.

1. Tung's first entry for 1899 is as follows:

Formerly, long before this year [1899], in the farming land on the bank of the Huan River, north of the village of Hsiao-t'un, located in the Anyang district of Honan Province, oracle bones (*chia ku*) were frequently found. The villagers treated them as things of medical value, so collected them and sold them to drugstores; they were generally known as dragon bones (*lung ku*). Li Ch'eng, a barber and a native of the village, made a business of dealing in dragon bones; he is now dead. The so-called dragon bones, are, in fact, largely oracle bones; and according to the folklore prevailing in Hsiao-t'un village, the majority of these bones bear inscriptions. The villagers sold them either retail or wholesale. In retail dealings, the dragon bones were first ground into a powder known by its native name as "knife points medicine" (*tao chien yo*), which Chinese medical practitioners considered effective in healing cuts and surgical wounds. The buyers in the wholesale market were usually managers of Chinese drugstores. The price charged was six cash per catty. The inscribed pieces at that time had no market value, and were considered worthless; so it was the usual practice among the sellers to polish off those inscriptions, before the dragon bones were brought to the market.

2. The second entry for 1899 is based upon an article by an author with the pen-name Hsi Weng, whose account, according to Tung Tso-pin, is incorrect in dating the event as happening one year earlier. The second entry:

In this year, Liu T'ieh-yün of Tan-t'u was visiting in the capital [Peking] as a house guest of Wang I-yung. The host of Liu T'ieh-yün was attacked by malarial fever. The doctor's prescriptions included an ingredient of decayed tortoise shell purchased at the drugstore Ta-jen-t'ang [name of the store] in Ts'ai-shih-k'ou [street name]. On the tortoise shells Liu T'ieh-yün saw seal characters (*chuan wen*), which he picked out and showed to his host; both of them were somewhat astonished at this discovery. Wang, a student of bronze inscriptions, immediately realized that these tortoise shells must be ancient. He went to the drugstore, to inquire about the source of supply of these ingredients. The manager told him that they came from T'ang-yin and Anyang of Honan province. They were sold at a very low price. . . . Liu T'ieh-yün went to the drugstores in the city and purchased them all.

This account differs in some detail from the previously mentioned episode concerning malaria in Wang I-yung's family. Tung includes it in his Chronicles since nobody is certain about what happened at the very beginning. This is the first mention of Liu T'ieh-yün (Fig. 2) whose subsequent importance to oracle bone scholarship will be discussed further on.

3. A third event, also recorded for 1899 in the revised Chronicles, is more or less general in nature, and is based upon Tung's conversations with Hsiao-t'un villagers. The Chronicles merely mention that a curio dealer by the name of Fan Wei-ch'ing traveled for the great collector Tuan Fang, a Manchu mandarin of culture and of experience in European contact. Fan roamed about with eyes wide open for any antiquity that might interest his lord. He stopped at Changte (Anyang) and found pieces of inscribed oracle bones, which Fan's sharp eyes realized as a source of great fortune. The story is still current that Viceroy Tuan Fang was so pleased with these new curiosities that he paid the dealer two and a half taels of silver per character for the inscribed bones. These rich rewards encouraged dealer Fan to take more field trips. Like the first two episodes, this story cannot be either confirmed or denied. At any rate Tuan Fang's collection, the story of which circulated only among curio dealers and peddlers, had no actual academic influence.

4. According to Tung's fourth entry for this year, this same dealer, Fan Wei-ch'ing, sold twelve tortoise shells to Wang I-yung, at a price of two taels per piece. Tung Tso-pin obtained this information from the unpublished lecture notes of James M. Menzies, a Presbyterian missionary, whose activity in collecting oracle bones during the 1920s will be discussed further. Menzies' own source for the information was the dealer Fan himself.

5. The final entry for 1899 in Tung's Chronicles is based upon two sources. The first is Liu T'ieh-yün.[7] The second is Lo Chên-yü's diary of a trip he made in 1914–15,[8] which included a visit to the village of Hsiao-t'un. Tung's brief statement of his fifth entry for the year is as follows:

According to Liu Tieh-yün's Preface to *T'ieh-yün ts'ang-kuei* [1903], tortoise shells were taken out of the soil in the year Chi Hai [1899] in the T'ang-yin district of Honan from the site of the ancient Yu-li. Fan, a dealer, wanted to monopolize the trade, so he kept the real provenance as a trade secret . . . on which Lo commented in his diary: "Thus was Liu cheated by the dealer as to the place of origin of these inscribed shells."

Figure 1. Wang I-yung

Figure 2. Liu T'ieh-yün

商遺先生册有九歲所攝景
宣統甲寅十二月王國維署

Figure 3. Lo Chên-yü

Lo Chên-yü (Fig. 3), as will be discussed below, is known as the man who discovered the provenance of the oracle bones and as the author of numerous distinguished paleographic studies.

The above five entries concerning the first knowledge of oracle bone inscriptions in Chinese learned circles represent the studied summary of Tung Tso-pin, who devoted his life to advancing scientific knowledge of the nature of these ancient inscriptions.

Although many points remain obscure, it is clear that Wang I-yung must be considered as the first man to recognize the scholarly value of the ancient characters inscribed on tortoise shells known as oracle bones. The biographical note on Wang I-yung in the *History of the Ch'ing Dynasty* includes the following comments: "I-yung's learning is wide; he is fond of bronze and stone inscriptions. Both Weng T'ung-ho and P'an Tsu-yin were profoundly impressed by the scope and depth of his classical and paleographical knowledge." [9] When the Boxer Movement reached its critical year, 1900, Wang I-yung committed suicide. It is generally accepted that the larger part of his collection of inscribed oracle bones passed into the hands of Liu T'ieh-yün, who had also, according to most specialists, purchased inscribed bones from the dealer Fan.

Liu Tieh-yün's diary, published in 1936, contains some additional information, probably not available to Tung Tso-pin when he revised his Chronicles, concerning both Liu's own early collecting activity and that of Wang I-yung.[10] One entry in the diary, for the twentieth day of the tenth month in the year *Hsin Ch'ou* (1901), reads as follows: "The dealer Chao Chih-chai sent me tortoise shells; there are some larger ones. In the evening I counted them; they amount to 1,300 pieces. What a rich collection!" From this entry Ch'en Meng-chia deduced that Liu Tieh-yün had his own collection as early as 1901.[11]

If Wang I-yung may be taken as the Charles Darwin of the new branch of Chinese paleography, Liu T'ieh-yün must rank, by common consent, as the Thomas Huxley. Liu is Wang I-yung's most important successor for two reasons. He not only continued the effort to collect the oracle bones (Ch'en Meng-chia estimated that his collection numbered 5,588 pieces as a minimum),[12] but he was actually the first man with the foresight to lithograph and publish the ink-squeezes of these totally unknown inscriptions.[13] In his six volumes, published in 1903, Liu reproduced 1,058 fragments of tortoise shell inscriptions, with forewords and preface by Lo Chên-yü, Wu Ch'ang-shou, and Liu T'ieh-yün himself—the earliest published documents discussing the nature and contents of the inscribed oracle bones.

One year later, the thirtieth year of the Kuang Hsü era, another eminent scholar, Sun I-jang, completed his first study of the inscriptions, but the manuscripts were not published till 1917.[14] This scholar was perhaps one of the most learned men of the final period of the Manchu dynasty. He was the distinguished editor of the last of the thirteen classics, *Chou-li,* about which he compiled and critically edited all the past comments, notes, and annotations, a gigantic task completed in 1899. When he first read Liu's *T'ieh-yün ts'ang-kuei* and saw the reproduced ink-squeezes, he remarked: "Unexpectedly, in my declining years, I am able to see these marvelous antique traces of ancient inscriptions which have fascinated me so much that I could not stop reading and studying uninterruptedly for two months, with notes and comments from time to time, till at last, I found some way to understand the meanings of these ancient documents!"

2 Exploratory Period

Collection, Deciphering, and Paleographic Studies of the Inscribed Oracle Bones

I HAVE, in the introductory chapter, summarized in a general way the circumstances in which the inscribed oracle bones first caught the attention of learned circles, especially among those who had attained a profound knowledge of paleography. The three scholars whose contributions were fundamental in building up this new branch of learning were, first, Wang I-yung, almost unanimously acknowledged as the man who initially recognized the importance of these newly discovered inscriptions; second, Liu T'ieh-yün, who not only continued the collection work of Wang, but, equally important, was the first man within the narrow pioneering circle who had the courage to lithograph and publish the ink-squeezes of those inscriptions, which spread the knowledge of these ancient and unknown inscriptions to a large group of scholars; and third, the eminent scholar Sun I-jang, whose *Ch'i-wen chü-li* represents the pioneering effort to make a scholarly inquiry into the structure and meanings of these inscriptions. The works of these three pioneers substantially supplemented one another, and together they laid a firm foundation for this new branch of Chinese paleography.

If these three had had no fellow workers or successors, the foundation they laid could have simply disappeared, like many early Chinese inventions and discoveries, being regarded as something occult, undeserving of serious attention in academic circles, a viewpoint to which some schools of Chinese epigraphy still held fast up to the time when scientific excavations had already started.[1] Fortunately both for the learned world in general and for Chinese paleography in particular, the publication of *T'ieh-yün ts'ang-kuei* successfully awakened classical scholars.

There followed a period of widespread efforts by many scholars to collect, to decipher, and to interpret these inscribed characters on the oracle bones. Here I think it is appropriate to give a general account of the various activities that took place between 1900 and 1928, when official excavations began. These can be considered under the following headings: (1) diggings; (2) collecting activities; and (3) publications and epigraphical works.

Private Diggings up to 1928

Our primary source of information here, as for so much of what took place in this period, is Tung Tso-pin, who both in his *Fifty Years of Studies in Oracle Inscriptions*[2] and especially in the revised edition of his Chronicles has given a detailed summary of these events.

Information gathered in Anyang convinced Tung that there had been at least nine private diggings for *tzŭ-ku-t'ou* (a local term for inscribed oracle bones) by the natives in and around Hsiao-t'un village, beginning with the twenty-fifth year of the Kuang Hsü era (1899–1900), the year when this worthless dragon bone gained a high value in the curio market. But the details of what Tung termed "the first digging" were however not given. The account merely mentions that after Wang I-yung's discovery, Fan Wei-ch'ing, a curio dealer from Shantung, went to Anyang searching for oracle bones and he paid two and one-half taels of silver per inscribed character, which according to the villagers was the prize Tuan

Fang offered. Concerning the second private digging, which took place in 1904, Tung's account gives more details. As the demand for *tzŭ-ku-t'ou* suddenly increased after Liu T'ieh-yün's lithographic reproduction of the ink-squeezes of the inscriptions, to meet the pressing market the villagers started digging in the northern part of a farm along the bank of the Huan River in 1904. The villagers still remembered, when scientific excavations started, that Chu K'un, one of the landlords who owned a portion of the village farms, had organized a big digging team and all the diggers stayed in a temporary camp specially erected for the participants. They kept on with this activity until a fight for the right of treasure hunting broke out between them and a rival party also organized by the villagers. A suit followed the fight, and the magistrate of the district stopped it by forbidding further digging.

It is impossible to say how many pieces of the inscribed bones were found during the second digging. Tung's memoir merely mentions that these new-found treasures were sold to a number of collectors, including Lo Chên-yü, Huang Chün, Hsü Fang, Frank H. Chalfant, Samuel Couling, and L. C. Hopkins.

Five years later, in 1909, the first year of the last emperor of the Manchu dynasty, the Hsüan T'ung era, when Chang Hsüeh-hsien, a rich villager who owned a great deal of land, was digging for sweet potatoes on his own farm right in front of the village, he discovered fragments of scapula in the shape of a horseshoe, which also bore inscriptions. It is said Chang reaped a rich harvest of oracle bones by digging potatoes.

The fourth digging did not take place till eleven years later, when in 1920 drought covered five provinces in north China and the villagers, pressed by hunger, were again forced to dig oracle bones. A large crowd, many participants being from neighboring villages, concentrated at the northern part of Hsiao-t'un, beside the Huan River, which the villagers knew to be the most productive site for hidden treasures.

The fifth digging occurred in 1923; it also took place on Chang Hsüeh-hsien's farm. Tung's memoir simply mentions the fact that two large inscribed bone plates (scapulae?) were obtained from this digging. In the following year, 1924, some villagers were building a wall of stamped earth, which required digging the needed material from the loess soils. In these diggings the villagers once more uncovered some *tzŭ-ku-t'ou*, which, according to village oral traditions, included some huge pieces. Most of the diggings of this year and the preceding year were sold to Mr. James M. Menzies who was stationed at Changte as a missionary.

Tung records that the seventh private digging took place in 1925. No name of any villager is mentioned. He simply records that the villagers were gathered in a large crowd and were engaged to dig in front of the village settlement by the side of the village road. Several baskets of *chia ku* were obtained. Some scapulae (Tung's term) seemed to be more than a foot (?) long. It is thought that all of these were sold to curio dealers from Shanghai.

The eighth private digging, which took place in 1926, is of some social and political interest for the early republican era. The story is that Chang Hsüeh-hsien, being a landowner and considered rich, was captured, kept a prisoner, and held by bandits for ransom. The villagers took this opportunity to negotiate with his family on the proposition of digging in Chang's vegetable garden. It was agreed that any worthy treasures uncovered were to be equally divided between the diggers and the owner. When the digging started, participants, numbered by several tens, were divided into three teams, all working in the same place and at the same time, each occupying an angle of a triangular piece of the same lot. They proceeded without any definite plan; naturally each team was eager to touch upon the hidden treasure first. But the search came to a dramatic end when the three parties reached a considerable depth, all concentrated toward the same hidden spot, so that they came in contact with one another. Suddenly the overlapping soil lumps collapsed, as occasionally happens in a mining shaft. The collapsed lumps buried alive four diggers, who were, however, rescued by members of the digging party. Thus the digging stopped. According to the oral tradition of this village, their findings were quite abundant; they were all bought by Mr. Menzies.

The ninth and the last private digging, before scientific archaeology started, took place in the spring of 1928 at the time of the northern expedition of the Nationalist army. There was some fighting in the Anyang area. One army was stationed on the southern bank of the Huan River. In the fighting period, the Hsiao-t'un village people could not till their land, and so, when the battle stopped in April, the villagers again gathered together to dig *tzŭ-ku-t'ou*. The crowd was a large one; they concentrated their effort by the roadside in front of the village threshing floor. The inscribed oracle bones dug out in this season were all sold to merchants from Shanghai and K'aifeng as recorded in Tung's chronicles.

Collecting Activities

As has been discussed in Chapter 1, the principal early collectors of inscribed oracle bones were Liu T'ieh-yün, who took over the major part of Wang I-yung's collection; Tuan Fang, the well-known collector of ancient bronzes, whose collection, whatever its origin or extent, was of no real scholarly influence; and Lo Chên-yü, who discovered the true provenance of these ancient scripts at Changte Fu.

In the years following the publication of *Tieh-yün ts'ang-kuei* there were probably dozens of collectors, both Chinese and foreign, who actively supported, and keenly competed in, the business of collecting the inscribed oracle bones. According to James M. Menzies, foreign scholars started collecting the oracle bone inscriptions as early as 1904.[3] The Reverend Frank H. Chalfant was probably the first foreign scholar to be involved in this activity, purchasing four hundred pieces for the Royal Asiatic Society in Shanghai. He was followed by the Reverend Samuel Couling and the Reverend Paul Bergen. Their purchases were later sold to several museums: the Carnegie Museum of Pittsburgh, the Royal Scottish Museum of Edinburgh, and the British Museum of London. Later, Mr. L. C. Hopkins of Great Britain also joined the collecting team; and soon afterwards Dr. Wilhelm of Ts'ingtao also participated, according to Tung's Chronicles. Meanwhile, in Japan, there developed an even greater enthusiasm for the collection and study of oracle bone inscriptions.[4] Concerning the various collections of this period, it is obvious that Tung's Chronicles are not as all-inclusive as his reports on private diggings. This is understandable since actual dealings were mostly in the hands of curio dealers, who, like most museum curators, prefer secret transactions. Still in Tung's Chronicles we do find quite a few important items relating to oracle bone collections on record. They are:

A. *1904–5.* Dealer Fan sold more than one thousand pieces to Tuan Fang, six hundred pieces to Huang Chün, and one thousand pieces to Hsü Fang. In the same year, Samuel Couling purchased many fragments, and Paul Bergen got more than seventy pieces which he presented to the White Wright Institute of Tsinan, but most of these latter are forgeries. L. C. Hopkins also collected eight hundred pieces this year. Dr. Wilhelm of Ts'ingtao gathered about seventy pieces and the Museum für Völkerkunde obtained more than seven hundred pieces. It is also recorded that the Anglo-Chinese College in Tientsin received a number of these inscribed bones as a gift from Wang I-yung's family.

B. *1909–10*. Japanese scholars also started collecting, led by Mr. Hayashi Taisuke who bought six hundred pieces this year; other Japanese collectors obtained more than three thousand pieces.

C. *1910–11*. Liu T'ieh-yün died in exile; his collection, according to Tung's Chronicles, passed into a number of hands: including Lo Chên-yü, Mrs. Hardoon, Yeh Yü-sheng, Central University, and Chen Chung-fan. The collection was evidently sold out or given away in piecemeal fashion since the Chronicles record that as late as 1926 Shang Ch'eng-tzu obtained twenty-five hundred pieces from Liu T'ieh-yün's original collection.

D. *1914*. James M. Menzies started collecting.

E. *1918*. The Japanese pioneer working on oracle bone inscriptions, Mr. Taisuke Hayashi, arrived at Anyang and purchased twenty pieces.

F. *1919*. Imitation pieces of oracle bone inscriptions appeared in great quantity in the curio market.

G. *1922*. Peking Government University received a gift of 463 fragments of oracle bone inscriptions from Ta-ku-chai, a curio shop in Peking.

H. *1927*. James M. Menzies purchased a large collection.

This collecting activity encouraged intense competition in the curio market in Peking, Shanghai, and Wei Hsien in Shantung province as well as Changte Fu in Honan. Since most dealings were secretive in nature, and in the hands of avaricious dealers and rich but ignorant collectors, the result was the appearance of an enormous quantity of imitation pieces. These spurious antiquities were produced in many places: Anyang, Peking, Wei Hsien, Shanghai, and so on. These forgeries, in the beginning at any rate, did probably earn the dealers quite a fortune. The author himself, in the years since the excavation started, has personally observed some of the forgeries in a number of well-known museums in both Europe and America.[5] And Tung Tso-pin, who made a special investigation of such forgery, actually made an effort to cultivate friendship with this talented group of men, and succeeded in winning an intimate acquaintance with one of the forgers, Lan Pao-kuang of Anyang, who, Tung said, was a real genius. He was an opium smoker, and only in the inspired moment would he show his craftsmanship by taking some uninscribed pieces found at Hsiao-t'un and producing a duplicate in exact detail. Tung told me further that Lan was a forger because he really enjoyed such work. As a matter of fact, he was a poor businessman. He sold all those imitation pieces for very small sums of money.

The appearance of the forgeries greatly disturbed the curio market, with two important results. On the one hand, the conservative school, who observed the authority of Hsü Shen's *Shuo-wen* dictionary with reverence and religious faith based upon a tradition of over a millennium, naturally took these forgeries as definite evidence to prove that all the so-called *chia ku wen* (oracle bone inscriptions) were pseudo-classic inscriptions, fabricated by a number of pretenders to scholarship to deceive the public at large. On the other hand, a few far-sighted scholars who were better informed and had examined the genuine pieces were pushed to work harder in order to find criteria by which to differentiate the genuine inscriptions from the forgeries. A pioneer in this field was the author of "Oracle Records from the Waste of Yin," Mr. James Mellon Menzies, the Canadian missionary. Menzies was first sent to Changte Fu in 1914, and, after World War I, was again stationed there from 1921 to 1927. He was thus in a position to learn, *in situ*, about the unearthing of oracle bones by the native diggers on his frequent visits to Hsiao-t'un.[6] This fortunate combination of an appropriate appointment and an inborn instinct for archaeology prepared the way for his special contribution to the oracle bone studies among the small community of foreign scholars.

At the same time, Chinese collectors developed a more discriminating and critical power to differentiate genuine pieces from the fabricated inscriptions.

To conclude our discussion of collecting activities, it can be said that from a commercial point of view, European and American collectors were more archaeologically conscious, and so were willing to pay a relatively high price for these new curiosities.[7] The Chinese scholars, however, were the ones who first became aware of the cultural value of these inscriptions; the second generation of *chia ku hsüeh,* as we will see in the following discussion, includes a number of scholars whose works have won international academic admiration because of their high standards of scholarship and erudition.

Publications and Epigraphical Works

Regarding books and articles, ink-squeeze reproductions, copying of original characters, and research works on the oracle bone inscriptions, Tung's Chronicles list 110 titles in Chinese, Japanese, and European languages published up to September 1928. These titles included 36 books: 30 by Chinese authors, 4 by Japanese, and the remaining 2 by an American and a Canadian, respectively. Among the 74 articles published, 41 were by Chinese and 9 by Japanese Sinologues, while in English no less than 19 articles appeared. There were 3 articles in German periodicals and 2 in French, of which one was a Chinese contribution, and the other was from the hand of the great French Sinologue Edouard Chavannes, who in 1911 wrote a summary review of Lo Chên-yü's *Yin-shang chên-pu wen-tzŭ k'ao*, published in Peking in the previous year. This lengthy note introduced both the book and the author to Western students of Sinology.[8] The Reverend Frank H. Chalfant's "Early Chinese Writings," published in 1906–7, was the earliest foreign-language study of the ancient inscriptions.[9]

The other articles in English, which were published mostly in the *Journal of the Royal Asiatic Society of Great Britain and Ireland*, were contributed by one single author, L. C. Hopkins, whose "Pictographic Reconnaissance," ran seven articles in this journal up to 1927. Meanwhile, in America, Germany, and Japan, Sinologues of this period also showed considerable interest in the studies as well as in collections of these newly discovered Chinese written records.

It was, however, in Japan that the new interest in the study developed most rapidly and intensively, although the published articles were not numerous. The work of Japanese scholars, including Taisuke Hayashi and Naito Torajiro, also had a great influence upon Chinese epigraphical studies. Tung's Chronicles record that in 1910 Taisuke mailed Lo Chên-yü his essay on *chia ku wen*. This penetrating essay, Lo remarked in a number of places, helped to make up what he had neglected in his forewords to Liu's *T'ieh-yün ts'ang-kuei*. It must be noted that both Lo Chên-yü and Wang Kuo-wei—the two most distinguished Chinese figures of this period who contributed abundantly and exerted the widest influence in the Chinese world of learning—both stayed in Japan for some time. Lo went to Japan soon after the revolution of 1911, while Wang was there for only a short stay. The Japanese contact, it seems to me, must have given to both men a tremendous stimulus, stirring up in them new ideas of approach, awakening in them an interest, historical as well as archaeological, hitherto deeply hidden in their subconscious. I do not pretend to give this as the underlying motive for their devotion to this study, which had been developed into an established branch of Chinese paleography; in their time there might have been other factors that served as a driving power to make these two scholars spend their lifetimes in this way.

Before turning to the research of these two pioneers, I would like to begin our summary of work by Chinese scholars with a more detailed discussion of the previously mentioned contributions of Sun I-jang. Sun first became acquainted with the oracle bone inscriptions by reading Liu T'ieh-yün's *T'ieh-yün ts'ang-kuei*. As early as 1904, only a year after the publication of Liu's work, Sun started examining, on the basis of his profound knowledge of bronze inscriptions, the individual characters of the oracle bone inscriptions. He labored continuously for two months, and his accumulated notes resulted in his study *Ch'i-wen chü-li* (Examples of Oracle Bone Inscriptions), although this study was not published until 1917. This pioneering effort to make a scholarly inquiry into the structure and meanings of the oracle bone inscriptions was organized according to the functional implications of individual characters: the calender system, methods of divinatory queries, events divined for, ghosts and spirits, and so on. There is one section on officialdom, another on various states. The section on *wen tzŭ* (written words) is the longest, constituting almost 50 percent of the complete work.[10]

In 1905–6 Sun I-jang wrote another book, *Ming yüan* (Origin, or Evolution, of Names), which he published at his own expense in 1906.[11] In this book Sun announced that his task was to trace the ancient Chinese scripts as they appeared in bronze inscriptions, oracle bone records, on stone drums of the Chou dynasty and petroglyphs of Kueichou province (considered at his time to be the Miao people's ancient scripts) and to compare them with the basic characters of *ku chou wen* which Hsü Shen found still current at his time. By these comparative studies, Sun aimed at finding out the origins and evolutionary changes of the more important words among nine thousand characters in Hsü Shen's dictionary.

It is remarkable to note that he dwelt specially on the origin of the numerals and traced with a great deal of accuracy the various numbers as they appeared and were still used in Chinese languages. Then he proceeded to discuss the original meaning of *hsiang hsing* characters, illustrated by a long list of names of animals and plants classified within the *hsiang hsing* category, such as the Chinese characters for horse (*ma*), ox (*niu*), sheep (*yang*), and so on. In discussing each example, the author usually cited bronze inscriptions and others from pre-Ch'in scripts together with any that had been found in the oracle bone inscriptions. In concluding each discussion he only commented whether it agreed with or differed from what was said in Hsü Shen's dictionary.

We shall have occasion to refer again to the works of Sun I-jang, but I would now like to turn to the next important scholar, Lo Chên-yü. Tung Tso-pin's revised Chronicles record that in 1902–3 Lo first came into contact with the inscribed oracle bones at the home of Liu T'ieh-yün.[12] The ink-squeezes of the oracle bone inscriptions impressed him so much that he remarked, at his first sight of these scripts: "Since the time of the Han dynasty, the most eminent epigraphers like Chang Ch'ang, Tu Yeh, Yang Hsung, and Hsü Shen never had such an opportunity to see these!" [13] So, it is clear that he was first introduced by Liu T'ieh-yün to this new learning.

Lo was so impressed by this discovery that he considered himself bound to circulate it, publicize it, and make it a permanent addition to the knowledge of ancient Chinese languages. The Chinese written language, he realized, after three millennia of history, had suffered too many changes, mutations, and erroneous interpretations. The language had in fact changed beyond any possible recognition of its original nature and of those characteristics that were in usage before the time of Ch'in Shih-huang-ti (the first emperor), who, as everybody knows, burned all the books in the thirty-fourth year of his reign (217 B.C.), only six years (221 B.C.) after the first unification of continental China. It is also a well-known historical fact that the first emperor issued the imperial command to standardize units of measurements, means of communication, and above all the written language in the first year of the unification. This command was soon followed by the famous imperial edict to bury alive all men of letters of this Confucian school (*ju*), and to burn all written documents except books dealing with magical practice, medical art, and tree plantings. It is also well known that the efforts to revive ancient learning in the earlier part of the following Han dynasty were in the beginning mixed in character; an effective search for ancient books started only after Han Wu-ti (140–86 B.C.) ascended the imperial throne. Emperor Wu issued an imperial edict to search for old books. At this time Chinese written characters, for a number of reasons, had already changed so much that they were radically different from what had been current in pre-Ch'in times.

There is no need to go further into the history of such changes, but it is important to bear in mind that these changes did take place in order to appreciate the importance of scholarly contributions after the recovery of the oracle bone inscriptions, especially those following the pioneering efforts of Wang I-yung, Liu T'ieh-yün, and Sun I-jang.

Inspired by the above-mentioned essay by Taisuke Hayashi, Lo Chên-yü decided to devote his leisure time to going over all the ink-squeezes of the oracle bone inscriptions in his keeping, and also those from the dealers who had been in Honan. He succeeded in seeing thousands of fragments of the inscribed tortoise shells and bones. Out of these collections he selected some seven hundred pieces distinguished by special characteristics, and with tireless efforts he devoted himself to the minute examination of the genuine specimens as well as the ink-squeezes. Finally he achieved two important results.

First, he was able to locate the exact place, namely the village Hsiao-t'un, on the outskirts of Anyang, where the oracle bones were being unearthed. Before Lo's time the curio dealers all kept the provenance a trade secret, but after diligent inquiry, cross-examination, and systematic searches, Lo finally discovered the place of origin of the ancient scripts. As mentioned in Chapter 1, Lo visited Changte Fu in 1915, keeping a diary account of his trip.

Second, by studying the genuine records, he also succeeded in discovering a list of names of the royal ancestors of the Shang dynasty, and thus began to understand that all these records were relics from the Yin-Shang dynasty. With these newly reached basic ideas in mind, he devoted three months' time to write the article *Yin-shang chên-pu wen-tzŭ k'ao* (On the Oracle Bone Inscriptions of the Yin-Shang Period), with a threefold purpose: "to correct historian's errors," "to trace the source of ancient Chinese written characters," and "to find out the methods of divination of the ancient Chinese," a statement which he made with some justifiable pride. In this article, Lo concludes: "I have solved the questions and doubts, which Taisuke's original contribution raised and left unanswered." This article, completed in 1910, was published under the imprint of Yü-chien-chai in the same year. In Tung's Chronicles, the subtitles of Lo's important paper are as follows:

I. Historical Studies (K'ao Shih)
 1. Capital city of the Yin
 2. Names and post-mortem honorific titles of the kings
II. Correcting Names (Chêng Ming)
 1. Identification of seal characters (*chou wen*) and ancient characters (*ku wen*)
 2. Pictographic characters (*hsiang hsing tzŭ*) are not limited by the number of strokes
 3. Comparative studies with bronze inscriptions
 4. Correcting errors of the *Shuo-wen* dictionary
III. Methods of Divination (Pu Fa)
 1. On making a query (*chên*)
 2. On inscription or incision (*ch'i*)
 3. On burning or scorching (*cho*)
 4. On applying ink (*chih mo*)
 5. On omens or crack signs (*chao ch'e*)
 6. On divination records (*pu-tz'ŭ*)
 7. On storage by burying (*mai ts'ang*)
 8. On scapulimancy (*ku pu*)
IV. Additional Discussions (Yü Lun)

The essay is published with a Preface and a Postscript.

It is to be noted that in Lo's Preface to this, his first important article on oracle bone inscriptions, he acknowledged several facts which are of historical importance in tracing the complicated early development of this branch of Chinese paleography, especially the mutual relations among Liu T'ieh-yün, Sun I-jang, and Lo Chên-yü. Lo's introductory remarks include some definite admissions: "My dear friend Sun I-jang (Sun Chung-yung) also investigated these inscriptions; his manuscripts were sent to me. It is regrettable to have to say that, in his study, he is unable to penetrate the mystery of these inscriptions. . . ." In the same Preface, Lo also admitted that the Foreword he wrote for Liu T'ieh-yün's *T'ieh-yün ts'ang-kuei* was hasty and by no means thorough. It is rather amusing to note that Lo found only shortcomings in Sun's original work, manuscripts of which, according to Lo's own statement, he had received from Sun I-jang before the latter's death. Further, Lo does not even mention Sun I-jang's second important work, the above-cited *Ming yüan,* which traced the evolution of a number of Chinese characters. Lo must have been familiar with this remarkable and original treatise.

It is therefore at least interesting to compare the contents of Lo's *Yin-shang chên-pu wen-tzŭ k'ao* with Sun's two earlier writings. There is hardly any doubt that, as far as the method of approach is concerned, Lo differs very little from his senior worker, who, for comparative purposes, made extensive use of his profound knowledge of bronze inscriptions, with which he compared the oracle bone inscriptions in great detail, and naturally not without fruitful results. After the example of Sun, Lo Chên-yü also took up some concrete examples of pictographs which represented animals to illustrate the *hsiang hsing tzŭ* in various stages, found in both bronze inscriptions and the oracle bone inscriptions. The examples given by Lo include the pictographs for sheep, horse, deer, pig, dog, and dragon. It is important to remember that in Sun's *Ming yüan* the list of pictographs chosen for special study also included horse, ox, sheep, pig, dog, tiger, deer, *k'uei* dragon, etc. It may be true that Lo approached the problem from a different angle; he aimed to show that the oracle bone pictographs were in a rapidly changing period and the pictorial stages were by no means standardized in a fixed form. But the examples he chose for illustrations clearly indicate that if Lo in his essay does show some new ideas and cover some new ground, it only means that he was taking advantage of his senior's unpublished materials as well as benefiting from the methods Sun I-jang developed in his pioneer study, *Ming yüan.*[14]

Lo Chên-yü, nevertheless, is a very important man, considering the various contributions he made to reinforce the firm foundation first laid by the three pioneers. He enjoyed good luck in the early days of collecting and studying the newly discovered epigraphical source materials. Through this opportunity as well as through his devotion to continuous research in the comparative studies of pre-Ch'in inscriptions, he came to a better understanding of oracle bone inscriptions, and produced the monumental publication, *Yin-hsü shu-ch'i ch'ien-pien* (Yin-hsü Oracle Bone Inscriptions, First Part) in the second year after the 1911 revolution. The four volumes of this work consisted of 2,229 ink-squeezes of oracle bone inscriptions, carefully selected by Lo himself out of his total collection of tens of thousands of fragments which included many new purchases in addition to Liu T'ieh-yün's major portion. These volumes were printed in collotype and published in Japan, on the finest paper. Three years later (1915) two volumes were added, known as *Yin-hsü shu-ch'i hou-pien;* these also were printed and published in Japan. One year before the publication of the *hou-pien,* Lo also completed and published an annotating volume with the title *Yin-hsü shu-ch'i k'ao-shih,* which was a translation of the inscriptions reproduced in *ch'ien-pien* into modern versions with explanatory notes. The manuscripts of this annotating volume were hand-copied by Lo's junior colleague, Professor Wang Kuo-wei, whose copy was lithographed and published. The annotating volume was divided into eight sections: (1) Capital Cities, (2) Kings, (3) Personal Names, (4) Geographical Terms, (5) Written Words, (6) Divination Records, (7) Ritual System, (8) Methods of Divination. It is prefaced by Lo Chên-yü, the author himself, with a Postscript by Wang Kuo-wei.[15] After another twelve years, a revised edition of the annotatory volume was published by the Oriental Society but without mention of the publisher or the place of publication. This new edition was one of the most noteworthy books on the oracle bone studies of this period. In this edition the annotation included a great many new investigations, of which the most valuable contributions were from Professor Wang Kuo-wei, who, as noted already, hand-copied Lo Chên-yü's first edition of annotations and transcriptions.

The contributions of Wang Kuo-wei, from a purely epigraphical viewpoint, are unanimously considered much more important for this period than Lo Chên-yü's summary notes, although Wang probably, in the early stage, received substantial help from Lo, his senior worker. Wang's work, however, depended upon the original materials which were collotyped in *Yin-hsü shu-ch'i ch'ien-pien,* which faithfully reproduced ink-squeezes of the oracle bone inscriptions from Lo's own collection.

Lo's own investigations and intelligent annotations of these carefully chosen materials were widely commented on by men of learning including some of the foremost Sinologues, and naturally exercised tremendous influence among the epigraphists of both the conservative and the liberal schools in the author's home land. The first edition of the annotatory volume included a list of deciphered characters, amounting to 485 individual words. In the revised edition of this volume, the list, according to Tung Tso-pin, expanded to 570.[16] This number constituted nearly 50 percent of the total number of individual characters inscribed in the oracle bones known at that time. Most of the deciphered characters on Lo's list included words referring to numerals, celestial stems, earthly branches, directions, animals, plants, geographical terms, utensils, and general terms concerning daily behavior, such as "come and go," "up and down," "walk and travel," "hunting and fishing," and so on. So they have tentatively served the basic needs of reading intelligently the contents of these ancient inscriptions. In the last section of his annotatory volume, Lo transcribed 707 items of the actual inscriptions, which according to Lo's standard, are intact and intelligible.[17] Lo organized these contents according to the types of events for which queries were made through divination. Lo's eight divisions are as follows:

TYPES OF EVENTS	NUMBER OF QUERIES
(a) Sacrifice (*ch'i*)	304
(b) Pray (*kao*)	15
(c) Sacrifice (*hsiang*)	4
(d) Going and Coming	123
(e) Hunting and Fishing	128
(f) War Expeditions	35
(g) Harvesting	21
(h) Weather	77
Total entries	707

The 707 entries that Lo in his *K'ao-shih* rendered into modern readings were originally sectioned on types of events recorded in these readable inscriptions. It is obvious that these events were concerned mainly with sacrifice (a-c), king's journey, (d) hunting and fishing, weather and harvesting; and also, warfare. These entries can be regrouped and calculated on a percentage basis:

	REGROUPED CATEGORIES	ORIGINAL CLASSIFICATION	NO. OF ENTRIES	PERCENT
I	Sacrificial Offerings	(a-c)	323	45.80
II	King's Journey	(d)	123	17.39
III	Hunting and Fishing	(e)	128	18.10
IV	Weather and Harvesting	(g-h)	98	13.80
V	War Expeditions	(f)	35	4.91
	Total entries		707	

The new edition of *K'ao-shih* published in 1927 considerably enlarged the list of deciphered vocabulary; it also augmented the number of readable items of inscribed records from *Yin-hsü shu-ch'i*. The number of deciphered words reached 671, while readable records amounted to 1,094 items which Lo divided into nine groups; the added group was named "Miscellaneous," while the other eight groups retained their original names. If they are calculated according to the above regroupings on a percentage basis, the following table shows the results:

		No. of Items	Percent of Total Entries
I	Sacrificial Offerings (a-c)	575	47.63
II	King's Journey (d)	177	14.66
III	Hunting and Fishing (e)	197	16.32
IV	Weather and Harvesting (g-h)	146	12.09
V	War Expeditions (f)	65	5.38
VI	Miscellaneous (i)	47	3.89
	Total entries	1207	99.97

Although the two percentage lists of events do show some differences, the extent of variation is relatively limited. The performance of sacrificial offerings to ancestors and other spirits no doubt constituted the major state event about which the Shang people had to consult the oracles and find an answer, while the other three groups—royal travels, hunting and fishing, harvesting and weather forecasts—were undoubtedly of equal importance; these four groups were probably the main occupations of a king's daily life. The war records, which constituted more than 5 percent of the readable records, represented state events also doubtlessly equal in importance to sacrificial performance; but their occurrences were naturally less frequent. There will be occasions later to discuss this group of records in more detail.

What has to be pointed out here particularly is the fact that Lo Chên-yü, with the help of Wang Kuo-wei, in these published volumes had succeeded in strengthening the foundation for a renewed study of Chinese epigraphy by demonstrating the evolutionary stages of Chinese written characters from the Yin-Shang period down to the late Han dynasty when Hsü Shen produced his *Shuo-wen* dictionary. In this gigantic task, they also accomplished some other important archaeological achievements in their study of the methods of divination, identification of the locations of the various capitals which the Shang dynasty occupied, and, above all, reconstruction of the genealogical tree of the royal family way back to the pre-dynastic time. The re-establishment of the succession of dynastic kings and pre-dynastic royal ancestors was mainly the work of Wang Kuo-wei, whose research covered readings of all the related records as well as the readable oracle bone entries. He was also the first scholar to succeed in piecing together the fragmentary ink-squeezes published in various reproductions into some complete documents, in which the ancestors were mentioned according to the order of succession when occasion for joint worship of all ancestors was to take place. Professor Wang, in two special articles published in 1917, built the genealogical tree of the Shang rulers, which he compared with three other important documents relating to the same matter.[18] Wang concluded:

According to Ssŭ-Ma Ch'ien's account, the Shang dynasty has thirty-one emperors (*ti*), ranking in seventeen generations. . . . What the oracle bone records have shown and proved is that the number of emperors as well as the generations in Ssŭ-Ma Ch'ien's record are the nearest to the correct list. The other two documents have both mis-recorded the number of generations.

The articles mentioned above represent the cream of his applied effort in his ingenious paleographic work in the course of his historical as well as epigraphical researches. To this day, his classical contributions have remained without any fundamental change. When Tung Tso-pin wrote his *Chia-ku-hsüeh wu-shih-nien* [19] in 1944, thirty-seven years later, Tung's list of Shang kings and their ancestors remained almost the same as those Wang first identified in 1917.

Wang's contributions to this new study started in 1915 and continued more than ten years till the time, after the example of Wang I-yung in 1900, that he terminated his life by drowning in the artificial lake of the Summer Palace built by the Empress Dowager Tz'ŭ-hsi. At that time, 1926, he had been teaching in the Research Institute of National Learning at Ts'inghua College.

Contemporaneously, there were at least half a dozen Chinese epigraphists who contributed to the advancement of this study. Among the Chinese contributions, two dictionaries deserve special notice. Wang Hsiang's *Fu-shih yin-ch'i lei-ts'uan*, published in 1921, included 873 deciphered characters; Shang Ch'eng-tzu's *Yin-hsü wen-tzŭ lei-pien,* published in 1923, included 789 deciphered characters. These dictionaries served an important purpose, not only in teaching beginners to approach ancient scripts but also in spreading this new knowledge to an enlarged circle among the Chinese intelligentsia.

Before concluding this chapter, something should be said about the attitude of Chang T'ai-yen (Ping-lin). Tung gives a vivid account of what he called the archenemy who stood in the way of developing the study of these newly discovered materials. And Chang T'ai-yen is important, because he was considered the most prominent epigraphist of his time and he was politically a revolutionary. Tung's account of Chang T'ai-yen's attitude toward the oracle bone inscriptions reads:

Chang T'ai-yen was one of those scholars who were skeptical of the oracle inscriptions and criticized any study of them. He maintained oracle inscriptions were not mentioned in the old documents and therefore the inscribed bones must be products of forgers of much later periods. It is most improbable, he argued, that shells and bones could have remained in the earth for three thousand years without decaying. Therefore Chang maintained that Lo Chên-yü, who believed in those inscriptions, must be thoroughly condemned.[20]

It is said that Chang's idea remained unchanged even after scientific excavation at Anyang confirmed the existence of these newly discovered precious documents. There is a graceful note on Chang T'ai-yen's innermost feeling toward these ancient relics which bear the Yin inscription related in this anecdote: "On one of Chang's birthdays, his chief disciple Huang Chi-kang sent him a birthday gift, oblong in shape and wrapped in red paper, which appeared to be box of edible delicacies; afterwards, when the old man tore off the wrappings, he found the four volumes of *Yin-hsü shu-ch'i ch'ien-pien* by Lo Chên-yü . . . ."

The anecdote end by merely mentioning that this birthday gift from his beloved disciple was not cast away; but the volumes found a place on the old man's bed, beside his pillow—evidently he actually read some of these condemned pseudo-inscriptions!

3 Field Method

As Demonstrated by Western Geologists, Paleontologists, and Archaeologists in China in the Early Twentieth Century

THIS CHAPTER is designed to give a general explanation of how Western learning in conjunction with traditional Chinese cultivation of antiquarian study confluently gave birth to archaeology in modern China.

It has often been questioned why, in the long tradition of Chinese culture, in which learning in general and antiquity as a special branch of study have enjoyed such a long history, investigation of the past never extended beyond the limits of book reading and treasure hunting. This pointed question undoubtedly deserves a certain amount of discussion. But if we go into the query at length, we may have to say a great deal about the traditional methods of learning, involving epistemology, philosophy, problems of value, and so on. This is definitely not the place to deal with all these big questions, although they are certainly in one way or another related to the query raised above. There is, however, a relatively simple answer, which can at least summarize Chinese traditional attitudes toward what is considered learning, and which may be helpful to those looking for a detailed explanation of the nature of the problem. Let us quote Mencius, in *T'eng-wen-kung:* "There is the saying, 'Some labour with their minds, and some labour with their strength. Those who labour with their minds govern others; those who labour with their strength are governed by others. . . .'" [1] Adherence to this maxim, and others like it, led to the following results:

1. Beginning with the Sung dynasty, every schoolboy's mentality had been molded by the sayings of Confucius and Mencius, which he has committed himself to memorize.

2. Once patternized, it becomes difficult to deviate from the standard.

3. There is a certain amount of self-satisfaction which all mental workers find in these sayings of Mencius quoted above—an egoism, that only modern psychology could adequately explain.

The general result of this education, as might be expected, is not only to accept the saying of Mencius as a general truth with regard to all social arrangements, but also to accept it as a standard for intellectual pursuits. To labor with the mind was gradually limited to book readings, especially after the invention of printing (which, as everybody knows, took place at least earlier than the Northern Sung dynasty).

On the other hand, if we take a look at the development of archaeology in the West, we find that at the close of the nineteenth century, anthropology had already developed into a special department of research, and archaeology under its influence also had gained status in the highly specialized prehistoric research inaugurated by the French prehistorian Jacques Boucher de Perthes (1788–1868), who started his search for evidences of human industry on the banks of the Somme as early as 1830,[2] nearly thirty years before the publication of Charles Darwin's *Origin of Species.* Yet as late as 1899, when D. G. Hogarth, director of the British school at Athens, still held the belief that archaeology of material evidences alone was the "Lesser Archaeology," the prevailing opinion was that only those finds which could be illuminated by literary documents, for example, those of Mariette, Layard, Newton, or Schliemann, constructed the "Greater Archaeology." [3]

From the beginning of this century, field workers in geology, paleontology, and archaeology spread across the world and field data gained importance by leaps and bounds. Old China, for centuries a hunting spot for European imperialism, was forced to open her door widely for whatever the "superior white power" liked to do, including field work in science. Geologists, geographers, and paleontologists as well as fortune hunters rushed to the Far East, particularly China. Among them were, as always, some real workers, a number of them true scientists, but, like political adventurers, they came and went freely without leaving the slightest trace on Chinese soil. Neither did they care, except, perhaps, for some missionary workers.

It was only after the revolution of 1911 that educated Chinese began to wake up. As it had in Europe, the "field method" as a way of learning established its influence on the Chinese mentality. The dual division of human labor set up by Mencius was "gone with the wind," together with the required reading of the "Four Books." [4]

The revolution gave rise to fundamental changes not only in the politics and social structure of Eastern Asia, but, even more importantly, in the mentality of the educated class, who gradually changed their outlook on life.

It was in the early Republican era, in 1916, that the Geological Survey under government order was first organized in Peking, as an agency of the Ministry of Agriculture and Commerce. This institution in its initial stage was fortunately in the hands of a well-known geologist educated in England, who combined mental vigor with a genius for scientific organization. Above all, he was dedicated to the promotion of Western science in his country; his name in English was V. K. Ting. [5]

With the Geological Survey as a center of his scientific activity, naturally Ting's first task was, as a matter of government policy and also for practical needs, to find mining deposits—of iron, coal, and other important minerals. To fulfill this official function, the newly established official organ certainly had plenty to do. Even more important to mention for our purposes, the surveying work was gradually extended to paleontology and still later to prehistoric archaeology. By this time university curricula already included departments of geology and paleontology so that university students also got acquainted with "field work" as a method of acquiring firsthand scientific knowledge. When Professor Wang Kuo-wei was asked (1925–26) to give a course on Chinese paleography in the Ts'inghua Research Institute of National Learning, he divided the course data into two major groups, which he called "book data" and "underground data." This may be taken as definite evidence that the influence of the field method of geological research had already reached the traditional scholars.

Since field method in Western science developed almost a century before its influence reached China, both the nature of problems investigated and techniques of operation had undergone, during the century, evolutionary changes. In fact the idea of "Evolution" itself, in scientific terms, became definite only within that century even in the West. But historically speaking, this basic idea, through the famous translation of Yen Fu, reached China earlier than other scientific conceptions and made a deeper impression on Chinese mentality than did any missionary attempts to introduce the West to China.[6]

So by the time the Geological Survey was first set up, the psychological attitude of the Chinese intelligentsia had already encompassed the idea of science in general, and the theory of evolution was already deep in their consciousness. Whatever difficulties the Geological Survey had to face were more or less matters of practical politics rather than ideology.

The Geological Survey in its early history achieved several important administrative results. The most important of these was the training of a number of field surveyors, who, in addition to the fundamental knowledge of geology and related sciences, had also to acquire the modern method of land surveying. Each surveyor had to possess the physical capacity to carry his own instruments and to walk on foot no matter how long the journey might be. This was of course a definite break with the traditional training of "scholars" in old China, who labored with their minds only.

It took quite a few years for V. K. Ting, the founder of the Survey, to accomplish the initial program. When the training of the first batch of surveyors was completed, he began to send them to the field for practical work. The author knew personally several of these first surveyors. They were all well-disciplined and hard workers; later on, each of them was assigned to a definite region for specialization. In surveying, as well as in geology and paleontology, most of them have rendered useful national service. To this group of pioneers, the field of not only geology but Western science in general in modern China owes a great debt indeed.

In the execution of this initial program, V. K. Ting was able to gain substantial support from a number of foreign scientists; some of them actually came to China and worked. The author would like to mention five whose reputation is international and who worked in north China and helped the Geological Survey directly or indirectly, in the formative stage: A. W. Grabau (American), J. G. Andersson (Swedish), Davidson Black (Canadian), J. F. Weidenreich (German), and Pierre Teilhard de Chardin (French).

The first two, A. W. Grabau and J. G. Andersson, are directly associated with the scientific work of the Survey; the next two, Davidson Black and J. F. Weidenreich, were directors of the Cenozoic Laboratory, also connected with the Survey. The last, Father Teilhard de Chardin, when he was in China, was working in a Catholic mission which was concerned more with science than with religion; so Pierre Teilhard is better known to the Chinese people as a paleontologist and archaeologist than as a priest.

In the early Republican era, especially between, say, 1915 and 1925, Peking was a city of new ideas, political and social as well as intellectual. Most of the scientists in the above list were in Peking and doing actual scientific research. Among them, Professor A. W. Grabau was commonly acknowledged to be the leader of the group by both leading Chinese scientists and the learned in the foreign community. His special task was to help the Survey publish scientific papers, especially *Paleontologia Sinica*. His official position was Professor of Geology at the National Peking Government University, and also, at the same time, he served as chief paleontologist of the Survey.[7]

The publication of *Paleontologia Sinica* helped to provide the capital of China with both a new branch of knowledge and a new method to acquire such knowledge. In this respect, it can be considered an altogether new feature as compared with traditional Chinese culture.

Most of these volumes were published in European languages, mainly English. The elementary idea of this publication, under the auspices of the Survey, was to bring scientific knowledge about its various finds to the attention of specialists and the scientific public. As far as educated circles in China were concerned, only a few specially trained individuals could be benefitted. But there is another aspect of the influence of these serial publications to be taken into consideration. They provided a model for the presentation of scientific data, as well as for methods of collection and preservation, in addition to accurate descriptions and cautious deductions—all these are of course familiar to scientific readers. In the course of time, when the younger generation of Chinese had mastered a European language and been initiated into modern science, they gradually looked toward these publications as a standard and a yardstick for measuring the value of various scientific activities in many branches of related research, especially in the fields of biology and archaeology. From a historical viewpoint, this development is important in the sense that there is no such model in traditional China. But it has remained a problem how to translate this model into the Chinese language, so that the average man in China, if he were interested, could easily understand and locate the source materials.

Let us take up the problem in a practical way. I propose to illustrate the nature of the problem by some analysis of the influence of the achievements of the five eminent scientists mentioned above.

Foremost among the five was A. W. Grabau, who worked the longest time and ended his life in Peking. He was the man who did the teaching in the university as well as editing the serial publications of *Paleontologia Sinica.*

It would be rather pretentious for me to comment upon Grabau's contributions to the science of geology and paleontology. Still, it may be said that his well-known theory of the polar drift, and the uplift of the Himalayan Mountains and the Tibetan Plateau in the Miocene period, which Grabau considered a phenomenon of crustal movement important and critical for the development of human origins, although it is now almost forgotten by the public, created a deep impression in scientific circles. The Natural History Museum of New York City sent several expeditions to Central Asia and Mongolia to hunt for man's ancestors on the basis of this theory. Although these expeditions did not achieve what they aimed at, there were many lateral results that were unexpected but nevertheless interesting and important, for instance, the discovery of dinosaur's eggs. Meantime, parallel endeavors undertaken by other groups of natural scientists made the amazing discovery of Sinanthropus Pekinensis near the ancient capital of China.

Grabau's scientific influence in educational circles, it seems to me, was much more important in his life time. He possessed a charming and fascinating personality, agreeable and attractive to all scientists gathered at that time in the city of Peking. Whether one liked his theories or not, it seemed to everybody a pleasure and a privilege to talk with the Grand Old Man. The first generation of Chinese geologists attached themselves to him affectionately, and the younger generation, most of whom were his disciples, loved and respected him. The author, merely an anthropologist by training and an archaeologist through opportunity, met Dr. Grabau only about a dozen times at most, yet the personality of this old man remains to this day an unforgettable impression. This point is important, because it is closely related to the growth of scientific mentality in the formative period of Chinese science, and his influence was naturally carried by his Chinese friends and Chinese pupils to a large learning circles, at a time when science was becoming immensely popular.

Dr. J. G. Andersson came to China in the early Republican era; he was engaged by the government to give practical advice on surveying China's mineral deposits. The story is still told that at that time all the big powers who had extraterritorial interests in China wanted to send their scientists to China with the idea of getting first-hand knowledge of China's mineral resources—especially coal and iron. The competition among the big powers for this job was very keen. The Chinese government, however, decided to choose an expert adviser from none of them, but gave the job to J. G. Andersson, a Swede, from a nation considered one of the few European countries without any imperialistic ambitions. The choice was made probably at the suggestion of Dr. V. K. Ting, director of the Geological Survey.

This was indeed a fortunate choice. J. G. Andersson came to China before A. W. Grabau. In the beginning, his work was entirely in the field, traveling in north China where mineral deposits were prospective. J. G. Andersson was however, not a narrow-minded technical expert. He had a broad intellectual background, and during his travels he always kept his eye open for anything of scientific interest. For this reason, his discoveries in his early wandering journey were numerous and of various natures. In *Children of the Yellow Earth,* a book for popular consumption in 1934, he had this to say in the Foreword:

By a series of fortunate circumstances I was on several occasions the pioneer. In 1914 I was the first to stumble upon the organic origin of a stromatolite ore. In 1918 I discovered collenia nodules and recognized their connection with similar "fossils" in the pre-Cambrian area of North America. In the same year we discovered the first Hipparion field in China made known to science. In 1919 we found the beaver fauna at Ertemte in Mongolia. 1921 was a red-letter year: the Neolithic dwelling-site at Yang Shao Ts'un, the Eocene mammals on the Yellow River, the Sha Kuo T'un cave deposit in Fengtien and still the more remarkable cave discovery at Chou K'ou Tien, which became world famous by the work of those who followed after us.[8]

Andersson's discoveries included many other items. Although most of these were geological and paleontological, what attracted him most seems to have been archaeological findings.

These archaeological discoveries are no doubt of great importance. What the author wishes to point out here is that Dr. Andersson was in fact the first Western scientist to demonstrate, by actual achievements, the effectiveness of the field method in the investigation of Chinese antiquity. As he stated himself, in these scientific travels he was frequently accompanied by well-trained junior assistants and a troop of untrained but intelligent workers. All his disciples followed the master faithfully and naturally also learned his method of working.

J. G. Andersson's scientific work started before the formal establishment of the Geological Survey in 1916. After this new, official organization began its field work under the able direction of Dr. V. K. Ting, Andersson's field collections were naturally encouraged and gained more publicity in scientific circles. He also received more substantial help financially, and obtained more trained assistants. An increasingly larger team of specialists could appreciate the merits of his various discoveries and evaluate the more abstract theoretical problems which Andersson had always kept in mind.

Among the various scientific achievements of this distinguished Swedish geologist, his archaeological discoveries in north China are perhaps best known to the general public. There are a number of reasons for the special reputation which he gained, and which he certainly deserved. The prehistoric site he excavated at Yang-shao in 1921 is remarkable because it is historically the first one uncovered in China. Before this discovery, only speculations about ancient China flourished, derived either from legendary accounts or from fantastic imagination. Second, the excavated materials of Yang-shao Culture indicated an advanced agricultural society, containing elements related not only to the traditional legendary accounts but, what is altogether novel, to central and western Asiatic prehistory. Third, the location of the Yangshao site is almost in the center of the Yellow River plain where the early history of China developed.

So, this discovery immediately attracted worldwide attention, including that of many conservative Chinese historians. The title of Andersson's first paper in Chinese and English, "An Early Chinese Culture," of course induced even the archaeologically uninitiated to pay some attention.[9] A further reason for the popular attention attached to this discovery was that similar to the appearance of oracle bone inscriptions in 1898–99: the time and the learning atmosphere in Peking in 1921 were just ready to accept such a discovery. Although there was no archaeological curriculum in the university, traditional antiquarian study under the influence of the May 4th movement of 1919, the student movement which initiated the intellectual modernization of China, had already advanced to a stage where scholars had full cognizance of the need for field work in the investigation of China's ancient past.

The detailed story of this first discovery of Chinese prehistory has already been told by Dr. Andersson himself in his *Children of the Yellow Earth,* in which a complete chapter is devoted to "We Discover the First Prehistoric Villages" (1934). Certain essential points in this chapter relate especially to the development of field methods in China's study of antiquity:

1. In 1920, Andersson sent his collector Liu Chang-shan to Loyang and the adjacent region to collect fossil vertebrates. Liu returned in December with a collection which included, in addition to the fossils, a large package of stone implements, consisting of several hundreds of stone axes, knives, and other artifacts. Liu told Andersson that all the stone artifacts were purchased from "the inhabitants of a single village," namely, Yangshao Ts'un. This led Andersson to investigate the site personally.

2. Yangshao Ts'un is a village in Mien-ch'ih Hsien. In 1921 Andersson went to Mien-ch'ih Hsien to further his investigation. He arrived on April 18, and then went to Yangshao Ts'un, six miles north of the district. The following account is Andersson's description of the site discovered in the village of Yangshao Ts'un.

About a km. south of village of Yang Shao Ts'un I had to traverse a great ravine, a real miniature canyon, which was subsequently a very notable feature of our topographical survey of the district. When I had reached the northern side of the ravine I saw in the side of a gully a very interesting section. At the bottom, the red Tertiary clay was exposed and it is with a distinct contact overlaid by a peculiar loose soil, full of ashes and containing fragments of pottery. It seemed not improbable that this might be the deposit from which the stone age implements had been derived. After some minutes' search, I found at the very bottom of the deposit a small piece of fine red ware with black painting on a beautifully polished surface . . . it therefore seemed to me inconceivable that such clay vessels could be found together with stone implements.

Somewhat dejected I felt that I had followed a track which would only lead me astray, and I thought it safer to return to my geological-paleontological research. . . .

Meanwhile I lay in the evenings and reflected on the Yang Shao Ts'un riddle. . . .

I decided to devote a whole day to a search in these ravine walls. . . . After a few hours' search, I extracted from the untouched ashy soil a fine example of the stone adze . . . "pen." . . . During the course of the day I made other interesting discoveries and it soon became clear that we here had to do with a deposit of unusual magnitude, rich in artifacts, especially fragments of pots, including the fine, polished polychrome ware to which I have referred above. . . .[10]

3. Andersson, when by a lucky chance he stumbled across the Yangshao prehistoric site, could not at the time of discovery recognize its real significance. This recognition came only on a subsequent trip to Peking where in the library of the Geological Survey he found the report by R. Pumpelly of the American geologist's 1903–4 expedition to Anau in Russian Turkestan.[11] From these reports, Andersson began to realize that painted pottery could have existed in protohistoric time. Then his enthusiasm for the puzzling discovery was greatly enhanced and he was able, with the enlightened encouragement of the director of the Geological Survey, to get the permission of the Chinese government, and the assistance of some trained geologists, to organize a digging party in the autumn of the same year (1921); the field work started toward the end of October. The results of the excavation are very well known through various reports, both technical and popular.

This epoch-making scientific endeavor in China marked the beginning of field archaeology in one of the oldest countries in Eurasia; it was almost half a century after French anthropologists had revealed painted pottery in Susa of Mesopotamia. But in Eastern Asia, which Western historians usually considered as an outskirt of Indo-European civilization, these findings once more reminded historians that East and West were not as separated as most people believed.

To return to the actual findings of Andersson's excavation at the prehistoric site of Yangshao Ts'un, the artifacts excavated were divisible into several groups. It was, however, the ceramic finds that excited world-wide interest. In this group of pot-sherds, the most striking ones are the painted pots as pointed out above. Later, these finds were sent to Sweden for special investigation, on which Dr. T. G. Arne issued a monographic report published by the Survey in 1925.[12] In Dr. Arne's report, all the painted pot-sherds are beautifully illustrated by color plates; some are reconstructed and the painted designs and other technical details are all given careful analysis; and when possible the sherds are compared with similar finds from other regions, especially those of Anau in Russian Turkestan. It is perhaps unnecessary to remind the reader that by this time, M. de Morgan's well-known discovery of Susa had been known to Western archaeologists for over thirty years.[13]

As far as archaeology in China is concerned the other type of Yangshao ceramics were even more interesting, and no less exciting in the light of the ancient history of China. I mean, of course, what is considered the more common type, known as the coarse gray ware. In this group, it was found that many kinds of tripods could be reconstructed, which have been classified as the *ting* or *li* type, corresponding in shape and structure to ancient Chinese bronzes of these shapes that had been recorded and described in the literature from the Chou dynasty onward for over two thousand years. The unearthing of clay-made *ting* and *li* convinced the conservative school among Chinese historians and antiquarians that field archaeology indeed held a key to the study of Chinese antiquities. In due course, I shall discuss the Yangshao discovery and its influence again. Here, however, it is more important to go on with the beneficial influence of some other foreign scientists who also worked in China at this time.

Next I should like to discuss Professor Davidson Black, who was a Canadian and was appointed Professor of Anatomy when the Peking Union Medical College (P.U.M.C.) was founded by the Rockefeller Foundation. Black's scientific work was mainly concerned with the investigation of the physical characteristics of the Chinese people. The anatomy department of P.U.M.C., like all other medical schools, started to accumulate skeletal materials of all dissected bodies as soon as the teaching of anatomy began such dissection, and the skeletal materials were deposited in the department in storage. When J. G. Andersson obtained permission to excavate at Yangshao Ts'un, he assigned the task of grave-digging to another geologist and paleontogist, Dr. Otto Zdansky, and at the same time he also invited Professor Davidson Black to visit the dig. According to Andersson, Black in "most important respects assisted in the investigation of the burial ground."

Later on, Andersson asked Professor Black to prepare a monographic study of these skeletal materials on which the latter cooperated enthusiastically.[14] Dr. Black compared in his professional way the prehistoric skeletons with the department's collection of those of the north China population, and also with some non-Chinese human bones; he applied extensively the biometric techniques developed in Karl Pearsons' laboratory in London. After a thorough analysis of the available and related materials, he came to the important conclusion that these prehistoric inhabitants of neolithic time showed an assemblage of physical characteristics in no respect markedly different from those of the present-day northern Chinese, except that some of the Kansu skeletons of the prehistoric period seemed to indicate some slight deviation.

Black's study of the physical traits of the northern Chinese remains, up to the present day, one of most frequently quoted papers on the physical anthropology of the Chinese, both because its quality is high, and because, as so often happens, anthropologists interested in this problem are comparatively rare.

Black's reputation, however, does not rest on this monograph alone. As is well known, he was the first scientist to study the remains of *Sinanthropus,* and he died in his laboratory while working on the Chou-k'ou-tien fossil man on March 15, 1934.

Peking man, the popular name of *Sinanthropus,* was discovered in the neighborhood of the city of Peking at Chou-k'ou-tien, also as a result of Dr. J. G. Andersson's wide interest in fossil collecting. Let us again read what Andersson says about the early part of the Chou-k'ou-tien exploration:

One day in February 1918 I met in Peking, J. McGregor Gibb, professor of chemistry at the mission university which at that time bore the somewhat pretentious title of Peking University. He knew that I was interested in fossils and consequently he told me that he had just been out at Chou K'ou Tien, about 50 km. southwest of Peking, a place which I have already described on a couple of occasions during my story.
. . . Professor Gibb had himself visited the place and had brought back to Peking various fragments of the bone-bearing clay. . . .
Gibb's description was so alluring that I visited the spot on the 22nd–23rd March in the same year.[15]

After he visited Chou-k'ou-tien, Andersson planned a systematic exploration. Eight years later in 1926, when the grandfather of the present King of Sweden, as Crown Prince, paid a visit to the capital of China, the discovery of the first indication of *Sinanthropus* was announced. At an academic reception for the royal visit, a number of eminent scholars gathered and read their learned papers—chiefly on archaeology. The well-known scholar Liang Ch'i-ch'ao was among them, but the remaining members of the audience were either foreign scholars or English-speaking Chinese professors. It was on this day that J. G. Andersson, on behalf of Professor C. Wiman, announced the latest result of the research work on the fossils collected at Chou-k'ou-tien by Zdansky as "the most important result of the whole of the Swedish work in China," [16] namely some hominid teeth.

The day of this meeting was October 22, 1926.

What followed was an internationally known scientific enterprise. Most important for China was the fact that, when scientists agree to cooperate, fruitful results seem to be a matter of course. The excavation at Chou-k'ou-tien was an example of truly international cooperation. Included were a number of distinguished scientists from America, Canada, Sweden, France, Great Britain, and Germany as well as the native Chinese. The organization was under the guiding hand of Dr. V. K. Ting who, with his experience and ingenuity, served as the honorary director of the Cenozoic Laboratory, of which the director was Professor Davidson Black. Dr. Black's scientific work was assisted by a Swedish scientist, Dr. Birger Bohlin, who was invited to start excavation at Chou-k'ou-tien, mainly with the aim of looking for fossil Hominidae. The Rockefeller Foundation financed the projected undertaking.

The scientific work carried at Chou-k'ou-tien lasted a long time. This gigantic task taught the budding generation of scientists in China several lessons of practical importance. While Dr. V. K. Ting helped to complete the initial stage of the Cenozoic Laboratory, it was the genius of its director, Professor Davidson Black, that guided the operation both in the difficult task of excavating rocky caves at Chou-k'ou-tien, and in systematically distributing the collection to competent scientists for specific studies. Above all, Professor Black himself took up the heavy task of investigating the fossil hominidae among the accumulated fossils from the limestone cave deposits at Chou-k'ou-tien.

After hewing and moving three thousand cubic meters of the cave deposits, Dr. Bohlin, a disciple trained by Professor C. Wiman from Sweden, on October 16, 1927, found a hominid tooth and personally handed this precious discovery to Dr. Black in P.U.M.C. three days later. This tooth was identified as the lower molar on

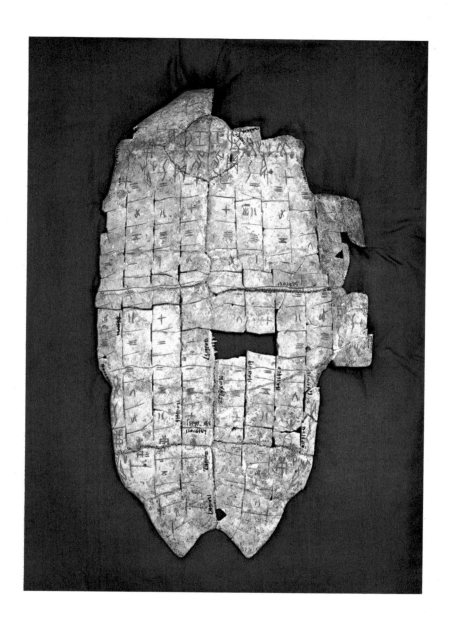

Plate 1. Inscribed tortoise shell from Hsiao-t'un

Plate 2. White pottery *tou*-dish

Plate 3. Marble horned bird

Plate 4. Marble owl

Plate 5. Marble tiger-headed monster

Plate 6. Music stone

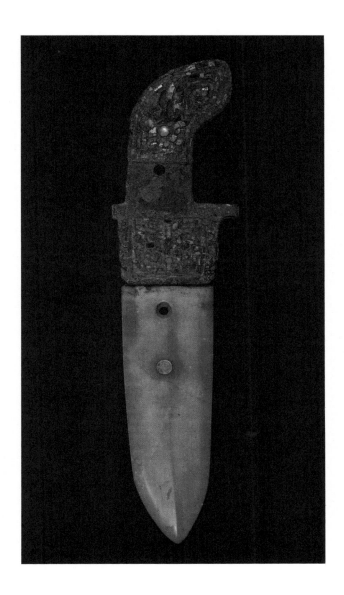

Plate 7. Jade halbert with bronze handle

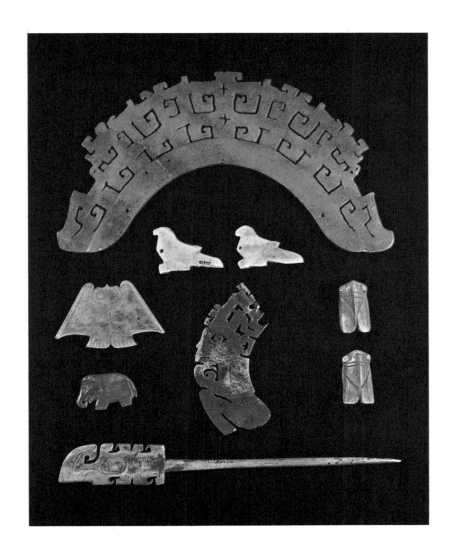

Plate 8. Precious stone artifacts: head ornament; pair of birds; bat; elephant; human figure in squatting position; cicadas; hairpin

Plate 9. Bronze tetrapod (*lu-ting*)

Plate 10. Bronze tetrapod (*niu-ting*)

Plate 11. The largest bronze tripod

Plate 12. Bronze *li*-tripod

Plate 13. Bronze *chia*-vessel

Plate 14. Bronze *chüeh*-cup

Plate 15. Bronze *ku*-beaker

Plate 16. Bronze *fang-i*–casket

Plate 17. Bronze *yu*-flask with a swinging handle

Plate 18. Pair of bronze *chih*-goblets

Plate 19. *Top:* bronze *yü*-basin; *bottom:* bronze *ssŭ-kuang* ▶

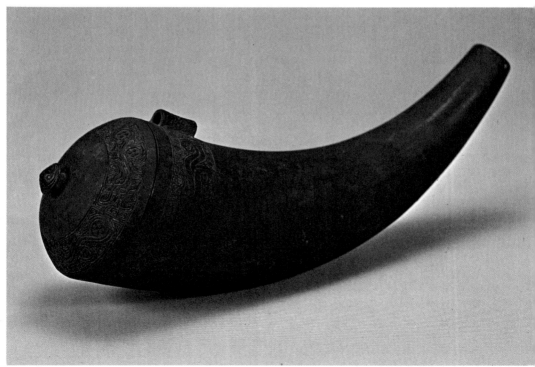

Plate 20. Bronze human mask

the left side; although somewhat worn, it was well preserved and complete with root. On the basis of this study, Davidson Black not only confirmed Wiman's identification; he went a step further in his ingenious speculation, and created a new hominid genus by naming it *Sinanthropus*, with the name of the species as *Pekinensis*.[17]

Continuing the field work, Bohlin was assisted in the next season by Dr. C. C. Young and W. C. Pei, both of whom played an important role in the Chou-k'ou-tien excavation.

To sum up, the scientific work carried out at Chou-k'ou-tien and in the Cenozoic Laboratory in Peking provided a tremendous stimulus to the younger generation of Chinese scientific researchers. Soon after, Young and Pei took up the field work at Chou-k'ou-tien following the departure of Dr. Bohlin. They were the discoverers of the first Peking Man's skull on December 2, 1929; this discovery was considered by many as the crowning achievement, fully justifying the enormous amount of money the Rockefeller Foundation had invested.

Dr. Black, after working continuously on the important discovery for half a dozen years, died of hard work in his own laboratory in P.U.M.C. as stated above. The necessity of finding a successor created a difficult problem. I have been informed that through V. K. Ting's recommendation, an international committee was organized, with Professor Elliot Smith as chairman, to select Black's successor. Dr. Franz Weidenreich was unanimously agreed upon by members of the selection committee, and received the appointment as director of the Cenozoic Laboratory to continue the important research.

If Davidson Black showed by his brilliant achievements his penetrating power in analyzing the fossil remains of Chou-k'ou-tien, Weidenreich, who succeeded him so competently, demonstrated a German thoroughness, which, in the eyes of the trained scientists of Oriental circles, had seldom been equalled by scientists of other nations. The successive volumes published in series D, *Paleontologia Sinica*, have fully proved these characteristics of German science. Weidenreich's scientific reports on *Sinanthropus* were not only masterpieces of anthropological reporting, they were also exemplary models of clarity and of minute, detailed examination both exhaustive and pointed. For Chinese workers, there is nothing in any European language concerning studies of human fossils comparable to these monographic reports on *Sinanthropus*.

As everybody knows, the valuable collection of Peking Man fossils were lost during World War II, and various efforts made to recover these important scientific specimens have all failed. Fortunately for the study of the early history of Hominidae, the complete reports by Davidson Black and Franz Weidenreich are available in most libraries all over the world.

The influence of the Chou-k'ou-tien excavation in China can hardly be exaggerated. In spite of many political changes, Chou-k'ou-tien has remained important to scientific workers to the present day.

Last, but certainly not least, the scientific work of the French paleontologist Pierre Teilhard de Chardin illustrated, for the budding generation of Western trained scientists in China, a number of characteristics typical of French mentality. It has been commonly agreed that the highly specialized study of man's remote past is a French science, in which French archaeologists have led the world for nearly a century. Father Teilhard, when he arrived at China in the early 1930s, had already acquired considerable experience in Western Europe. He was in fact associated with the ill-fated work on the notorious *Eoanthropus,* which was proved to be a forgery. I believe it was for this reason that on October 22, 1926, when J. G. Andersson announced the discovery of the hominid tooth at Chou-k'ou-tien, Teilhard was the only person in the audience who cast some doubt and thought that the fossil specimen as illustrated by the lantern slides might prove to be the tooth of "a beast of prey." He wrote a note to Dr. Andersson stating his skepticism of Wiman's identification.

If later finds proved that Teilhard had misjudged—as he himself of course agreed—it only serves to indicate how open-minded a first rate scientist can and should be!

Teilhard's main scientific work in China was widespread both in subject and in geographic region. His field work and studies covered many kinds of scientific tasks, including paleontology, prehistoric archaeology, geological stratification, glaciology, and so on.

Père Teilhard came to the Far East at the invitation of Father Emile Licent, founder of the Huang-Ho-Pai-Ho Museum in Tientsin. Father Licent in 1920, through his exploration in northwestern China, had discovered at Ch'ing-yang Fu in eastern Kansu province a rich deposit of the Hipparion Fauna. Removing the loess which covered the Hipparion clay, Licent found at the bottom of the loess formation pieces of quartz which appeared to him to have been modified by human hand. In 1922 Licent, acting on information from other Catholic priests working in Mongolia, went to Sjara-Osso-Gol. There he found another bone deposit which looked so promising that he decided to invite Teilhard de Chardin from Paris to join the scientific investigation of these deposits in northwestern China and the Ordos region of Inner Mongolia.

The archaelogical explorations of the two Catholic fathers—at Ninghsia Fu, Shui-tung-kou, and Sjara-Osso-Gol, where they discovered old stone cultural deposits including many hundreds of kgs. of stone implements, mixed with charcoal—are well known to European prehistorians, as the results of their diggings were published in French. The stone implements from these paleolithic sites at Sjara-Osso-Gol are mostly made of red quartzite and silicious limestone, which are said to be commonly found in the rubble deposited in gravels of the cultural stratum. Some of the implements —scrapers, drills, and blades—are of considerable size, reaching 17cm. in length.

The main conclusion of their study of these important discoveries and associated fauna was that this culture belongs to the Pleistocene period, during which the loess deposits were formed.

These French scientists worked in splendid isolation, communicating only with their fellow workers in Paris, and their publications appeared only in French. The author had the fortune to meet Teilhard de Chardin in 1924–25 at the home of Dr. V. K. Ting. Later on, when the Catholic scientist joined the newly organized Geological Society of China, we met more frequently. At that time Père Teilhard became known to geological and paleontological circles in Peking and Tientsin, and came to be considered the "youngest and the most brilliant 'paleontologist'" in north China, a comment made by A. W. Grabau when Teilhard received the Grabau Medal.

Père Teilhard was invited to be a regular member of the Cenozoic Laboratory and frequently visited Chou-k'ou-tien when the excavation was in progress. Dr. C. C. Young was his closest coworker in China. For instance, they jointly made a study of the fauna discovered from the Anyang excavations. Teilhard's whole interest seemed to be concentrated on "Early Man in China," which he investigated from both a geological and a paleontological angle in addition to his excellent research on prehistoric artifacts. While he was still in Peking, he wrote a memoir with this title, published by the Institut de Géobiologie (Peking), in 1941.

Teilhard's influence on the spread of science in China was indeed many-sided. He seldom talked. What was exemplary was the manner in which he did his scientific research. When the author was in charge of the Anyang excavation, Père Teilhard and Dr. C. C. Young paid us a visit. They spent a few hours on the spot, carefully examining our method of working and recording. While he was there, he happened to pick up a fragment of animal tooth tinged with green color, and commented, "This is a tiger tooth, evidently buried together with some bronze." Then he examined the stone implements recovered from the excavation. He took a long look at the sample of "what is called a green stone axe" without saying a word. When his opinion was asked, he remarked: "This kind of stone axe seems to be very widely spread in north China. Wherever it is found in north China, it is petrologically the same and of the same shape!" Père Teilhard was a field scientist; although a man of few words he was both charming and dignified; whenever he did speak, his words indicated a profound knowledge. He had a quick mind, and, above all, he was always inspiring and could on occasion be witty and full of humor.

His personality touched Chinese men of science deeply, although only a few had the privilege of knowing him. His *Early Man in China* was indeed a classic among all the popular books of science published in this period in China.

I have given a somewhat detailed description of five eminent men of science and some of their closest associates. This does not mean that there were no other scientific visitors working in this area when China began to take Western learning, particularly science, seriously, and to demonstrate a conscious wish to incorporate the teaching of science into the Chinese educational system. In geological science, there were men like Otto Zdansky and Walter Granger; in geography, Sven Hedin; in archaelogy, N. C. Nelson, Henri Breuil, and so on, who all made contributions to the building up of modern science in China. But the service of Grabau, Andersson, Black, Weidenrich, and Teilhard de Chardin is distinguished from that of others by their close contact with Chinese minds. This contact was naturally much more contagious than written reports; consequently the cumulative effects soon become overwhelming and irresistible.

4 Early Period

of Planned Digging in Anyang

In the first three chapters, the historical background that led to the development of modern archaeology in China has been related, with special reference to the discovery of the oracle bone inscriptions by antiquarians educated in China's traditional disciplines and to the exemplary influence exerted by European scientists who did actual field work in China. At the time that these two sets of research activities converged, the new generation of the Chinese renaissance found modern archaeology quite acceptable.

Fu Ssŭ-nien was appointed acting director of the Institute of History and Philology of the National Academy in May 1928, when he was also dean of the school of Arts of Chungshan University in Canton. Fu had been one of the leading spirits in the May 4th movement, deeply learned in all the Chinese classical studies, but alertly critical, and revolutionary against the old educational system. After the May 4th movement he went to Europe (1919–26), studying in both England and Germany, not aiming at a degree, but devouring and absorbing Western ideas that interested him. He returned to China in 1927, the year that the Nationalists established Nanking as the capital of China. Chungshan University was at that time a center of learning which attracted all the younger men with new ideas.

When Fu was given the task of creating a research institute in history and philology, his quick-witted mind created a slogan frequently quoted by contemporary scholars. A free translation would be:

> Up to the very top of the blue heaven
> down to the bottom of the yellow spring,
> move (your) hands, move (your) feet,
> search for source materials!"

This slogan in the original Chinese is couched in two phrases of seven characters each, like a poetic couplet. The first phrase is a quotation from the well-known poem of Po Chü-i, "The Ever Lasting Wrong," and the second was coined to lay emphasis on "Labor with Strength," that is, "walking and moving to search for source materials." Fu's long study in Western Europe had shown him that what was deficient in Chinese traditional education was the artificial division between body and mind. He was convinced that unless this barrier was torn down, there was no hope of achieving a new way to obtain scientific knowledge. In his early days in Europe, he had registered in a department of psychology, but he did not stay with it to become a specialist. This introductory training, however, was evidently sufficient to provide him with an understanding of the intricate relationship between man's body and man's mind, and impressed on his adolescent consciousness the basic idea that the root of the human soul is deeply buried in the whole frame of his bodily structure which modern medical science is devoted to examining in detail, while modern psychology specializes in studying the mental aspect.

Fu was a noted man of letters before he went to Europe. After the European contact in the period following World War I, he exemplified those Chinese scholars who had considered the problem of cultural differences between the East and the West and had made concrete recommendations to amalgamate the twin systems. He created his slogan and expounded it in detail in the Foreword to the first issue of the *Bulletin of the Institute of History and Philology*, published while he was still in Canton and the institute was still in a preparatory stage.[1] The slogan worked, for Fu possessed, in addition to his profound classical learning, a penetrating knowledge of Western science. He was also one of the ablest administrators among scholars of his generation.

Fu's slogan, it must be emphasized, did not stop with words. It has actually been the fundamental policy governing the research work carried on for over forty years by the institute he founded.

While the institute was still in the preparatory stage, the acting director sent Tung Tso-pin to Anyang for a preliminary investigation of the site long noted for its production of the inscribed oracle bones. At this time (1928), many epigraphists, among whom Lo Chên-yü was the leader, believed that thirty years' continued search for the *chia-ku-wen* had recovered all the buried treasure. Further searches were bound to fail and it would be foolish to attempt them.

Fu, one of the few gifted with an understanding of modern archaeology and scientific technology, did not take that current notion for granted. Tung Tso-pin was not a university graduate; he was, in 1928, just over thirty years old and a natural follower of the May 4th movement, full of new ideas and eager to search for materials for his own study. Director Fu sent him to Anyang for a preliminary investigation for two simple reasons: Tung was a native of Honan, which would facilitate his work in a number of ways, and he was intellectually alert, although not an antiquarian even in the traditional sense.

In fact, neither of the two scholars—Director Fu, who initiated the idea of field operations at Anyang, nor Tung Tso-pin, who was sent there because he was a native of Honan with an inborn intelligence and receptive mind—had any experience in modern archaeology. Tung stated in his report that his job had been to look at the site and find out whether there were still some oracle bones worth digging, or whether the site was really exhausted as Lo Chên-yü and his cohorts believed.

For this purpose, prior to his first official visit to the site, Tung made an unofficial, personal visit to reconnoiter conditions there. After he arrived at Anyang on August 12, 1928, he first visited a number of the local gentry, among whom were the director of the middle school of Changte, the owners of several antiquities shops, and the man noted for his forgeries of the unknown inscriptions—

Lan Pao-kuang. In these visits, Tung obtained a great deal of information about general conditions and about local opinions current in the city concerning the oracle bones. On the next day, he paid a personal visit to the village of Hsiao-t'un, accompanied by a guide. There, many villagers showed him tiny fragments of inscribed bones for sale; he purchased more than one hundred such broken fragments at the price of three silver dollars. The villagers told Tung that in the past when curio dealers came to the village to buy they did not care for these small fragments which the local folk, however, picked up and stored at home. So at the time of Tung's first visit to Hsiao-t'un, almost every home in the village had some "tzŭ-ku-t'ou" in its keeping. Occasionally there appeared some larger pieces for which the owner would ask a price of four to five dollars per piece, which Tung then considered exorbitant.

Meanwhile Tung hired a young boy from the village who guided him to a place where oracle bones had been dug out. The place located by the youthful guide was a mound of heaped-up sand which at first impressed Tung as contradictory to what Lo Chên-yü had described in his 1915 visit. Both Lo's diary account and the information Tung got from the director of the middle school in the city agreed that the localities where oracle bones might be hidden were to be found on the cultivated cotton farms. The sandy mound by the side of the Huan River was nonproductive land for farming. But while examining a particular spot on the western side of the sandy mound and near the cotton field, Tung discovered several newly refilled holes which had obviously been dug recently, and by the side of one of the three refilled pits, he picked up a fragment of oracle bone without inscriptions. This piece of evidence gathered at the spot, together with what the villagers had offered for sale and the information Tung had collected in the city, led him to the important conclusion that the hidden treasure of inscribed oracle bones at Hsiao-t'un had not, as Lo Chên-yü and his followers maintained, been completely exhausted. Tung believed, after his first preparatory visit to Hsiao-t'un, that the site was still worth digging. So he reported, and he also planned a preliminary excavation.

After reading the report of Tung's first preparatory Anyang trip, Director Fu Ssŭ-nien, without the least hesitation, took the immediate steps needed to begin a preliminary digging at Hsiao-t'un. This new venture, although not enormously expensive, had no budget. After considerable negotiation with the headquarters of the National Academy, Fu Ssŭ-nien succeeded in getting the necessary support: a sum of one thousand dollars in Chinese National Currency, at that time by no means a small sum. Even with this amount of money, the field workers had to pay for all their equipment, including surveying and photographic instruments and other necessary materials. In due time Tung was able to organize a band of workers, partly voluntary and partly paid, including six principal members who in one capacity or another cooperated with him in accomplishing the first official season (October 7–31, 1928).[2] This preliminary digging conducted by Tung Tso-pin in October 1928 has always been referred to as the first season of the Anyang excavations.

Tung arrived at Anyang on October 7, 1928, armed with the necessary official documents from the central government in Nanking and the provincial government at K'aifeng. The provincial government of Honan had selected two officials to accompany Tung Tso-pin to the Anyang district in order to facilitate his work. The full report of Tung's first official trip to Anyang was printed by lithograph in K'aifeng in the winter and later reprinted as the first article in the four issues of *Preliminary Reports of Excavations at Anyang* (1929 Dec.–1933 June).[3] Tung's report after the first official trip not only concluded the antiquarian period of armchair studies of old curiosities, but, what is more important, paved the way for systematic excavation of these famous ruins.

It is of great interest and historical importance to note some of the concrete results of this first trial digging and also some of the opinions expressed by the participants. Let us see first what was done in the experimental exploration of this famous site. The main points are:

1. The party carried out the first surveying work.

2. Three locations were selected for actual digging. Two (Sections I and II) were on a farm northeast of the village of Hsiao-t'un, near the west bank of the Huan River which partly surrounds the farming area of this village. Another locality (Section III) was within the village itself.

3. Of the 784 pieces of inscribed oracle bones dug out, 555 were tortoise shells and 229 were scapular bones of cattle. In addition, there were more than a thousand fragments of uninscribed bones.

4. Besides the oracle bones, the other finds included:

Bored bone implements	56
Animal bones	62
Human skeltons	3
Shell and cowry fragments	96
Stones or jades	42
Bronze fragments	11
Iron fragments	10
Potteries	49

5. The scope and extension of the excavation, according to the preliminary surveying work, might cover the whole area of the farmland north and northeast of the village and the village site itself; it might be extended far to the south.

6. The Waste of Yin seemed to have been formed after the region suffered some big flood, originating, according to Tung's interpretation, from the Yellow River, which at that time followed a course quite close to Hsiao-t'un.

7. The inscribed oracle bones were excavated from the following pits in the three localities where trial diggings were made:

SECTION I	Pit 9
SECTION II	Pits 26, 33
SECTION III	Pits 35, 36, 37

Tung hand-copied the 392 pieces of oracle bones with inscriptions: he also made a number of comments, which were reprinted with his general report in the *Preliminary Reports of Excavations at Anyang* (see Fig. 4).

After the preliminary diggings led by Tung Tso-pin, the author played the leading role in the Anyang excavations, which lasted in the field for nearly nine years. Accordingly, the following account must be partly autobiographical.

I did not meet Fu Ssŭ-nien until 1928, when he had already made a national reputation after the May 4th movement. I was studying in the United States between 1918 and 1923, and was deeply absorbed in several branches of social science—psychology, sociology, and anthropology. Returning home after five years of study, I accepted a teaching position at the newly established Nankai University in Tientsin where I worked for two years (1923–25).

As I had lived in Peking since the Manchu days, when I taught in Tientsin I constantly traveled between the two cities—Peking and Tientsin. Since anthropology was quite a novel subject at that

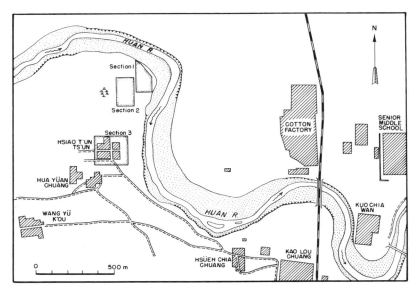

Figure 4. First sketch map by Tung Tso-pin

time in the university curriculum, a number of men of learning in these two cities became somewhat curious about me, and I was frequently invited to attend learned meetings and social occasions in both cities. After a short period of initiation, I gained the friendship of many specialists whom I had admired for a long time. I was soon introduced to Dr. V. K. Ting (Ting Wen-chiang), Dr. W. H. Weng (Weng Wen-hao), and Dr. Hu Shih, and was also inducted into membership in the Geological Society of China. As a member of this learned society, I naturally had every opportunity to get acquainted not only with many geologists but also with a number of visiting scientists—geographers, paleontologists, archaeologists, and so forth.

V. K. Ting, no longer heading the Geological Survey at this time, was managing a coal mining company with headquarters in Tientsin. His keen interest in anthropology led him to interest himself in my work and he advised me to miss no opportunity to go to the field for data collecting. When the discovery of the Hsin-cheng bronzes was reported in the newspapers, he urged me to go to Hsin-cheng to dig, and obtained two hundred dollars in China National Currency for field expenses.[4]

So I did; but the results of the dig were not very encouraging, and I recovered only some human skeletal materials, since the bronzes and jades had all been plundered previously. This initial experience did not draw me seriously to the science of archaeology; however, it taught me the lesson that in doing such works, one certainly has to pay a great deal of attention to current political and social conditions.

In 1924–25, my second year of teaching in Nankai, I met Mr. Carl Whiting Bishop in Peking, who represented the Freer Gallery of Art there, and was looking for an opportunity to do some scientific excavations in China. Soon we became friends. Mr. Bishop wrote to me in this academic year and inquired whether I might consider joining his field team to do some archaeological excavation. After careful consideration and advice from friends, I responded to Mr. Bishop's offer by suggesting two conditions that seemed to me important: first, that field excavations, if I were to engage in them without misgivings, should be done in cooperation with a Chinese learned body and under its auspices; and second, that I be excused from any obligation to export the artifacts from such digging—my hint being that studies of such finds should be done in China.[5]

For a long time I had no answer from Mr. Bishop. Later, when I happened to meet him again on a social occasion, he was very cordial and approached me courteously to talk again about his proposition. In this informal conversation he told me that the Freer Gallery of Art would not ask me to do anything I might consider unpatriotic. Since political and social conditions were changing so rapidly, why not work together on an experimental basis? Mr. Bishop was one of the few Americans in Peking who impressed me as friendly and sincere. Since his offer fitted in with my idea of academic research, I agreed to take up the job "on an experimental basis." This happened in the spring of 1925, when J. G. Andersson's prehistoric discoveries were already the talk of the academic circles in Peking and Tientsin.

Earlier in the same year, Ts'inghua College founded a research center for what was known at that time as "national learning," a term for which the modern English equivalent is "Chinese Studies." I had the honor to be invited by the newly established Ts'inghua Research Institute of National Learning to serve as an instructor, in company with a faculty composed of such eminent scholars as Liang Ch'i-ch'ao, Wang Kuo-wei, Chen Yin-k'o, and Chao Yüan-ren. My specific duty was to teach anthropology. It was about this same time that the Freer Gallery of Art, through its field representative

Mr. Bishop, also agreed to employ me as a member of its field team in China with the understanding mentioned above.

In the winter of 1925, the Freer Gallery of Art and the Ts'inghua Research Institute jointly dispatched me to do some field work, giving me the power to choose whatever place I wished. The senior member of the Ts'inghua faculty, Professor Liang Ch'i ch'ao, was a great enthusiast for field archaeology and offered to introduce me to Yen Hsi-shan, the model governor of Shansi province, where the political administration was the best known, and peace and order had long prevailed. I chose Shansi for my first archaeological trip after careful consultation with friends familiar with China's current political and social conditions.

It was indeed a great fortune for me when the geologist F. L. Yüan (Yüan Fu-li), who had accompanied J. G. Andersson in his Yang-shao diggings, on hearing about my proposed archaeological trip to Shansi, volunteered to accompany me. Both the Geological Survey and the Freer Gallery of Art consented. Yüan and I left for Shansi in the winter of 1925–26. We settled our course of reconnaissance on the way. At that time, neither the politicians nor the general public knew anything about science, not to mention scientific archaeology. So, on this first trip, I had to spend much time negotiating with administrators and local people. Whatever social and political advantages I enjoyed were, in most cases, given to me either by my senior colleague or by sheer personal luck.

Yüan and I decided, after reaching Taiyüan, to go south and explore the archaeological possibilities mainly along the Fên River valley north to the Yellow River, which serves as the southern border of Shansi province. There was already a paved road, and mules, camel-chairs, rickshas, and mule-carts were the available means of transportation. We decided to start the detailed reconnaissance from P'ing-yang Fu (or Lin-fên Hsien) southward. At this place, a mule for each of us was hired to transport the luggage, the surveying and photographic equipment, as well as the human burden. Shansi pack mules are famous for their endurance; they can keep up a steady rate of traveling twenty-five miles a day carrying over three hundred pounds even if the journey covers the ascent and descent of mountainous regions. This was exactly what we needed.

On mule-back, Yüan and I wandered from Lin-fen southward for about a month's time. In the course of our daily observations, the chief discoveries were three prehistoric sites with painted pottery, in addition to many historic sites of great archaeological value. Having reported the details and especially the new discoveries to the Ts'inghua Research Institute and the Freer Gallery of Art in Washington, D.C., I was asked to return to Shansi again for some digging. Both the Freer and Ts'inghua agreed to let me choose the first site for excavation. As Mr. Yüan's service was greatly appreciated by the two cooperating institutions, the two of us again went to Shansi in the autumn of 1926. After the necessary official papers and letters of introduction had been obtained, F. L. Yüan and I agreed to choose for our first dig Hsi-yin Ts'un, located at Hsia Hsien, one of the three prehistoric sites with painted pottery discovered during our reconnaissance trip. We made this choice for the following reasons:

1. A prehistoric site contains nothing metallic, so suspicions of treasure-hunting might be avoided.

2. Any burials that might be uncovered would relate to unknown tombs of the past, and therefore attract little attention, so that public opinion against grave digging would be reduced to the minimum.

3. The discovery of Yang-shao culture had already demonstrated beyond a doubt the importance of this prehistoric culture.

In addition, my fellow worker, Mr. Yüan, the geologist, had acquired a great deal of field experience in the excavation of the Yang-shao site, which he had surveyed.

There is no need for me to go any further with the story of my first excavation of the prehistoric site at Hsi-yin Ts'un, since the work has been reported in both Chinese and English. Of the artifacts collected at this site, the best known is an artificially cut silk cocoon which was identified by a specialist at the Smithsonian Institution as *Bombyx Mori*.[6]

The excavation of the Hsi-yin Ts'un prehistoric site, although it attracted little attention at a time when political revolution was in progress in China, achieved for me a personal reputation as the first archaeologist in China whose method of working was modern, and whose scope of interest extended far beyond historical time. The director of the Freer Gallery of Art, after learning what I had done, indicated through Mr. Bishop his wish to have an interview with me and invited me to Washington, D.C.

I went to Washington in the summer of 1928 and had a very pleasant interview with Director John E. Lodge. After some talk, he promised to continue his support of further cooperative efforts between a Chinese institute of learning and the Freer Gallery of Art in any new project in Chinese archaeology.

I returned to China via Europe, Egypt, and India. When I arrived at Hong Kong for the first time in my life, I was very anxious to pay a visit to the city of Canton, where I had never been before. In 1928 this city was the center of all sorts of revolutionary activities. According to the sailing schedule of the P. and O. boat which I was taking to Shanghai, the stop at Hong Kong harbor was to last three days, so I figured that I could easily pay a short visit to Canton within the time limit. This I did.

Once in Canton, I was soon taken to see Fu Ssŭ-nien, who was, at the time, looking forward to meeting me. The first thing he asked was whether I would like to take charge of the Archaeological Section in the Institute of History and Philology, which he was organizing. He told me what Tung Tso-pin had found in Anyang; I also informed him of my engagement with the Freer. There seemed to exist little difference of opinion, since the director of the Freer Gallery of Art had just approved such cooperation on an experimental basis.

So I started planning for the program of the Archaeological Section of the Institute of History and Philology of the Academia Sinica in the winter of 1928–29. Naturally, this necessitated that I learn as much as possible about the site of the Waste of Yin in Anyang. My immediate task, after returning home to Peking, was to take a trip to K'aifeng to confer with Tung Tso-pin, whom I had never met before. He had, of course, already been informed by Director Fu Ssŭ-nien of my appointment. In K'aifeng I learned all that Tung could tell me about the current conditions of Hsiao-t'un site, and the results of his trial digging. My impression remains vivid to this day of my first conference with this charming and admirable colleague. He possessed an alert and witty mind, full of practical wisdom. His main academic interest and recent success both seemed to have convinced him that there were still hidden oracle bones worth digging.

After the informal K'aifeng conference, Tung and I agreed to go to Anyang after the Chinese New Year for another trial digging. We also reached an understanding that Tung was to study the written records while I was to take care of all other artifacts. This understanding has proved, in the course of time, important for our personal relationship as well as for teamwork. For Tung, as the first pioneer to explore this site, deserved the opportunity to study the most important group of scientific discoveries and the inscribed oracle bones were the key-finds of the collections from the Anyany excavations. Furthermore, Tung's qualifications for the epigraphic investigation was beyond any question.

On the basis of my personal contact with Tung Tso-pin and his written reports, I was provided with a general knowledge of the current condition of the site. And, on the basis of this general understanding, it seemed to me that:

1. The site at Hsiao-t'un was evidently the last capital of the Yin-Shang dynasty.

2. Although the size and scope of the remains were uncertain, an area where inscribed oracle bones were unearthed must have been an important center of the captial site.

3. Together with the inscribed oracle bones, there might well be many other kinds of artifacts found in the underground deposits. These might have coexisted with the inscribed oracle bones, or be even earlier, or possibly later, depending of course upon a number of depository conditions.

I planned the program for the spring of 1929, the second season at Hsiao-t'un and the first time that I took charge of the field work in Anyang, with these three hypotheses in mind. Since the Freer Gallery of Art had agreed to support my field work under the auspices of a Chinese institute of learning, there was no financial problem. The concrete work which I, after consultation with Tung Tso-pin, decided to adopt consisted of the following procedures:

1. To employ a competent surveyor to survey the site, so that a detailed topographical map with Hsiao-t'un Ts'un as the center might be accurately drawn.

2. To continue trial diggings by means of trenching at a number of localities within the site, the main purpose being to obtain a clear understanding of the stratification under the surface, and find out the true nature of the deposit where oracle bones might remain still intact.

3. To keep systematic records and registration of every artifact which might be dug out, with its exact location, nature of the surrounding deposit and stratification, and also the exact time of its appearance.

4. To have every participant in charge keep a personal diary of what he observed and what occurred in the field.

In the spring season of 1929, the excavation was carried through as planned. In Hsiao-t'un village more oracle bones (685 fragments) were found. The investigation of the underground conditions was made in three different localities: (1) south of the village; (2) in the village yard; and (3) in a wheat and cotton farm north of the village settlement. We concluded the season by packing a great number of excavated artifacts in cases and transporting them to Peking for study. At this time the Institute of History and Philology had already moved its headquarters to Peking. Director Fu Ssŭ-nien decided to issue a preliminary report for the general public; the first paper I contributed was an analysis of underground conditions.[7] In this paper I drew one important conclusion, based upon the observations and excavations made during the spring diggings, namely that the underground deposits are divisible into three main strata: (1) the main cultural deposits from the Yin-Shang period, overlaid by (2) the scattered but nevertheless numerous tombs of the Sui-T'ang dynasties (589–906 A.D.);[8] these cemeteries being again covered by (3) a surface layer of modern deposits. We also discovered a number of underground caves and caches, filled mostly with remains of the Yin-Shang time—composed of pot-sherds, stone implements, and animal bones, occasionally some broken pieces or even fragments of jade, and so on. These finds were duly registered and were all carried back to the headquarters in Peking for study. Still the most important group among the artifacts uncovered during this season are the inscribed oracle bones, which were found in the locality within the village settlements, very near the place where Tung Tso-pin had found similar relics during the previous season.

During this second expedition to Anyang a topographical survey of this important site, with Hsiao-t'un as the center, was begun. As nobody could say anything definite about the size of the site, we temporarily limited the surveying work to the region within which oracle bones had either been found by excavation or were said to have been turned up according to village tradition. This first topographical map, surveyed by Mr. Chang Wei-jan, was completed in the autumn of 1929, during the third season of the Anyang expedition (see Fig. 5). Another item of the field work, which I initiated in the second season, was to keep a systematic record of the ceramic collection, an arduous task that was continued uninterruptedly for the ensuing fourteen seasons of the Anyang excavations, but, as might be expected, with several revolutionary changes in both the method of recording and the criteria of classifications.

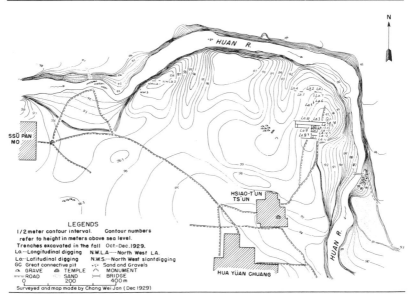

Figure 5. Topographical map of Hsiao-t'un and its immediate vicinity

To what extent the present surface condition of the cotton and wheat farm northeast of Hsiao-t'un village represented what had appeared in the Yin-Shang dynasty, nobody could guess. But the present surface topography was the task of the field worker to map out accurately.

After my party started its field work, we had the first impression that the village was located on a more or less flat piece of land, with the wheat and cotton farms to its northeast, about 180,000 square meters in size, rising gradually toward the north and the east. An accurate survey revealed that the surface rose some 3–4 meters higher. The highest points were in one place near the bank of the Huan River to the east. Near the river bank to the north, there is another raised area, which is also 2–3 meters higher than the village settlement; but it is separated from the eastern higher surface by a strip of depression. This depressed surface may have served, during the rainy season, to convey flood waters toward the Huan River. West of the northern mounds, there existed in 1929 an elongated, deep-sunken channel. This channel-like depression from Hua-yüan-chuang runs almost directly to the Huan River on the north and serves as a boundary line of the cotton and wheat farms of Hsiao-t'un village. The villagers called it a "water ditch." This water ditch seemed also to have been a western boundary line of the oracle treasure deposits according to the village tradition. All *tzŭ-ku-t'ou*, according to those who knew the locations of the deposits, were found in localities east of the "water ditch." After the survey we found that the lowest level of the ditch depression was in fact not much lower than the ground level of the village settlement at Hsiao-t'un.

The two mounds which rose nearly two or three meters above the village settlement and the water ditch on the western border of the wheat and cotton farm at the northwest were the general surface appearance at the time of my first visit. These preliminary observations helped me also in planning the third season's work, which started October 1929. Another digging party, organized and backed by the Honan provincial government under the inspiration of the old treasure-hunting tradition, interfered with our third season's works for three weeks. This political interference was soon settled, but the treasure-hunting tradition dies hard. For this reason some of us moved actively to request the central government to pass an Antiquities Protection Law with provisions for the protection of sites and monuments of historical value, including rules regulating export of national treasures and conditions governing scientific excavations. The first article of the law, proposed and later adopted, was for the government to declare that all underground antiquities are national treasures, which no private individual or party has any right to dig. After several years of general discussion, the law was finally passed by the Legislative Yüan (June, 1930). Included in this law were rules regulating official excavations, which were however supplemented much later. It is interesting to note that certificate number one with official permission to excavate was issued jointly by the Ministry of Interior and the Ministry of Education in the spring of 1935 to Academia Sinica, when the Anyang excavation was in its eleventh season.[9]

The implications of this law had an important bearing on the progress of the field work in Anyang, for the field archaeologist had to face, in addition to complicated technological problems, certain formidable nontechnical, social and political barriers in a tradition-bound country such as China was during the period of our excavation.

Having pacified the rival party from the provincial government by means of administrative arguments as well as rapprochement, we resumed excavation on November 15, 1929. In the beginning of the season, my plan for the field had been to scrape the entire surface of the site by what I termed "carpet rolling" method. But when I was interrupted by the rival party organized with local official backing, I was forced to adopt a method of approach that would be more adjustable as circumstances might require. So I started anew and planned more systematic trenchings over the wheat and cotton farmland northeast of Hsiao-t'un village.

Near the western half of this land, I planned one long vertical trench, running N.S., and six parallel horizontal trenches running E.W., in order to explore the distribution of the main deposits in the whole site underneath the farmland. As for the portion within the village, the underground conditions had already been examined on a preliminary basis in the preceding spring season.

The findings of the third season, despite the interruption of the field work for more than three weeks, were more encouraging than originally expected. The results fully justified the basic idea that the important centers of the Yin-Shang cultural remains lay somewhere underneath the cotton-wheat farms northeast of the village between the water ditch northwest of the village and the Huan River valley on the eastern and northern border.

While the vertical trenches in the north-south direction had exposed important underground sections of general deposits, the six parallel trenchings, fifteen meters apart cut across mainly from the vertical trenching eastward, had definitely hit the core. Between trench H13 and trench H13.5, near the vertical north-south cut, we discovered an almost intact deposit, which in fact turned out to be the most important deposit of the Yin-Shang culture. Later on, this locality was known as the Ta-lien-k'eng, or "Ta-lien pit."

The details of the first discovery and of the gradual extension of this dig were reported in a special article in *PREA*.[10] Let me summarize the important new discoveries and also their bearings on the course of the field events in our archaeological work on the site. It must be understood clearly that the accomplishment of the third season's work was by no means limited to the discovery of the Ta-lien-k'eng alone. The following summary therefore includes the fruitful results of the whole season.

What to the working team seemed to be of primary importance was the exposure of a definite stratification series portraying the underground condition. This became significant after a study comparing a stratified section over a burial of the Sui dynasty with the intact layers of the Ta-lien-k'eng revealed these main points: above the Yin-Shang cultural deposit there was a sort of protective layer, brownish to black in color, hard to break, and sometimes varying in thickness from one to two meters thick. This protective layer was usually barren of any cultural content, containing not even fragmentary pot-sherds. In the case of the Sui-T'ang burials, however, which were sometimes found at a depth of more than three meters, the overlying soil usually showed a stratification completely deficient in the protective layer as described above.

Even more interesting were, of course, the objects and artifacts discovered during this season. Since I personally supervised the digging of the Ta-lien-k'eng, I am able to describe from my own experience the various stages of the gradual exposure of this important deposit.

The Ta-lien-k'eng was located about fifty meters southwest of the raised mound near the west bank of the Huan River; its exposure was the result of the trenching of horizontal trench thirteen (H13) and its extension northwards, immediately after the underground stratum indicated signs of an intact deposit. The following field records (registered from the surface layer downward) serve as an example to illustrate the method of field registration:

1. The top layer, 0–0.40m.; soil mixed; one net sinker found.

2. Second layer, 0.40–0.87m.; soil yellowish-black; a stone knife the only find.

3. Third layer, 0.87–1.40m.; soil turned brown; no artifacts.

4. Fourth layer, 1.40–1.85m.; soil color same as above, but more compact and hard to break; mixed with rubbish of casting, and a specimen of one cowry shell.

5. Fifth layer, 1.85–2.10m.; soil gradually blackened, very hard; a few pot-sherds, some casting rubbish, a piece of carved sandstone.

6. Sixth layer, 2.10–2.40m.; soil very black and harder; in northeast corner, mixed with patches of yellow sand and sediments containing many fragments of burned clay and casting rubbish.

7. Seventh layer, 2.40–2.65m.; soil condition continued as (6), but below 2.65m., the northeast corner, changed to grayish ashy color and became less hard; more pot-sherds, and fragments of inscribed oracle bones began to appear; fragments of human skull also found.

8. Eighth layer, 2.65–2.80m.; soil color grayish-yellow, with deeper chrome at northeast corner; many kinds of pot-sherds, string-

impressed in red and black; also some with squareshaped relief in black and red; and other varieties of pottery sherds. Many of the sherds carried incised ornaments. Other artifacts: inscribed bones, shells, stone knives and pebbles, deer horns, human skeleton fragments, casting molds, also stone axes and other fragments of stone mixed within the remains.

9. Ninth layer, 2.80–2.95m.; soil completely gray in color; potsherds as above; in addition, inscribed oracle bones, carved bone artifacts, carved stone artifacts, carved ivories—many specimens.

10. Tenth layer, 2.90–3.20m.; soil color still grayish-yellow, but near the bottom of this layer at the depth of 3.10m. the yellow soil appeared; and south of this loessic soil, a heap of black charcoal was found, mixed with pot-sherds of the gray, red, and black varieties, bearing incised and string impressions; also skulls, casting molds, pebbles, bone awls, stone implements, oracle bones with or without inscriptions and lapis lazuli, etc.

11. Eleventh layer, 3.20–3.30m.; mixed yellow and black soil, artifacts rare. Below the depth of 3.30m., the floor of the upper portion seemed to have been reached except in the southeastern corner where a semicircle of black soil remained.

It is a critical observation that below the eleventh layer, at a depth of 3.30 meters below the present surface, a floor space covered by a layer of black earth over clean sandy yellow soil seemed to be untouched by any later intrusion. This floor space evidently might have served as the floor of a dwelling place, or of a storage pit. What was more exciting was the fact that below this floor, at the 3.30 meter level, still another underground deposit appeared in a deeper circular pit that went down more than three meters further below the bottom of the Ta-lien-k'eng. At the bottom of this lower circular pit—whose diameter was nearly two meters—were found heaps of oracle bones, and some nearly complete inscribed shells whose importance was set forth by Tung Tso-pin later in a special article.[11]

From this circular pit and another rectangular pit near its western side—these twin pits constituting the subterranean cache underneath the superlayer of the Ta-lien-k'eng—we discovered hidden treasures which were the richest harvest of the season's work. Most of the discoveries had been unknown before. These new discoveries at the Ta-lien-k'eng together with the deposits of the twin lower pits proved one definitive point: that is, that the following artifacts were definitely contemporaneous with the inscribed oracle bones: (1) uninscribed oracle bones as well as nearly complete specimens of inscribed tortoise shells; (2) many kinds of animal bones; (3) many types of pottery: white, glazed, red, and gray; (4) carved bones and stones; (5) carved ivories; (6) deep storage pits which might sink down below the surface more than ten meters; (7) coexistence of stone and bronze tools; (8) molds for casting bronzes; and (9) other associated finds.

The importance of these associated finds, individually and as a group, was widely realized as soon as the underground conditions were made known. This recognition was advantageous to our continuing efforts in the Anyang excavations.

Among these new discoveries, the glazed pottery, white pottery, and bronze molds attracted international attention and gave rise to worldwide discussion. But it was the unique find of painted pottery sherds, never duplicated in later diggings, which aroused a hot debate among Chinese historians and archaeologists. The point at issue, to be brief, was the relationship between the neolithic Yangshao culture and the Bronze Age Yin-Shang culture as revealed in the deposit at Hsiao-t'un. The discussion lasted a number of years, since it involved the fundamental question concerning the origin of early Chinese culture.[12]

The Anyang excavation stopped for a year in 1930, when the Archaeological Section of the Institute of History and Philology extended its field activity to the Shantung province. At a place near the provincial capital Tsinan, a new phase of neolithic culture—the Black Pottery Lungshan Culture—had been discovered by Ginding Wu (Wu Chin-ting), a graduate student of mine from the Ts'inghua Research Institute of National Learning. The field staff of the Archaeological Section was sent to Tsinan and excavated the site of Ch'êng-tzŭ-yai for a season. The Black Pottery Culture here discovered for the first time in north China stirred deeply not only those scholars whose special interest was in ancient China but also the new generation of field archaeologists, especially those who had been paying close attention to the discoveries and circumstances of excavation at Anyang.

Meanwhile, there were other occurrences in 1930 that affected both the organization of the field work and the program of planned digging of the Hsiao-t'un site. What concerned me particularly was the failure of the Institute of History and Philology and the Freer Gallery of Art to reach an agreement on continuing archaeological excavation in north China. When this regrettable cessation of the cooperative undertaking happened, my position became obviously untenable. So I resigned my Freer Gallery job, after the completion of all the field work assigned to me. I had worked, from 1925 to 1930, for five continuous years with the understanding described above and in the hope that some agreement might be reached between a national institute of China with the Freer Gallery of Art of Washington, D.C., to promote archaeological science as well as Sino-American friendship in academic works. This failure naturally disheartened me greatly.

A number of friends who appreciated my field work extended their help by asking the China Foundation for some financial assistance for the Anyang excavation, which was soon achieved. Beginning in the autumn of 1930, I received the China Foundation appointment as Research Professor in Chinese Archaeology, a chair endowed specially to the Institute of History and Philology of the Academia Sinica. In addition, an annual sum of ten thousand silver dollars for three years was granted to the institute for field expenses.

So the fourth season of the Anyang excavation opened in the spring of 1931; it was already more than a year after the Archaeological Section had stopped field work at Hsiao-t'un in the winter of 1929. The field party for the fourth season of digging was organized on a new basis and included a larger number of archaeologists. I went to the field also with a more advanced understanding of the nature of the site as well as a number of new ideas; and many new and better-trained assistants were on my staff.

Beginning in this fourth season, the site, which we had surveyed in 1929, was divided into five subareas, each of which was excavated under the supervision of a trained and experienced archaeologist who was assisted by a number of junior assistants and many trained diggers. Most of the staff members had greatly benefited from their participation in the excavation of Ch'êng-tzŭ-yai, where the uncovered artifacts had included interesting specimens of oracle bones which had been used in scapulimancy, but bore no inscriptions. Surrounding the site at Ch'êng-tzŭ-yai, a ruined wall had been found, which was built of pounded earth. A careful examination of the pounded earth reminded those with experience in the Anyang diggings of the amazing similarity to strata found at Hsiao-t'un in the first three seasons, which at the time had been interpreted both by Tung Tso-pin and Chang Wei-jan as layers of flood sediments.

So the excavation of the Ch'êng-tzŭ-yai site provided some radical new ideas for major reinterpretations of our past problems at

Anyang, thus making a very important contribution to the advancement of the field work there. I had been personally greatly encouraged both by the China Foundation appointment and by the discovery of the Lungshan culture at Ch'êng-tzǔ-yai, for whose excavation I had been mainly responsible.

With the additional knowledge gained in the Shantung field work, I began to speculate that scapulimancy not only existed in north China in prehistoric times but was also widespread. And, since legendary accounts about the early history of the Shang dynasty do mention the fact that the dynasty moved its capital five times after the founding—the locations of these capitals had been a favorite theme for students of the ancient history of China—it seemed possible to me that the newly discovered Lungshan culture might have been the immediate predecessor of the Shang civilization. At least, scapulimancy definitely provided a link between the Shang civilization and that of the preceding prehistoric culture in north China.

With all these new ideas in my mind and a reinforced staff, I was encouraged to plan expanded field work in Anyang for the fourth season. The important decision, taken after detailed discussion with members of the Archaeological Section and the director, was to excavate the Hsiao-t'un site in its totality by the carpet-rolling method. I felt confident that we had found the key and by mapping the pounded earth areas would be able to trace the architectural foundations of the Yin-Shang dynasty in the Waste of Yin.

The field staff included the old staff members (those who had participated in the first three seasons)—Tung Tso-pin, Kuo Pao-chün, Wang Hsiang, and Li Chi—as well as new members—Liang Ssǔ-yung, Li Kuang-yü, Wu Gin-ding (Chin-ting), and Liu Yü-hsia. Beginning in this season, Mr. Shih Chang-ju and Mr. Liu Yao also joined the Anyang field work as student workers.

One method of tackling the site (looking particularly for undisturbed pounded earth area) in the fourth season was outlined by Shih Chang-ju in his Archaeological Chronology published in 1952 (see also Fig. 6).[13]

In this season, the site was redivided into five subareas, A, B, C, D, E. The locations of the five subareas are as follows:
Subarea A, west of the vertical trench of 1929 (3rd season),
Subarea B, east of the vertical trench between horizontal trenches 11 and 14,

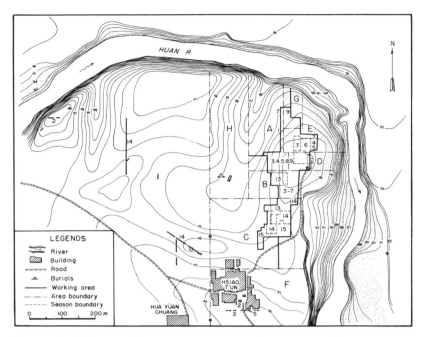

Figure 6. Subareas of excavation in Hsiao-t'un

Subarea C, south of horizontal trench 11,
Subarea D, east of the Ta-lien-k'eng,
Subarea E, north of the horizontal trench 14.

At the conclusion of the season's work, it was found out that
Subarea A had been disturbed the most; between H13 and H14
frequent diggings had been carried out in the past. Subarea B, by
contrast, had preserved a great deal of pounded earth surface,
which had not been found in the Subarea A. Experience in excavating this subarea convinced all field workers that our earlier interpretation of the pounded earth as flood sediments had been wrong.
In Subarea C, a location which villagers in the past had never
cared to dig, we also found extensive evidence of pounded earth,
similar to what had been found in the Subarea B; the same was
true of the Subarea D.

Subarea E was somewhat different. In this locality two untouched, underground storage caves were uncovered, which we
denominated respectively as E16 and E10. E16 was filled with
both bronze weapons and inscribed oracle bones, while in E10

heaps of large animal bones were stored. A whale's scapula and vertebrae and, even more interesting, the lower jaw of an elephant, were found in this group of remains. Shih's summary for this season stated:

The excavated area is more than fourteen hundred square meters. With the exception of the exposure of a large area of pounded earth, the discoveries included a large number of circular caches, twenty-five huge underground dwelling spaces, eighteen burials. The storage pits were carved out and reshaped with plastered walls; in the building corners of these sunken pits, there were foothold cavities in the vertical rows. In the storage cells of E16 were found some very valuable artifacts: bronze spearheads, bronze halberts, molds for bronze casting, carved bones, together with pot-sherds and a great number of inscribed oracle bones (781 pieces). There was also a number of burials of the Sui-T'ang dynasties . . . found in this season all over the excavated area.

The new planning introduced in the fourth season proved not only workable but also successful in that both the findings and the carpet-rolling method proved their soundness by the substantial results of two months' hard work. At the end of this season, my colleagues and I decided that whatever financial difficulties we might have to meet with, the new idea of tracing architectural foundations of the Yin-Shang dynasty should be followed till we could gain some solid basis for a reconstruction of the architecture of this almost forgotten dynasty. The guideline of this basic work, already proved sound, was to make a thorough study of the extensive areas of pounded earth already discovered and to continue to trace this extension. This new procedure, that is, the tracing of the pounded earth, proved to be time-consuming: it needed not only patience and technical experience, but also a great deal of imaginative power to appreciate the significance of this protracted project, which, after a long period of work, proved its lasting value.

Meanwhile, the fourth season field party, besides conducting the excavations at the Hsiao-t'un village site, found excess energy to explore other promising sites nearby in the Huan River valley. Liang Ssŭ-yung and Wu Gin-ding together with Liu Yao started digging at Hou-kang, a mound very near to the railway. Wu and Li Kuang-yü also carried some field work in Ssŭ-p'an-mo, west of Hsiao-t'un. The excavation at Hou-kang under Liang continued during several seasons and proved to be very important; it showed for the first time a stratified series of the painted pottery, black pottery, and the Anyang culture deposits laid down in definite sequence. In succeeding seasons, the exploratory digs were made as far west as T'ung-lo-chai, where a pure Black Pottery Culture site was discovered. But more important findings—important in being more closely related to the Hsiao-t'un Yin-Shang culture—were made in the ninth season (1934) of our Anyang digging in the village of Hou-chia-chuang. Here, on the other (north) bank of the Huan River from Hsiao-t'un, for the first time in the course of the Anyang excavations inscribed oracle bones were found elsewhere than Hsiao-t'un.

However, in the immediate ensuing seasons of the Anyang field work—from the fifth to the ninth—the main excavations were still concentrated at Hsiao-t'un, with tracing the architectural foundations of the Yin-Shang dynasty as the main purpose of our project. The five successive seasons were carried through between October 1931 and March 1934; the personnel of the field party and the man in charge also changed from time to time:

SEASON	PERIOD	LEADER	FIELD STAFF
Fifth	Nov. 7–Dec. 19, 1931	Tung Tso-pin	Kuo Pao-chün Liu Yü-hsia Wang Hsiang
Sixth	Apr. 1–May 31, 1932	Li Chi	Tung Tso-pin Wu Gin-ding Liu Yü-hsia Wang Hsiang Chou Yin-hsüeh Li Kuang-yü
Seventh	Oct. 19–Dec. 15, 1932	Tung Tso-pin	Shih Chang-ju Li Kuang-yü
Eighth	Oct. 20–Dec. 25, 1932	Kuo Pao-chün	Li Chin-tan Liu Yao Shih Chang-ju Li Kuang-yü
Ninth	March 9–Apr. 1, 1934	Tung Tso-pin	Li Chin-tan Shih Chang-ju

In the fifth season, a more definite area with pounded earth appeared in Subareas B and E. A terrace, composed of more or less pure clean yellow soil, was uncovered in the E. The discovery of this terrace, square in cross-section and oriented to magnetic north but undercut by later intrusion, seemed to me at that time very important, so I went to the field to take charge in the ensuing sixth season. In that season, a further important discovery concerning architectural engineering was made, namely that rows of untrimmed boulder-stone of moderate size were regularly arranged along the edges of the pounded earth. They were obviously the foundation stones for supporting pillars. These untrimmed boulders, ranged in rows along the borders of the regular-shaped foundation surfaces, occurred very frequently.[14]

This discovery made us realize that similar boulders varying in size, which had been frequently met with in past seasons, might also have served some architectural purpose. In this way, the tracing work naturally grew more and more meaningful.

From the seventh season to the ninth season, the field work was led alternatively by Tung Tso-pin and Kuo Pao-chün. The main purpose of the field operation was still to continue tracing the architectural foundations, and also to investigate other underground structures. Efforts in these seasons were more concentrated on an intensive study of the various stages of development of the "pounded earth methods," since it was evident that mastery of this technique was the basic training for civil engineers of the Yin-Shang period. In this study, our field men learned a good deal of the technology of the civil engineer, as practiced in China more than three thousand years ago.

5 The Royal Tombs

Their Discovery and Systematic Excavation

THERE SEEMS to be little question that the custom of elaborate burial of the rich and powerful was universal all over the ancient world, and that it was based on the belief in another world where man could continue to live on after his death in a way not altogether different from his life on earth. Though this practice was shaped in many different ways according to the mores and folkways that happened to dominate a particular region, its foundation remained the same: namely, the persistent human desire for and faith in a post-mortem existence.

As to when the idea of burying the dead started, it seems that no archaeologist has yet been able to provide a definite answer. It is definite, however, that in the neolithic period, interment was already commonplace, as was the custom of entombing burial goods with the dead body to accompany it to the other world.

Prehistoric investigations also indicate that the practice of elaborate burials certainly developed after man's exploitation of metals and the development of the caste system and of slavery. Of course the stages of social and political organization differed in various regions at various times, but the basic idea persisted: it was the duty of the heir to provide those luxuries and necessities which the deceased might need in his existence as a spirit or ghost or whatever other shape he might assume.

In the case of China, J. G. Andersson's discovery of neolithic burials has already been referred to in Chapter 3. Nils Palmgren, in his monograph on Kansu mortuary urns, has given a detailed description of all the buried painted pottery vessels found in the prehistoric graves in Kansu province.[1] These potteries, whether excavated or purchased, provided the earliest evidence found by archaeologists that the neolithic Chinese, like neolithic peoples in other parts of world, believed in the dual existence of man. Later investigations have fully confirmed the dualistic faith of neolithic China. Neolithic sites in Honan, Shansi, and Kansu, more scientifically excavated, have exposed both a living quarter and a separate quarter for a cemetery among the ruins.[2] The burial goods from these neolithic sites are mainly pottery, animal bones, and stone implements. They vary a great deal from grave to grave in both quality and quantity. Whether the variation is an indication of wealth or power or both is not at all clear. But it is significant that such differentiation already existed in prehistoric China; the range of such variation widens in the course of time till the Bronze Age, when huge tombs, palatial in size and luxury, began to be built.

The custom of elaborate burials was criticized as early as pre-Ch'in China, and vehemently condemned and ridiculed by many schools of philosophy, especially by the Moists and Taoists. Mo-tzǔ and Chuang-tzǔ's attacks on elaborate burials are both well known. This tradition, however, was preserved by Confucian emphasis on "Li," translated as "ritualism" by some, "propriety" by others. In the original Chinese sense, the term "Li" connotes, of course, a great deal more than either "ritualism" or "propriety." It is a sort of Confucian canonization of the current moral code about manners and customs prevailing in ancient China. The origin of "Li" as a code is usually attributed to Chou Kung, the famous brother of the founder of the Chou dynasty, Chou Wu Wang, an idol of the Confucian school and worshiped as one of the saints in traditional Confucianism.

In the first nine seasons of excavation of the Anyang sites, none of the burials located in Hsiao-t'un could in any respect be considered "elaborate," although a number of them, untouched by tomb robbers, contained beautiful bronzes, especially of the *ku* and *chüeh* types. It was in the adjacent regions of the Waste of Yin that the field teams first came upon tombs of huge size—when in the eighth season (1933) they were doing some further excavation at Hou-Kang, where Liang Ssŭ-yung discovered a stratified sequence of the Yangshao, the Lungshan, and the historical Yin-Shang cultures.[3] The first big tomb found in Hou-Kang had been almost completely sacked when our archaeologists reopened it. This work, nevertheless, served as the earliest evidence to indicate that systematic searches might locate tombs of large size, even royal cemeteries. The field workers in Anyang after 1931 were all well acquainted with the textures and appearance of "the pounded earth," which they came across frequently. When the opening of the Hou-Kang tomb confirmed that the same technique of *pisé* (pounded earth) engineering was used in building large tombs, naturally a guideline was provided. The Anyang field team, therefore, by hard labor and accumulated experience, found a key for their search for cemetery sites of the Yin-Shang dynasty in the neighboring regions.

Meanwhile, the treasure-hunting tradition persisted in spite of the promulgation of the Antiquities Protection Law by the central government. In Anyang, although the Academia Sinica excavations under the legal protection provided by the local government progressed without hindrance, illegal treasure-hunting and tomb-robbings took place whenever possible. This treasure-hunting tradition is shared by the East and West alike regardless of religion or law; so wherever buried treasure was located, hunters rushed like a crowd rushing for gold.

Anyang had been noted for ancient bronzes as early as the Northern Sung dynasty.[4] Once the scientific digging started, several foreign newspapers became interested; among them, the *Illustrated London News* gave much space to our Anyang discoveries, which immediately attracted world-wide attention.[5] One of the evil effects of such publicity was the encouragement of private diggings, which immediately became contagious even among the missionaries in China. Lawless plundering activities flourished everywhere in north China, and in Anyang as soon as the season for our official excavations closed, illegal treasure-hunting immediately became active. It was through these plundering activities that the royal cemetery at Hou-chia-chuang was first made known. The details of this discovery were of course entirely lost. Every visitor to the Nezu Art Museum in Tokyo must have been deeply impressed by three huge strangely shaped *ho* wine ewers, with heights of 71.2cm., 72.1cm., and 73.2cm., respectively. They are all said to come from Anyang, although Seiichi Mizuno did not mention them in his catalogue of Yin-hsü bronzes.[6] The story circulated in Anyang amounts to this:

The time may have been as early as 1933; private diggings near the village Hou-chia-chuang resulted in a rich harvest of huge bronzes and other treasures. Especially notorious were the three bronzes—of unknown shape but unusual size—that were immediately sold in the curio market, which of course made the chief digger suddenly rich. Although the definite conditions were unknown, those who shared the spoils naturally could not keep their mouths as closed as the chief plunderer. So, news of his ill-gotten wealth very soon became widely known not only in the adjacent villages, but also circulated in Anyang city. Some of the Academia Sinica employees within a short period learned a great deal about this "lucky digging." The younger archaeologists of our expedition immediately got busy and naturally reported to the leader in charge of the excavation. The time was October 1934, when the tenth expedition to Anyang was just getting ready to start work under the leadership of Liang Ssŭ-yung.

In the tenth season, the original plan had been to continue tracing the building foundations of the Yin-Shang period, as in the previous three seasons, with further explorations of adjacent regions in the Huan River valley. When Liang Ssŭ-yung heard the story of the recent plundering of a Bronze Age tomb and learned the approximate location near the village of Hou-chia-chuang, he took immediate steps to move his men, and to concentrate all the efforts of the field team under his command to find out whether a real cemetery site might be discovered. This was indeed a momentous decision!

In this season, Liang was assisted by five experienced younger archaeologists: Shih Chang-ju, Liu Yao, Ch'i Yen-p'ei, Hu Fu-lin, and Yin Huan-chang—all well trained in field techniques, and full of enthusiasm for trying to find the exact location of the cemetery. They successfully located the cemetery site and, choosing a slightly raised mound northwest of the village settlement of Hou-chia-chuang, known locally as Hsi-pei-kang (meaning "north-west mound"), the field team started a trial digging, and exposed a number of huge tombs. This encouraging revelation induced Liang to concentrate all the available money and manpower to explore the entire dimension of this remarkable site. In three months' time (Oct. 3–Dec. 30), the excavated area covered more than three thousand square meters of land surface. A modern village road divided the site into two sections more than one hundred meters apart. The subarea on the west side of the road was named the western section, and that on the eastern side of the road the eastern section. Later on, the underground distribution of the excavated burials proved to fall handily into this dual division.

At the close of the first season's work at the Hou-chia-chuang cemetery, the results were more encouraging than had been expected. The important discoveries were these: (1) four huge tombs, all located in the western section; sixty-three burials of ordinary size, all located in the eastern section; (2) buried bodies, in a number of different postures (prone, face-up, contracted, skulls only, etc.); (3) many well-preserved bronzes from the small graves; (4) carved stone artifacts from huge tombs, some as high as 36cm.; and (5) numerous jade ornaments, carved bones, and white potteries. The artifacts, as a whole, were better made and better preserved than those from Hsiao-t'un; but all were clearly part of the Yin-Shang culture, corresponding in time with the inscribed oracle bone period; there existed little doubt in the mind of the excavators that the huge tombs of the western section, which were only partly uncovered at the close of the tenth season, were unquestionably some royal burials of the most powerful group of the ruling Yin-Shang dynasty.

In planning for the second season's field work at the Hsi-pei-kang cemetery of Hou-chia-chuang (the eleventh season of our Anyang excavation), Liang showed his unusual farsightedness and perspective, as well as a powerful grasp of practical details. I fully supported his project for the Hou-chia-chuang field work, but it also created some financial difficulties. The budget requested a sum between twenty thousand and thirty thousand silver dollars, which was far beyond the limit of the regular allowance to the research institute. At that time, I was also acting for Director Fu Ssŭ-nien, besides my duty as Chief of the Archaeological Section. Luckily, however, Dr. V. K. Ting was the Director General of the

Academia Sinica. Ting, with his broad learning, had in the past always shown a great deal of interest in field archaeology and was now in a position to help by practical means the realization of Liang's brilliant project. He made the timely proposal of inviting the National Central Museum to participate in this undertaking. The idea was that the National Central Museum would share a part of the field expense of the Hou-chia-chuang excavation with the understanding that the artifacts, after the completion of our studies, were to be permanently deposited in the museum, which was at that time erecting its building in the capital on a magnificent scale with an endowment from the British Indemnity Fund.

This eleventh Anyang expedition, in the spring of 1933, can be taken in retrospect as the climax of our field work. The financial costs were great, but, more impressive, the results were the richest. The expedition represented the best-organized team work and also the highest executive efficiency. More important for the general public, the achievements successfully confirmed the truth that scientific archaeology not only promotes verifiable knowledge, but also provides an assured means to find buried treasures and give them legal protection.

The eleventh season lasted ninety-seven days (March 10–June 15, 1935). Liang had seven assistants from the Archaeological Section. In addition, Ts'inghua University sent a graduate student, Hsia Nai, to Anyang to learn field archaeology, before sending him to England.

The field work of the second excavation at the Hsi-pei-kang cemetery site covered about eight thousand square meters. Four huge tombs of the western section were completely cleared, and 411 small burials in the eastern were opened. The depth of the huge tombs is between twelve and thirteen meters. It was definitely established that the smaller burials were sacrificial in nature; many of these sacrificial tombs contained merely skulls or headless skeletons, which provide, of course, definite evidence of human sacrifices. In excavating the huge tombs, it gradually became clear that these tombs had been ransacked more than once in the past, so before the clearance reached the bottom, everybody in the field was already aware that no intact hidden treasure could be expected. Nevertheless, discoveries made in nooks and corners, which had escaped the attention of the earlier plunderers, were already astonishing. Especially precious were those findings of delicate impressions left by perishable materials like bamboo, wood fibers, and so on, which only trained archaeologists could trace. More substantial artifacts like marble carvings and many bronze articles of unusual size, as well as delicate and fine jade work and so forth, though not *in situ*, were frequently recovered in the refilled earth of the earlier robbed tunnels.

The excavation of this season attracted a number of eminent visitors. Among them, Professor Paul Pelliot, accompanied by Director Fu Ssŭ-nien, was guest of honor at Hou-chia-chuang for a special visit (see Fig. 7).

The work was continued for another season (autumn 1935), at Hsi-pei-kang, on an even larger scale than that of the second season. The workmen engaged reached five hundred per day, the largest number ever employed in the history of Chinese field archaeology up to that time. The excavated area covered 9,600 square meters. More huge tombs in the western sections were opened; altogether there are seven regular tombs in the western section besides an unfinished huge pit (see Fig. 8). In addition, nearly eight hundred small burials in the eastern section were cleared. At the close of this season's work, the results once more indicated that all the huge tombs, like those opened in the first

Figure 7. Fu Ssŭ-nien, Paul Pelliot, and Liang Ssŭ-yung at one of the Hou-chia-chuang tombs

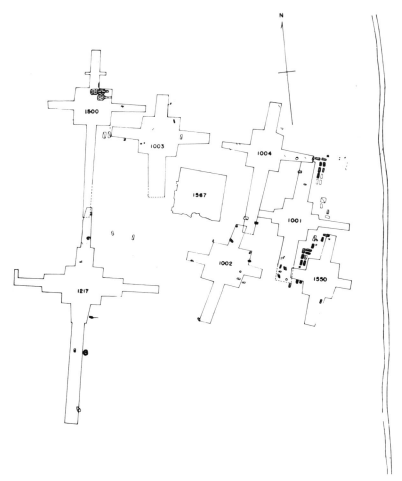

Figure 8. Seven big tombs and one pit in the western section of Hou-chia-chuang (see legend for Fig. 9)

two seasons, had more than once been plundered. The earliest sacking started probably as early as the Chou dynasty; at least, it took place before the Eastern Han period, since a tomb of Eastern Han was discovered on the top of the refilled plundered tomb. As in the previous seasons, artifacts discovered were nevertheless rich, and in many cases unexpected. So, in addition to a great deal of detailed knowledge of the structure of the gigantic tombs and the engineering skill of the Yin-Shang dynasty, the exposure of the material culture of this dynasty constituted a real revelation.

Professor Kao Ch'ü-hsün summarized the three seasons' diggings at the Hsi-pei-kang of Hou-chia-chuang in the following terms: [7]

During the three seasons of the excavations of the cemetery site at Hsi-pei-kang, north of Hou-chia-chuang, 1,267 tombs were opened. . . . Of these opened tombs, . . . 1,232 tombs are of the Yin-Shang dynasty. [Kao later pointed out that some of the small tombs might belong to a later age, although they culturally pertained to the Shang dynasty.] These Yin-Shang tombs are distributed underground in a very orderly fashion; but no mounds or other conspicuous marks above the ground surface are visible or could have existed! . . .

Of the 1,232 Yin-Shang tombs, 10 are large-scale big underground structures, one of which is obviously an unfinished tomb—without any passage like the other nine. . . . All the rest—1,221 in exact number— of the opened burials are small graves but evidently related to the 10 big tombs in one way or another.

Of the 10 large tombs, 7 are located in the western section of Hsi-pei-kang cemetery, 3 in the eastern section. . . . They are all N.S. oriented with the northern passage inclining towards the east a few degrees. . . . In the case of the minor burials—the 1,221 small tombs—, only 104 of them are found in the western section, while all the others, 1,117 in number, are all located in the eastern section of the cemetery. . . . [See Fig. 9].

Liang's idea, after the third season's excavation of the Hou-chia-chuang cemetery, was to pause for a short period to examine the amazing new discoveries and unusual finds, so that there might be sufficient deliberation for further planning to continue the excavation. But, alas! who could predict that this promising enterprise should suddenly be ended by the Japanese invasion of 1937!

It is certainly important and necessary to give a general account of the scientific contributions from these excavations to our knowledge of ancient Chinese culture and the early history of China. In my Preface to Volume 2 of the Hou-chia-chuang series, I have pointed out the more salient features in the following remarks:

I should mention in this short preface the more important contributions from these excavations to our knowledge of the history of Ancient China. It is obviously impossible to itemize these contributions in any numerical order. If I should arrange the following features in an order, it could only represent the sequence of our gradual recognition of the historical value of these various features, which are:

Figure 9. Western and eastern sections of Hsi-pei-kang, the cemetery site of Hou-chia-chuang

1. The planking method of earth pounding (*pan-chu*) as the main technical skill of the civil engineer in the Yin-Shang dynasty; neither bricks nor stones were used as building materials.

2. The building of the huge tomb (Esp. HPKM 1004) as an illustration of the burial custom of the privileged class and of the large-scale control of man power of the dead man's heir.

3. Definite evidence of the practice of human sacrifice.

4. Artifacts, which have survived many sackings, serve as material evidence of the stage of economic development and artistic achievement attained by ancient China in the later part of the second milliennium B.C.

5. Various examples of stone carving from the big tombs, although moderate in size, are amazing in the sense that they were totally unknown previously.

6. The numerous specimens of weapons and ritual vessels provide a starting point for a scientific study of metallurgical craftsmanship in Yin-Shang China.[8]

I also mentioned, in this Preface, that the knowledge and importance of some of the features listed above were germinated in the group mind of the field team, long before the cemetery site was first discovered. But these hypotheses did not develop into assured knowledge until they were confirmed by the Hsi-pei-kang excavations.

I would like to expound these items with some concrete illustrations.

Perhaps the best starting point is to outline the main features of one of the huge tombs excavated in the western section of the cemetery site, where seven of these gigantic, complete tomb structures were successively opened in these seasons. Four of these in the eastern part of this section and two in the western part show definite structural sequence in the crosscuttings of the passage corridors attached to each tomb. The one in the middle-west portion, HPKM 1003, together with an unfinished pit in this section, shows no structural relationship with any of the other six tombs.

HPKM 1004, which is located in the eastern part of the western section of the cemetery, may be taken here as a sample to illustrate the size and general structure of the royal tombs discovered in Hou-chia-chuang. The detailed report of the excavation of this huge tomb was published in the third series of Archaeologia Sinica, based on the original manuscripts of Liang Ssŭ-yung, edited and supplemented by Professor Kao Ch'ü-hsün.[9]

Let us first see the essential features of the tomb's structure.

Location, Size, and Structure

HPKM 1004 is located on the eastern portion of the western section of the cemetery; its exact location is northwest of HPKM 1001; its eastern passage corridor cuts the northern corridor of HPKM 1001, while its southern passage corridor is cut by the northern passage corridor of HPKM 1002. These two crosscuttings definitely indicate that HPKM 1004 was built after HPKM 1001, and before HPKM 1002.

As for the size, the various midline measurements are shown in the following table:

MAIN PIT AT THE CENTER	AT THE MOUTH	AT THE BOTTOM
Measured areas	284.61m.^{2}	142.52m.^{2}
Midline measurements N.S.	17.90m.	13.20m.
E.W.	15.90m.	10.80m.
Depth of the central pit (at the center)	12.00–12.20m.	
Midline of southern corridor		31.40m.
Midline of northern corridor		14.10m.
Midline of eastern corridor		15.00m.
Midline of western corridor		13.80m.

The central pit alone, according to the measurements above, contains nearly two thousand cubic meters of compact soil, which had to be dug out in the course of clearing. It was soon found, when the excavation was in progress, that all the huge tombs had been sacked more than once, before modern tomb robbers intruded. The past sackings were so thorough that at least the earliest plunderers clearly reached the wooden chamber and took away all the buried treasures they could find; however, they did not care for the buried goods in the corridors. Those stored in the passage corridors were stolen later, some of them perhaps only recently. For modern archaeological purposes, cleaning up the refilled huge tombs proved to be a burdensome business, but not entirely unrewarding. In the first place, the tomb structure is itself an important study, and, second, refilled tombs frequently included precious artifacts that the earlier tomb robbers were too ignorant to appreciate. It is true also that, as a general rule, no tomb robbers, past or present, are in the mood to do a 100 percent clean job; so there are always nooks and corners that have been neglected. The Hou-chia-chuang excavations have once more proved this generalization.

In the case of HPKM 1004, the outline of structure of the central pit at the cross-section is nearly square, but somewhat longer in the north-south direction than in the dimension from east to west. So, as the pit goes down, the dimension of the pit gradually shrinks in size, and at the bottom, which appeared at the depth of 12.00–12.20 meters from the surface, the size shrinks to 15.20 × 16.30m.; thus the whole huge pit, when drawn on scale, looks like a Chinese square peck for measuring rice and wheat. At the bottom of this deep-sunken pit is a wooden chamber. The wooden chamber of tomb HPKM 1004 was still preserved sufficiently for a reconstruction of the original. Leading to the wooden chamber at the bottom of the central pit are the four sloping passage corridors from the four directions; some of these are stepped, others merely sloping. The one from the south, which measures 31.40m. long from the upper end near the surface soil down to the southern entrance at the central pit at the bottom, is the longest of the four, while the other three passages to the east, west, and north are all less than half the distance of the southern corridor; they are naturally also more steep.

The Wooden Chamber

The floors of the wooden chambers, some of which still leave visible traces, are clearly composed of long wooden beams, 20–30cm. in dimension; and the side walls are nearly three meters high. Whether these chambers were also roofed by timbers is however not very clear. But there is no question that these chambers must have been roofed. And, also, there must have been an entrance door facing the south, which passed directly into the southern passage corridor. Evidence also shows that inside the wooden chamber, the walls might have been elaborately decorated by painting, carving, or inlaying, or even stucco, presumably as extravagant as the inside of a palace. As the side walls of the central pit have been found usually smooth and well plastered, while the wooden chamber is much smaller than the bottom size of the hollowed pit, there obviously existed a distance between the wall of the pit and the wall of the wooden chamber, which was filled in by layers of pounded earth.

Professor Kao Ch'ü-hsün illustrates the wooden chamber of HPKM 1004 as reconstructed in Figure 10. The measured dimensions at the bottom of the pit are 13.2 × 10.0m.; the reconstructed wooden chamber at the bottom occupies the maximum dimension of 9.00 × 8.50m. only, including all the side chamber, so there is an average of more than one meter's distance between the wall of the central pit and the wall of the wooden chamber. The empty space that separated the wooden chamber from the pit wall, before the tomb was closed up, had to be filled in by pounding the soil up to the top of the roof, layer after layer, with the exception of the southern entrance. There is scarcely any doubt that this pisé work definitely took place long before the final closure of the tomb. There is also reason to believe that this part of filling-in engineering might have been the final phase of the construction of the tomb, a finishing touch after the completion of the building of the wooden chamber. When the filling-in was completed, the regular burial, that is, the conveyance of the royal coffin into the wooden chamber, may have taken place, although the means are still uncertain. The method of transportation for the dead body might have been a specially constructed carriage, or an ox-drawn cart.

There seems to be no question that once the dead body was placed within the wooden chamber, a sacrificial ceremony started. The ritual procedure may have taken a long time; it must have been a time-consuming business, judging by the extraordinary

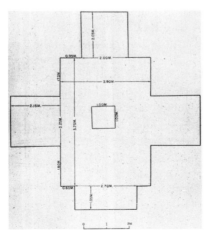

Figure 10. The floor of the wooden chamber of HPKM 1004

number of burial treasures and the total number of human sacrifices. Also, according to pre-Ch'in tradition, the custom of three years' mourning by the heir started in the Yin-Shang dynasty, although many historians may still be skeptical on this point.

Early Plunderings

In opening HPKM 1004, the archaeologists observed that long before modern treasure hunters cast their eyes on this group of royal tombs, they were plundered in early periods more than once —in the case of HPKM 1004, definitely twice. In the previous tomb-robbings, diggings were evidently carried out in a systematic manner; traces of the early diggings reach down to 12 meters deep, much lower than the present water level. The plunderers obviously knew the exact location where the buried treasures were hidden underneath, as they drilled their tunnels almost exactly on the top of the wooden chamber—slightly deviating northward in the case of HPKM 1004. So the first sacking—if we take HPKM 1004 as instance—scooped out nearly 90 percent of the buried treasures, leaving what they believed to be only trifles.

The refilled robbing tunnels are in a way also interesting for a modern archaeologist to trace. By careful examination of the traces of the previous plunderings and the refilled caves one can learn the technique of the robbers' procedure. More important, one might also acquire some information by which to judge approximately when the plunderings occurred. In the case of tomb HPKM 1004, the drilling by the early plunderers for some reason ran a little toward the north; as a consequence, a small part near the southern wall of the pit was left untouched. The result was that the two magnificent bronze tetrapods were left buried there till our field team reopened the tomb in 1934 (see Fig. 11).

Offerings and Human Sacrifices

From the refilled tunnels in all the big tombs in both the western and eastern sections, many important artifacts have been recovered; but as they were not found *in situ*, it is impossible to say whether they originally belonged to the tomb where they were found. Fortunately, as mentioned above, there are nooks and

Figure 11. Two of the big bronzes *in situ*, HPKM 1004

corners which early plunderers overlooked, and in these intact and usually out of the way places, occasionally some lucky finds, like the two huge bronze tetrapods in HPKM 1004, were occasionally found *in situ*.

The original report on HPKM 1004 describes the exact location of these two bronze tetrapods in the southern side of the central pit of this tomb near the entrance of the southern passage corridor at a depth from the modern surface of 8.1 meters, a little less than 2 meters above the roof of the wooden chamber. They constitute the fourth intact layer of depository furniture found in this untouched portion. Below this layer, our archaeologists discovered a bundle of 360 bronze spearheads at the depth of 9.60–9.85m. (see Fig. 12); the second layer of deposit below was bronze helmets, which according to later accounting were as many as 141, and mixed with the helmets in the deposit were also spearheads and halberts. The bottom layer, that is, the first layer, was located near the bottom of the pit at almost 12.0m. below the modern surface. In this layer were found articles originally made of perishable materials, which had almost completely disappeared at the time of discovery. Still our field archaeologists were able to trace out four individual artifacts; they apparently were parts of a carriage, judging by the decorative trace left on the soil, in which the pigments and the copper rust had left deeply impressed marks in the soil.

Finds as given above are comparatively rare; still they occur here and there in almost every big tomb in both sections. And in the case of the small sacrificial tombs, there were many which remained intact when our field team started systematic excavation.

Among the minor tombs, located mainly in the eastern section of the HPKM cemetery, 439 were undisturbed by early grave robbers, and 419 were partly destroyed; all the rest had been completely destroyed by tomb thiefs. Of this total number of small tombs only 104 were located in the western section; the majority of them, 1,117 in number, were found in the eastern section.

Among the opened small tombs—1,046 in number—643 can be classified according to their contents and other features, namely: [10]

Type I. Human bones	Number
a. Single complete skeleton	131
b. Multiple complete skeletons	57
c. Skull and skeletal part separated	52
d. Skulls only	209
e. Post-cranial skeleton only	192
f. Infants in urns	9

Type II. Animals	Number
a. Horse burials	20
b. Elephant burials	2
c. Other animals (including birds)	?

Type III. Miscellaneous	Number
a. Carriage	2
b. Vessels	1

A casual examination of the above list is sufficient to show that these minor burials are in fact the pits for sacrificial offerings. Among the human burials alone, the over four hundred which have been exposed in which the dead bodies were definitely mutilated before burial (the c., d., and e. subtypes according to the

Figure 12. A large number of spearheads discovered *in situ*, HPKM 1004

above classification), certainly proves the existence of the practice of human sacrifice in the Yin-Shang dynasty. It may be justifiably deduced, as our archaeologists have done, that all the small tombs are sacrificial tombs.

One of the most incontestable confirmations of this barbarous custom was found in the very bottom of the deep sunken pit, far below the floor of the wooden chamber in HPKM 1001, where no less than nine underfloor sacrificial human pits had remained intact for our archaeologists to clear in 1935. The wooden ground floor was sufficiently well preserved to indicate that early plunderings did not reach deeper than this floor. When they discovered the nine burial pits underneath the floor, located in the center and four corners, the field archaeologists concluded that these were the skeletons of the guards placed there to protect the dead master against subterranean evil spirits. Even more interesting to an archaeologist is that all the nine pits indicate: (1) a definite position—one at the center, two at each of four corners of the wooden chamber floor, (2) the bodies were all contracted, either prone or on the side, (3) each was accompanied by a dog skeleton, and

(4) each burial had a halbert weapon—the *ko*—a standard Chinese weapon. Most noticeable is the fact that while the halberts uncovered in all the four corner pits were all made of bronze, the central pit alone contained a stone halbert.[11]

Even more astonishing were the disclosures that in all the large tombs, both in the central pit above the level of the wooden chambers and in the passage corridors, the mutilated skeletons and skulls were found in groups, layer after layer, repeated in the accumulated strata of the pounded earth that filled up the central pit as well as the various passages. It is almost impossible to make an account of the number of victims slaughtered for each of the royal tombs, as all the tombs were sacked more than once before our team started the clearing; many of skeletal remains of the victims must have been already destroyed.

Important Finds

Among the various and abundant artifacts recovered from the Hou-chia-chuang cemetery site, the group that commanded the most attention and was considered unique and unexpected was a series of stone carvings of both realistic and mythical types, such as turtles, frogs, human figures, and tiger-headed, eagle-headed, and double-faced monsters. Most of these relatively large stone carvings were excavated from HPKM 1001, but unfortunately only from the refilled sacked pockets, so that it was impossible to say exactly what their positions had been *in situ* in the original tomb. It is even difficult to judge whether these artistic stone artifacts were originally buried in these big tombs where they were uncovered, as there is reason to believe that these sacked areas were refilled from mixed dumps of soils from a number of graves plundered at the same time. In the special reports on these tombs, a number of instances show that fragments of one article, which had been broken into several pieces, had been deposited in the refills of several different tombs.[12]

While the finds from the refilling of HPKM 1001 exhibit a long list of stone sculptures, the most interesting example to professional archaeologists is the one found in the filling-in deposit of the plundering tunnels from HPKM 1004. This is a fragment of a human figure in the kneeling-sitting posture, exactly resembling the formal posture of a modern Japanese sitting at home on the *tatami* (see Fig. 13).

Figure 13. Reconstruction of a human figure in the kneeling-sitting posture

I personally made a special study of this particular figure years later and found out that the posture represented by this stone figure was historically known as *seiza* in the Japanese language; but the original Chinese term for it is *cheng-tso*, meaning "correct seating," especially on Chinese ceremonial occasions, as during the emperor's reception of an official audience. Ancient China kept this "correct seating" posture up to the end of the Han dynasty, while the Japanese *seiza* can be traced only to the middle of the fourteenth century A.D. through the Korean influence.

Another group of important artifacts is a series of beautifully impressed traces left on the soil in brilliant red and other colors, sometimes inlaid by colored stone and shells; these are from articles made of perishable materials like fabrics of hemp and silk in wooden and bamboo frames, especially lacquered wooden utensils, and so on. These articles were probably painted in brilliant mineral pigments that were better preserved in the buried soil than the major substance of the original articles. The field men referred to these "traces" as "decorated clay." In HPKM 1001, findings of decorated clay were very extensive; they also appeared in other big tombs. Our field men cut off these clay lumps with great care and packed them in specially made boxes sent to headquarters for study. Some of the designs left on the impressed clay remain clear and vivid; they have provided a rich source of materials for investigating the development of decorative art of this period.

In this connection, mention should also be made about an intact group, discovered in the western corridor of HPKM 1217, the original traces of a drum and a musical stone *in situ* (see Figs. 56 and 57).[13] The decayed and disintegrated drum still kept its original shape as well as the marks of snake skin as the drum head; the musical stone (*ch'in*) was well preserved, although somewhat imperfectly made.

The bronze vessels and weapons, which appeared abundantly, were on the whole much better preserved and were originally certainly better made. If we remember that all the finds made during our excavations were only the relatively few lucky survivals of past systematic and thorough-going plunderings, we can imagine how extravagant these elaborate burials must have been, not to mention the enormous amount of human labor commandeered to build these excessively huge mausoleums.

6 Last Three Seasons of Field Work

in Hsiao-t'un before World War II

THE JAPANESE invasion of China in the summer of 1937 suspended the excavations which had been planned in 1928 by trained archaeologists under the able leadership of Director Fu Ssŭ-nien of the Institute of History and Philology, Academia Sinica, and which had continued thereafter for nine years with only occasional interruptions. This Japanese invasion was the prelude to the worldwide conflict known as World War II. Western historians are still in the habit of dating the outbreak of World War II from Hitler's challenge to Western Europe, neglecting altogether the early phase of this global warfare in the Far Eastern theater. As a matter of historical truth, it seems almost impossible to divide this tragic story.

Since the Anyang excavation was a scientific enterprise undertaken by the Academia Sinica under the aegis of the National Government in Nanking, it was forced to discontinue active field work in Anyang after the Japanese invaded north China.

Before this happened in 1937, the Anyang expedition had worked for another three seasons following Liang Ssŭ-yung's decision to stop the field operation at the Hsi-pei-kang royal cemetery of Hou-chia-chuang in the winter of 1935. The field work of these three seasons, known respectively as the thirteenth, fourteenth, and fifteenth seasons of the Anyang expedition, was concentrated at the Hsiao-t'un site, carrying out in a systematic manner the carpet-rolling method of tracing the building foundations in the last capital of the Yin-Shang dynasty. The schedules of the field operations and the varying composition of the working staffs are tabulated on the following page.

In carrying out this method of digging during the last three seasons, there were naturally places to which special efforts were more intensively applied, namely where pounded earth was found to be more extensive and where past plunderings were comparatively rare, relative to the finds of the past nine seasons. So the field labor of these three seasons was almost all concentrated in Subareas B and C. Each of these two subareas was again, by surveying instruments, redivided into a number of parts of the same size, 40m. × 40m. with a surface area of 1,600 square meters. In the map, these parts were further divided into sections; each section measured 100 square meters (10m. × 10m.), which constituted the smallest unit of the more detailed surveying area, all of which were given a serial number in a definite order, such as C126, etc., which means section 126 in Subarea C.

Also beginning with the thirteenth season, serial numbers were given to the underground pits and burial sites, with the English capital letter "H" (*hui-k'eng* , "pits") to signify the former and "M" (*mu*, "burials") for the latter, such as H127, or M164.

Our main purpose during the last three seasons of field operation was to complete the excavation of the architectural foundations built during the period of the oracle bone inscriptions. The detailed procedures, however, naturally varied in accordance with the progress of the excavations and the underground conditions, which differed from place to place. For instance, the technique and appearance of the "pounded earth" were found to be by no means uniform. Some sections had been pounded merely for the purpose of leveling up a depressed area, others for building independent walls; the most common remains were those designed as foundations of surface buildings. For wall building, planning would be needed before starting to pound the earth. In foundation building,

Season	Period	Leaders	Field Staff	Digging Activities
Thirteenth	March 18–June 24, 1936	Kuo Pao-chün Shih Chang-ju	Li Chin-tan Wang Hsiang Ch'i Yen-p'ei Kao Ch'ü-hsün Yin Huan-chang P'an Ch'üeh	14 Chinese acres excavated; 127 caves and caches; 181 burials. Foundations without border, but with pillar stones. Water ditches under the foundations. H127 discovered.
Fourteenth	Sept. 20–Dec. 31, 1936	Liang Ssŭ-yung Shih Chang-ju	Wang Hsiang Kao Ch'ü-hsün Yin Huan-chang Four others	60 trenchings; excavating an area of 3590m.^{2}; 26 foundations; 122 caves and caches, 132 burials; underground ditches.
Fifteenth	March 16–June 19, 1937	Shih Chang-ju	Wang Hsiang Kao Ch'ü-hsün P'an Ch'üeh Four others	37 trenchings; excavating 3,700m.^{2}; foundations units 20, caves and caches 220; underground ditches 120m. long, gates located with human sacrifices in kneeling position, many artifacts.

there evidently was some sort of architectural "blueprint" to follow, for the ground first had to be leveled by filling in any underground pits or caches wherever they might occur and also by scraping down to the level all raised areas. Ever since the field party had discovered the main function of the pisé technique during the fourth season, the technology of earth-pounding had been studied with great care. The field workers were all aware of the fact that some pisé areas might be several meters deep, whereas others were so thin that only one layer of stamped earth measuring less than 20 cm. in thickness remained on the surface. Further, they concluded that this technology was developed probably only after the Shang dynasty moved the capital to Anyang. In the course of field operations, they discovered that the pisé layer, no matter how deep it might be, was frequently underlaid by other architectural features—subterranean dwellings, cache pits, and channeled water ditches, or by burials and other prehistoric remains. Such subterranean constructions, according to Professor Shih Chang-ju, were part of the early Shang dynasty culture; they were built before King P'an Keng moved the capital here.

Let us examine some of these pre-Yin architectural features which were found under the pounded earth area (see also more extended discussion in Chap. 10).

Underground Dwellings and Cache-Pits for Storage Purposes

In the last three seasons of our expeditions to Anyang before World War II, a larger area was excavated than in all the diggings of the previous nine seasons. The total area uncovered amounted to more than twelve thousand square meters, while the area dug in the first nine seasons had been just a little over eight thousand square meters. If we compare the number of underground cache-pits or dwellings, the total number discovered in the first nine seasons was only 123, but in the last three seasons 479 of these underground structures were cleared. Seemingly of even greater importance were the disclosures of a regular system of water-ditches, strengthened by wooden piles on both banks of the channel, definitely built in the pre-pisé period of the Shang dynasty. These ditch-channels were no doubt designed when subterranean pits and semiunderground dwellings were the general habitations of the population.

These cache-pits and subterranean dwellings, according to Professor Shih Chang-ju, were divisible into several classes of which the main categories are as follows:

Round or Oval Tou-*Pits* (*Fig. 14*)

These subterranean holes were sometimes paired like joined double rooms. Some of the pits were very shallow, not more than 1 meter deep below the modern surface. But the deeper pits might go down from 7 to 10 meters and even deeper. The latter pits usually had vertical rows of foothold niches on the side walls, either opposite each other or on the same side. Professor Shih divided this group into six subtypes. The first two subtypes with flat bottoms or irregular bases were all shallow, their diameter being about 1½ meters, usually found above the pisé foundation. But the more deeply cut pits—usually more than 3 meters in depth—were in most cases built below the pisé and therefore antedated the stamped earth period. Shih redivided the deeper *tou*-pits into four subtypes, according to the arrangement of the foothold niches. These pits were usually designed for storage purposes. And, according to Professor Shih, most of these *tou* storage pits uncovered during our diggings were located on the western side of the Hsiao-t'un site.

Rectangular or Square Chiao-*Cellars* (*Fig. 15*)

The depth of these underground structures varied from 1.10 meters to more than 10 meters; and for ascent and descent there were foothold niches cut in the walls as in the previous group. Similarly, most of the deep *chiao*-cellars were built earlier than the period of pounded earth, but the shallower ones were evidently constructed later. The majority of these *chiao*-cellars were like the round pits, deep and evidently also used for storage purposes as they were comparatively narrow—the total area of the surface at the base being seldom larger than 4 square meters.

The Hsüeh-*Pits* (*Fig. 16*)

This group consisted of a number of large, but usually shallow, subterranean pit dwellings. Many of these underground dwellings

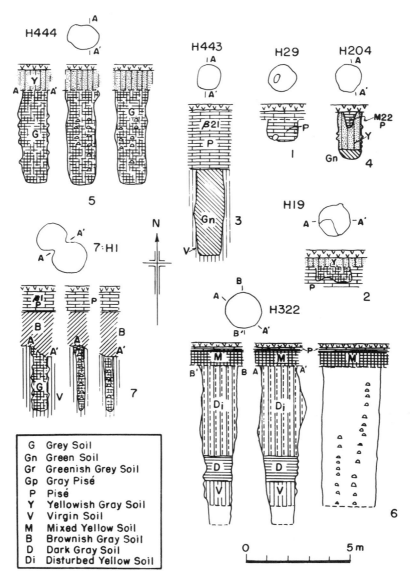

Figure 14. *Tou*-pits

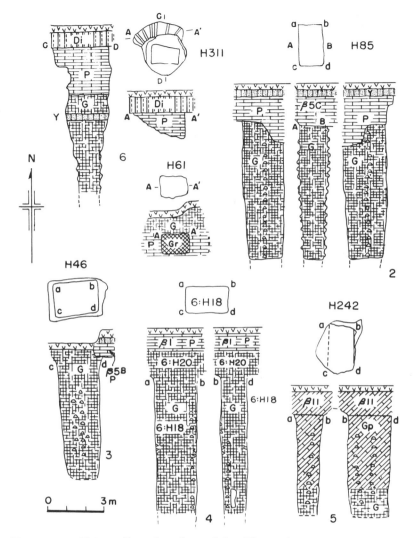

Figure 15. *Chiao*-cellars (see legend for Fig. 14).

still retained a flight of steps, either along the pit walls or at the center. The floors were often flat, and in some cases divided into two parts. The ground plan of the entire dwelling might be round, oval, or rectangular (see discussion on pp. 175–79). Most of the pits had a floor size larger than 10 square meters, the size of the largest

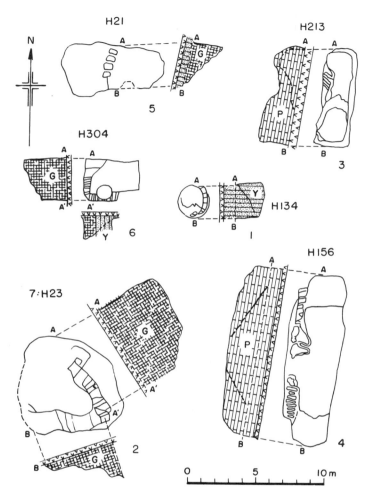

Figure 16. *Hsüeh*-pits (see legend for Fig. 14)

might exceed 30 square meters. The average underground depth was between 2 and 3 meters but in one rare instance (7:H23) it went down to almost 6 meters with a stairway of seventeen steps.

Professor Shih remarked that this group of underground pit dwellings had been found, in the majority of cases, underneath the foundations built by the pounded earth method. This obviously indicated that they were the earlier habitations of the local peoples. Further, Shih remarked that judging by the average depth of these *hsüeh*-pits, which was only about 2 meters, the walls of these dwellings must have extended above the ground surface and consequently the roofs would have been well above ground.

Semiunderground Dwellings

Finally Shih also added another group of what he called "semisubterranean dwellings," of which the underground portions were less than 1 meter deep, and round, oval, square, or rectangular in cross section. The diameter of this group of structures, if round-shaped, was usually more than 3 meters. If rectangular or square, the floor areas varied between 20 and 30 square meters. A peculiarity of these semisubterranean dwellings was the fact that postholes were usually found on the margin of the bases of these underground pits, indicating that wooden pillars were provided for wall-building and supporting the roof of the house above the land surface.

The fact that many of these four groups of underground structures were located under the pisé foundations led Shih to conclude in a special article that as noted above the majority were remains left here by the earlier inhabitants before King P'an Keng moved the Shang capital to this locality.[1] There were, however, exceptions; in the course of continued excavations, many deep-sunken pits and cellars were found to be contemporaneous with the pisé foundations; these pits or cellars were built either for storage or, as I interpreted them in an early article, for sacrificial purposes.[2] Very few subterranean dwellings *per se* were found after the introduction of the pisé. It seems quite clear that most of the living quarters were built above the ground surface once this place became the capital of the Empire. Except for sacrificial burials, it is almost certain that no temples or palaces were ever built underground after King P'an Keng developed the city into a capital.

In the final three seasons, field excavations on a large scale systematically exposed the extensive architectural foundations of the altars, temples, palaces, workshops, and dwelling houses all over the areas northeast of Hsiao-t'un village, which were reported in *PREA*. Chapter 10 will cover all these discoveries and discuss possible reconstructions, since they constitute one of the major archaeological contributions to our knowledge of Shang history.

Certain other important field observations should first, however, be related. What I have in mind is the definite establishment of the cultural sequences of the underground deposits at Hsiao-t'un, determined through the accumulated evidence gathered by the field workers throughout the expeditions from 1928 through 1937, culminating in the final seasons. These established archaeological sequences can be noted briefly in the following order:

1. The most basic depository remains indicated that the earliest inhabitants of the Hsiao-t'un site were the prehistoric folk who lived in subterranean dwellings and who had already developed the Lungshan or Black Pottery Culture.

2. Succeeding the Lungshan Culture were a large series of underground pits, cellars, and subterranean dwellings of the early Shang period before this place was chosen as the capital of the kingdom in King P'an Keng's period.

3. The period of Yin-Shang with Anyang as capital was the time when the pisé method of construction was introduced and extensive surface buildings became abundant.

4. After the downfall of the Yin-Shang dynasty, the remains were mainly burials.

Significant Discoveries in the Thirteenth, Fourteenth, and Fifteenth Seasons of the Anyang Expeditions

The number of findings and unexpected discoveries in the last three seasons at Hsiao-t'un exceeded the expectations of every experienced participant in the field work, including all the old-timers among the diggers. Let me itemize the more important groups of these findings made in the final phase of the Anyang expedition from the summer season of 1936 to the end of June of 1937. Of these groups, I shall choose those which were not only in themselves significant, but which also provided new data for the solution of some older historical problems:

GROUP A. IMPORTANT AND UNEXPECTED DISCOVERIES IN THE LAST THREE SEASONS

1. Chariot burials
2. Underground deposit of archives of inscribed oracle bone documents (H127)

GROUP B. PROBLEMS SOLVED BY THE ACCUMULATION OF OBSERVA-
TIONS AND MATERIAL EVIDENCE

1. Human sacrifice
2. Fauna and flora
3. Ceramic collections
4. Evolutionary stages of the subterranean pits and dwellings
5. Orientations and sizes of foundations of surface buildings

Group A lists finds made by chance whereas those listed under Group B were the result of planned scientific recording and gradual accumulations of collected data. In this chapter, I shall go into some detail about the surprise findings, namely Group A. The items in the second category will be for the most part discussed later, but let me first make brief mention of their chief characteristics, the methods of their collection, and the circumstances of their discoveries.

I have listed "Human sacrifice" as number one in Group B for a special reason. Chapter 5 above refers to evidence that this barbarian practice existed all over the Old and New World in the Bronze Age. The account in that chapter concerning human sacrifice could be taken to imply that this practice was confined to sacrificial rituals connected with funerals. As a matter of fact this was what the field archaeologists believed at the beginning. But evidence unearthed in the last three seasons at Hsiao-t'un definitely proved that human sacrifices were also customary for other purposes: they were made in connection with such activities as laying building foundations, and the annual worship of various spirits, whether abstract, such as river gods, or concrete idols. This deserves some description: for example, such instances were found in tracing the foundations in subarea B7.

Only the left side of the Subarea B7 foundation was traced out; the right side had already been submerged by the Huan River, which bounded the Hsiao-t'un farm on the east. The part of the pounded foundation that was traced out measured no less than forty meters in the east-west direction and over thirty meters north-south. Within this portion of the foundation in section B7 were discovered a series of sacrificial pits, arranged apparently in some order, on the southern side of the pounded earth. Each of these pits was given an individual name-symbol according to Shih's report, as follows:

Sacrificial pits	Contents
M 230	5 oxen
M 229	1 dog, 2 sheep
M 96	3 oxen
M 106	11 dogs
M 141	2 dogs, 1 sheep
M 94	3 dogs
M 105	3 dogs, 3 sheep
M 140	3 oxen
M 168	1 kneeling man, facing north

Summarizing the above list, Shih said that altogether ten oxen, six sheep, twenty dogs, and one human being were found in this row of sacrificial pits. Even more surprising was evidence disclosed near the door of the building where Shih found more pits, which he described as sacrificial pits connected with "earth-breaking rituals" when the erection of the front gate or door was to take place. According to Shih's account, three more human beings were sacrificed and buried here. These additional pits were located on the right, left, and at the center where the foundations for the doorposts were to be laid. Each of these three sacrificial victims was found in a special burial and in a kneeling posture, accompanied in every case by a halbert. A fourth victim was found further south, right in front of the gate. This front guard, so to speak, was equipped with both a shield and a spear; he was also buried in a kneeling posture, facing north.

Professor Chang Ping-chüan, in an article based upon oracle bone records, classified the sacrificial offerings recorded in these inscriptions according to the kind of victims and the number used on each occasion.[3] Each of these accounts is related to the sacrificial offering to a particular ancestral spirit, or other idol, like a river god, mountain spirit and so on. Chang found in these accounts that the victims offered might be ox, sheep, pig, dog, human being, deer, elephant, tortoise, and even rhinoceros. He found out also that the ox, sheep, pig, and dog were evidently domesticated and perhaps some of them were specially reserved for this particular purpose. As for human beings, Chang cited a special record to show that at least some of the human victims were captives. Even more interesting as recorded in these inscriptions is the number of victims employed, which varied considerably. Chang collated in his article the number of oxen cited as being offered as sacrifices with the number of citations as follows:

NUMBER OF OXEN USED	NUMBER OF TIMES RECORDED IN ORACLE BONE INSCRIPTIONS
indefinite	33
1	23
2	23
3	17
4	6
5	13
6	3
7	2
8	1
9	8
10	21
15	1
20	3
30	10
40	2
50	5
100	6
300	2
1,000	1

The number of sheep, dogs, and pigs employed for sacrificial purposes also varied a great deal but none of these victims exceeded one hundred in a single offering. As for tortoises, deer, and elephants or rhinoceroses, all were comparatively rare. In the case of human victims, however, according to Chang, there is at least one record that gives the number as three hundred, and another records the number as one thousand, but generally the number varies like the list of oxen above. Whether the isolated instances of three hundred and one thousand human victims could be interpreted in any other way remains a problem that can be solved only by new data.

The other four items of field data under category B are all of fundamental archaeological significance, as each of them—fauna and flora, ceramic collections, various stages of underground construction, and different orientations of surface buildings—has provided basic materials which illustrate concretely the ways of life during the initial historical period in the last quarter of the second millennium B.C., when Chinese civilization was still in the making.

Special monographs and articles devoted to studies of fauna and of ceramic materials from this site were issued many years ago; let me mention some of the results briefly here.

In a special monograph on mammalian remains, Pierre Teilhard de Chardin and C. C. Young identified no less than twenty-four species from the mammalian collections made by the various Anyang expeditions in the early period, which had been sent to the Cenozoic Laboratory for special investigations.[4] The twenty-four species identified by Teilhard and Young are divisible into almost twenty genera: namely, *Canis* (dog), *Ursus* (bear), *Meles* (badger), *Felis* (tiger), *Catacea* (whale), *Epimys* (rat), *Rhizomys* (bamboo rats), *Lepus* (hare), *Tapirus* (tapir), *Equus* (horse), *Sus* (pig), *Hydropotes* (water deer), *Pseudaxis* (Sika deer), *Elaphurus* (David deer), *Ovis* (goat), *Capra* (domesticated goat), *Bos* (ox), *Bubalus* (water buffalo), *Elephas* (elephant), *Macacus* (monkey).

One of the most interesting conclusions drawn by these two eminent paleontologists was that "the Anyang citizens [of the Yin-Shang period] were industrious commercial and agricultural people, working bone extensively for economic purposes, and that in addition, they regarded the hunting of big game as a royal achievement. These conditions explain why the faunistical remains recovered from the ruins of the city are so abundant, so various, and so heterogeneous."

The two authors also recognized three distinct groups among the examined mammals: (1) the wild indigenous group, (2) the domesticated local group, and (3) the foreign imported groups. The raccoon-dog, the bear, the badger, the tiger, the panther, the common rat, the bamboo rat, the hare, the water deer, and the Sika deer are examples of the indigenous wild animals. For the domesticated group, the authors named the dog, the sheep, and the goat; the *Elaphurus* (deer), the *Bos* (ox), the water buffalo, and the *Macacus* (monkey) were also included in this group.

For the definitely foreign, imported group, only a small list is given, which includes the whale, the elephant, the tapir, and a small bear. Regarding this last group, the authors had this to say:

Bones of whale could easily be collected anywhere along the closest seashore. Elephant and Tapir, on the contrary, seem to have been imported alive from the south. An extensive trade between Anyang and southern China is proven by the discovery in the ruins of the city of ingots of tin and also of an enormous quantity of *Lamprotula* shells. This thick *Unicnid* (used for its mother-of-pearl) has become rare ever since the Upper Pleistocene in N. China. It was therefore probably brought to Anyang from the Yangtze valley . . . [p. 56].

The authors discussed with great erudition the history of mammalian fauna in north China and, at the end, drew the further conclusion that the water-buffalo was possibly domesticated in China in early prehistoric times, as the ancestral type of buffaloes was traceable to the Pleistocene Age. At any rate, buffaloes were found to be as abundant as oxen in the later excavations at Anyang. Whether they were offered in sacrificial rites is, however, not yet definitely determined.

New data resulting from investigations in subsequent seasons have added to the list of mammals found in Anyang. Especially interesting is the bone of a peacock, which was evidently an immigrant from the south. It should also be noted that horses were found in great number in later excavations.

Our attempt to study the flora was, unavoidably, a miserable failure. We had made a collection of wood charcoal from the excavations, amounting to thousands of test tubes. This precious collection, if it had been duly investigated by authorities like Father Teilhard, might have provided the fundamental data for our knowledge of Yin-Shang botany in the neighborhood of Anyang and would certainly have given us some ideas about the climatic environment of this period. But these data disappeared and were irrecoverably lost to science during the war.

We were, however, more fortunate with our ceramic collections, which I myself took great pains to register, classify, and catalogue, and finally brought together into a corpus. My monograph on Anyang pottery was published in 1956 and includes the entire corpus of Yin-hsü pottery.[5] Although I will go into more detail on the technological and decorative aspects of these ceramics in Chapters 11 and 12, here I would like to briefly mention some of the main characteristics of this collection.

The total number of registered pot-sherds was nearly a quarter of a million. Of this enormous amount, nearly 80 percent were collected during the last three seasons at Hsiao-t'un when, through accumulated experience, all members of the field staff were familiar with the up-to-date criteria of classification and registration. Mr. Wang Hsiang, who had been from the very beginning of the Anyang excavation assigned to the special task of pottery collection, was able, before his departure for wartime service, to give a full report containing a classified list of the total collection in the field. The field team, after returning from the thrilling experience of excavating the royal tombs at Hou-chia-chuang and enriched by the great quantity of precious white potteries they had found there in the royal cemetery, had gained a deeper insight into the craftsmanship and technology of the ceramic industry of the Yin-Shang era. It may be said that all the members of the field staff had a full knowledge of the typical Yin-Shang ceramics, divisible into the following four classes by their outside appearance alone:

CLASS 1   Gray pottery, nearly 90% of the total collection
CLASS 2   Red pottery, about 6.86% of the total collection
CLASS 3   White pottery, about 0.27% of the total collection
CLASS 4   Hard wares, about 1.73% of the total collection

In addition to these four typical Yin-Shang products, there were also a fifth and a sixth group: black pottery and painted pottery. Although the white pottery of Yin-Shang period, which has long been considered typical of the ceramic products of this epoch, was highly valued by collectors, from a purely technological viewpoint, however, the hard wares, many of which were covered with a thin layer of primitive glaze, were really a great discovery, totally unknown before. When this was first announced in the newspapers, the veteran British Sinologue and antiquarian, Professor Perceval Yetts, immediately wrote to me and announced it to the Royal Asiatic Society in London. Our archaeological collection included several nearly complete specimens of both the white pottery and the glazed hard wares. Many of the archaeologists of this institute have always cherished the idea that these specimens are even more valuable than the more spectacular field collection of bronzes, including the huge tetrapods from the royal tombs.

Leaving Group B, subgroups 4 and 5 for later chapters, I shall devote the remaining portion of this chapter to some descriptions of what I consider the two major unexpected discoveries of Group A, all made in the last three seasons of the Anyang excavation. Let me relate them in order.

Chariot Burials

Paleographers knew long ago that wheeled vehicles had existed in the Shang dynasty. During the Anyang excavations, decorative pieces made of bronze and apparently intended for some parts of chariots were found frequently in early diggings at Hsiao-t'un, and disassembled carts had been discovered in the royal tombs at Hou-chia-chuang more than once. All these findings were important indications of the existence of wheeled vehicles during the Shang dynasty, but they could hardly serve for any systematic reconstruction of the original model of this important means of transportation. It was not until the thirteenth season, and on the thirteenth day of April in 1936, that Professor Kao Ch'ü-hsün, in charge of clearing Subarea C in Hsiao-t'un, first discovered underneath a layer of pounded earth a distinct boundary line marked by traces of brilliant red lacquer. This led to the discovery of M20. This particular subsection was known as C74; here the boundary line was found at about 0.80–1.00m. below the existing surface. When the surface pisé layer was scraped away, an elongated pit 2.90 × 1.80m. appeared. This was the famous chariot pit, M20, of Hsiao-t'un, in which some complete chariots with four horses had been buried and were found almost intact (Fig. 17).

M20 of Hsiao-t'un, discovered at C74, proved to be only one of the five chariot burials in this section: the other four were located respectively at C72, C73, and C120 as Figure 18 shows. These five chariot burials were found very close to one another and apparently in some kind of order, which led Shih to recognize in later studies that they were sacrificial burials offered for a definite purpose. But the other four pits had been disturbed either by later intrusion or by subsequent construction. Only M20 remained more or less intact. Still, when it was opened, it was found that the overlying pounded earth and the underground moisture had damaged the skeletal remains of both animals and men, and that such perishable materials as wooden frames and leather bindings had already decayed to such a degree that only traces of outlines could be perceived. The metallic gadgets and stone pieces and some bones had survived the centuries intact. Nevertheless it was possible for the field men to get approximately accurate records by means of photographing and sketching *in situ*. To this day, M20 remains one of the few assemblages of the earliest field data on

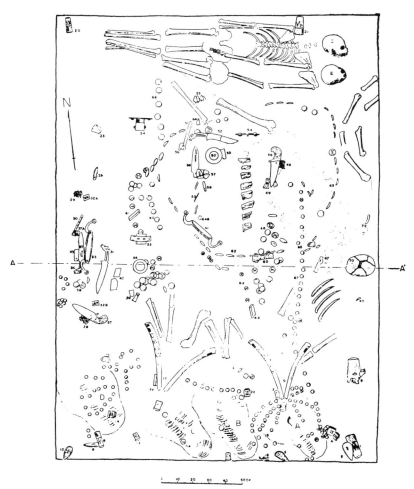

Figure 17. M20, the chariot pit of Hsiao-t'un

which could be based a study of the history of the "wheeled?" vehicle in ancient China.

I have put a question mark following the term "wheeled," because actually when this pit, M20, was opened, there were found four horses, three human bodies, and traces of chariots but not the slightest indication of a wheel. The field records, fortunately, were taken and kept in good order, and after years of continuous studies, a number of archaeologists and antiquarians concluded that M20 contained two-wheeled chariots from which the wheels had been

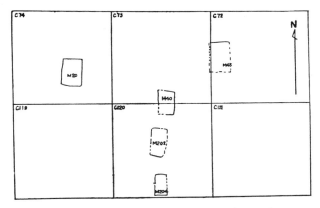

Figure 18. Distribution and locations of the chariot pits

taken and probably buried somewhere else, analogous to the custom of burying the human head and body separately.

Still the painstaking excavation of M20 helped to preserve together the essential parts of the main structure of the chariot body which could serve as basic data for later reconstruction. In this pit, the field workers found the following in order: (1) three human skeletons; (2) four horse skeletons; (3) decorated pieces for horse heads and bodies; (4) bronze devices from the chariot body: bronze terminals for both the shaft and axles; (5) weapons: three sets of halberts, small swords, and arrowheads; (6) bells for horses; (7) whips; (8) traces of wooden frames and leather bindings of shafts and axles; (9) yokes and cross-bars; and (10) a stone *pi*-disc and other miscellany. The remains and artifacts recovered from M20 were studied by half a dozen specialists during the war and long after. But it was not until 1970 that Professor Shih Chang-ju was able to publish his reconstruction, based on his continuous study of these original data, which, with his permission, I reproduce in this summary.[6]

I have no intention of going into details about Professor Shih's reconstruction of this important vehicle and its significance in the study of the history of early Chinese culture. I am aware of recent discoveries, similar in nature to M20 of Hsiao-t'un. Whether detailed comparisons will confirm Shih's reconstruction is an interesting speculation. Be that as it may, the excavation and research of M20 constitute a historical landmark signaling the beginning of the study of the "wheeled vehicle" in ancient China.

Shih's reconstruction (Fig. 19) shows one of the chariots buried

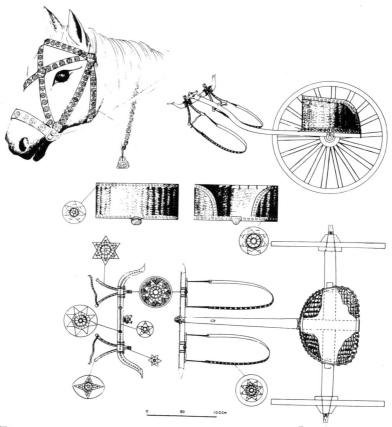

Figure 19. Reconstruction of chariot and head of horse

in M20, with a single shaft and a bow-shaped crosspiece suspended from it near its front end. Attached to the crosspiece on either side were found the two forked bronze yokes for the two horses harnessed on the right and left of the shaft-tree. The pieces that decorated the terminals of the axle, the shaft, and the yokes were cast in bronze. These bronzes, although all dismantled when found, were apparently in their correct positions relative to the original structure of a chariot drawn by two horses. It is of course important to note that although wheels were not found, the axle was definitely buried together with the under-carriage. This would mean that the axle

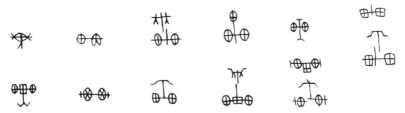

Figure 20. Oracle bone characters for "chariot"

did not turn with the wheels but was constructed as an integral unit of the under-carriage.

Further interesting evidence is supplied by the contemporary pictographs for wheeled vehicle. Of the fourteen sample specimens of this character in the oracle bone inscriptions, *ch'ê* (車), given in Professor Li Hsiao-ting's *Dictionary*,[7] eleven varieties are presented (Fig. 20). It is possible that the form of the pictograph character for wheeled vehicle was undergoing rapid changes, parallel with the progress of the actual structural designs in this period. Shih holds that there are at least two different types of wheeled chariots which can be reconstructed on the archaeological evidence collected from Hsiao-t'un.

Underground Deposit of Archives (H127)

The crowning achievement and, popularly considered, the greatest success of fifteen seasons' excavations in Anyang under the auspices of Academia Sinica was the discovery of H127, an underground storage pit at Hsiao-t'un filled with thousands of inscribed tortoise shells. This discovery was made on June 12, 1936, the day when the season's work was to have closed according to the original schedule. It was in the thirteenth season, which had followed three successful expeditions to excavate the royal tombs at Hou-chia-chuang. In the middle of June, the Anyang summer is hot and the noon heat is sometimes unbearable, so the usual schedule is to stop the field work in summer. The following is a translation of the account of what happened on that day:

According to the pre-arranged schedule, June 12 was to be the last day of this season. But, at 4 P.M. on June 12, numerous tortoise shells suddenly appeared in H127. When we ended the day at 5:30 P.M., the digging party had cleared in one hour and a half only half a cubic meter of closely packed tortoise shells which, according to a rough counting, already amounted to no less than 3,760 fragments of tortoise shells. Indeed, this is a respectable number, in view of past experience! Naturally we postponed the work for one more day, anticipating that the extra time would be sufficient for the completion and clearance of the contents of this amazing archive! But, indeed, facts are stranger than fiction. The actual pleasure of discovery far exceeded our anticipations! The contents of H127 were, unlike the other underground deposits, found to be by no means mixed and disorderly; on the contrary they had been accumulated in an orderly fashion, so it became obvious that a new method of excavation and recording was needed. . . .[8]

Very fortunately the archaeologist in charge of H127 was Mr. Wang Hsiang, who, in addition to his long experience with the Anyang diggings, was also one of the most ingenious field workers. Wang spent the whole extra day extended to him cutting the hidden documents loose from the burying soil. When the sun declined again the next day the whole day's labor had apparently only succeeded in scratching the surface of the hidden treasure. It became immediately clear that trying to take out the oracle bones piece by piece was not the right procedure. Unanimously all the archaeologists in the field agreed to scoop out the whole mass in one big lump.

Once decided, the new method was immediately closely followed. The labor of cutting loose the complete mass of those hidden documents from the soil took four days and four nights, all the members of the field staff working continuously without a moment's interruption. Meanwhile the news was communicated to the Nanking headquarters; and I, as chief of the Archaeological Section, immediately went to Anyang to conduct the final operation to the finish.

As there was no modern equipment in Anyang to handle such a heavy weight, how to move this hidden archive mass, which weighed over three tons, became the next difficult problem for the field workers. The huge mass was packed in heavy wooden planks and fastened firmly by iron straps. But to lift one single box weighing over three tons proved to be extremely difficult by local methods, not to mention moving it to the railway station although the distance was only a few miles. At that time, there was no modern road to speak of, nor any motor transportation.

Nevertheless the combined ingenuity of our field archaeologists and the local diggers finally solved the problem of transportation, still mainly by means of local tools plus a great deal of human labor. The heavy box was finally transported to the railway station on July 4. It took another eight days before this mass of buried documents from H127 was finally safely delivered to the headquarters of the Institute of History and Philology in Nanking for more detailed studies and investigations; the day of arrival was July 12, 1936.

Hu Hou-hsüan, assistant to Tung Tso-pin, was given the task of disassembling the mass of inscribed tortoise shells, which were closely stuck to one another after their three millennia of underground deposit. After many months of hard labor, Hu pointed out what he called the ten "Characteristics of the H127 Inscribed Oracle Bones," as follows: [9]

1. Most of the records are datable to the times of King P'an Keng and King Wu Ting, especially the latter. Hu inferred that this archive must have been closed and stored away in Wu Ting's time.

2. Quite a number of the tortoise shells still retain the original writing in vermilion, indicating definitely that oracle bone inscriptions were first written by brush, and only later incised.

3. Many inscriptions are filled with vermilion or black pigments in the incised marks.

4. Oracle crack signs, signifying luck or evil, are often trimmed artificially.

5. Carapaces of tortoises are frequently bisected for divinatory purposes; these fragments, when they are complete, are usually punctuated with a perforation at the end of the piece.

6. The sources of the tortoises are frequently noted on a selected portion of the tortoise shell.

7. Shells of a number of extra large tortoises, probably imported from the south, occur among this accumulated mass.

8. The total number of inscribed pieces in the mass is 17,096; of this enormous number of inscribed oracle bones only 8 fragments are from ox scapulae, all the others (17,088) are from tortoise shells.

9. The burying of these documents, Hu inferred, was intentional.

10. Hu further figured that, in previous diggings, only four shells from Ta-lien-k'eng in the third season, and nine tortoise shells from Hou-chia-chuang in the ninth season, had been recovered. But, this time, from H127 alone, over three hundred inscribed tortoise shells were restorable! It was indeed an unprecedented achievement.[10]

Tung Tso-pin, in the prefatory note to the second volume on

Anyang inscriptions, had this to say: "Truly this event [the H127 discovery] should be written with large characters and deserves particular notice! It is indeed a miracle among achievements, taking all the fifteen seasons' work into consideration." [11] Tung further quoted Shih's following passage from the article cited above:

"The field number for the pit is H127 (at C113) . . . the upper and surface layer is a huge but shallow cavity (H117): underneath pit H117 was found another pit, H121 . . . and H127. The uppermost part of H127 pit appeared 1.70 meters below the modern surface; which showed signs of having been somewhat intruded, but not obviously.
   The diameter of H127 at the upper opening is 1.80m., the depth of the pit is six meters from the surface. The upper deposit was filled with greyish soil, the bottom layer was greenish soil, and between these two layers were the accumulated inscribed oracle bones and shells,[12] which constitute the middle layer with a thickness of 1.60 meters. A human skeleton was also found accompanying these documented antiquities. . . .

Shih's account was written five years after the discovery, when the Institute of History and Philology had moved its headquarters to Kunming, Yünnan province, during the Japanese invasion; the exact date of Shih's article is March 1940. It was a time, in the middle of Japan's invasion of China, when the whole nation was engaged in a life and death struggle. Shih was able to put on record this memorable event not only as an eye-witness but also as the man in charge of the field operations. So even Tung Tso-pin had to rely upon this information for his detailed studies.
   If I conclude this chapter with this account, it is understandable. When Director Fu Ssŭ-nien originated the idea of taking Anyang as the first site to test the theory and methods of modern archaeology, he was mainly inspired by the well-known fact that in this region, the earliest written Chinese records had already been found. In other words, the main purpose of Fu's decision was to find out whether inscribed oracle bones still existed in the soil. And, indeed, the H127 shell-archive was discovered in the summer of 1936 after more than eight years of persistent labor guided by means of scientific method; it crowned an enterprise based on reasoning and on accumulated field experience! It was not luck that gave us the findings of H127. They were definitely the fruit of planned and accumulated scientific labor.
   From a purely archaeological viewpoint, the discovery of the H127 archive was only one among a number of amazing achievements in the various Anyang expeditions which I have briefly de-

scribed. In fact, the thirteenth, the fourteenth, and the fifteenth expeditions resulted in a large number of accumulated field records as well as material discoveries and field data of the highest value by any scientific standard, and these have provided the basic materials for the understanding of the true nature of the Anyang culture up to the present time!

Still, H127 stands out conspicuously as one of the climaxes which seems to have given us a kind of spiritual satisfaction beyond all others! So, speaking not just from a purely scientific viewpoint but with the memory of our elation, I consider it a fitting and proper subject to close this chapter on the field operations in the last three seasons.

7 Wartime Efforts

to Continue the Anyang Research

By THE SUMMER of 1937, it became inevitable that the Japanese militarists, encouraged by their political and military successes since the Meiji era, would continue their expansion and their aggressive policy toward China until, like Genghis Khan and Nurhachi, they had swallowed the whole territory of Southeastern and Eastern Asia. Although the revolutionary government established in Nanking by the followers of Dr. Sun Yat-sen was militarily still far inferior to the Japanese army and navy, and therefore unable to engage the Japanese on a large scale, the policy makers of the Nanking government nevertheless decided to resist the Japanese invasion, and adopted the tactics of a small-scale but long-drawn-out war of resistance.

The eight-year resistance war is now recognized as an important initial phase of World War II with which modern historians are at least not totally unacquainted. This chapter will give a general outline of what happened in this period to the important archaeological collections from the fifteen expeditions of field work in Anyang, considered by many to represent one of the most distinguished scientific achievements sponsored by the Nationalist Government in Nanking.

When the elder statesmen of the Nationalists had originated the idea of establishing a national research academy, they had laid emphasis first of all upon physical and natural sciences; so the physics, chemistry, engineering, geology, and meteorology institutes were the first five to be established in Nanking and Shanghai. The Institute of History and Philology was inaugurated later, chiefly through the efforts of its founder, Fu Ssŭ-nien, as already described in Chapter 4.

Less than ten years after the establishment of the Nanking government, the Japanese invasion of China actually started, following the failure of repeated negotiations. The policy of long resistance, announced in Nanking, was unanimously supported by the whole nation.

Despite the chaos of wartime, the policy of scientific education was still maintained though it naturally suffered reduction and many changes. Active research could not be promoted. Still, in spite of all difficulties, the government gave full consideration to individual and collective efforts in this direction.

First of all, while engaged in military mobilization, the government still managed to assign a certain amount of transport to move national treasures and scientific equipment to inland China, mainly to the west and southwest but also to the northwest—Szechwan, Yünnan, Kwangsi provinces, and so on, via the Yangtze River, the Lunghai Railway, and public highways in various regions.

The main portion of the collections and the library of the Institute of History and Philology were, through the energy and historical insight of a few leaders, for the most part successfully transported to several destinations: Chungking, Kunming, and finally Li-chuang, a town in the western part of Szechwan province, on the southern bank of the Yangtze River. Before it settled at Li-chuang, the institute first migrated to Kunming and stayed in or near that capital city of Yünnan province for more than a year (1938–40). Needless to say, in the course of moving these national treasures, which included scientific records and equipment, there were overwhelming difficulties to overcome and inevitable losses suffered due to chaotic wartime conditions despite the efforts of the organization and of its individual members who were carrying out their assigned duties as best they could. All these difficulties and losses have been recorded in one way or another, either privately or in official documents.

A serious loss I should not omit to mention was the dispersal of our talented younger archaeologists, trained by more than half a dozen years in the field. Some time in November 1937, when almost all the members of the Archaeological Section of the Institute of History and Philology were gathered at Ch'angsha in a wayside inn, each member declared what he would like to do during the war. The result of this gathering was that some left the institute for war work, and some went to wander around; but the majority, including all the senior members, decided to follow the migration of the institute wherever it might lead, according to the drift of the time.

When the institute first settled in Kunming in the early part of the war, the members were actually able to resume some research work. During the latter part of the Kunming days, the headquarters of the institute was moved from the city to a nearby suburban village, known as Lung-ch'üen Cheng, where most of the archaeological collections and the books were actually set out on shelves. The three senior archaeologists took the lead in working on the Anyang finds: Liang Ssŭ-yung was engaged in a preliminary survey of the Hou-chia-chuang digging records; Tung Tso-pin devoted himself to the continued study of the oracle bone inscriptions, assisted by Hu Hou-hsüan; I myself undertook a detailed study of the shapes and decorations of the Anyang ceramics and examined all the types of specimens with the able assistance of Dr. Wu Gin-ding, who returned from London to join us and was appointed a curator of the National Central Museum, of which I was still in charge during wartime. At the same time, the human skeletal materials were handed to Dr. Woo Ting-liang, chief of the Anthropological Section of the institute. Dr. Woo, as a well-trained biometrician, was regarded as the specialist best qualified to handle the precious collection of skeletal materials from the Anyang excavations. The major portion of these materials had also been taken to Yünnan for further study.

Research on the Hsiao-t'un and Hou-chia-chuang archaeological collections continued for about a year and a half—from September 1938 to June 1940, when the institute had to move again. During this period there was a great deal of concentrated labor on the Anyang materials, and a firm basis was laid for the official publication of these scientific records. These academic achievements, although not directly related to actual warfare, were indicative of the kind of scientific accomplishment that trained individuals were capable of attaining even in a time of national crisis. I should therefore like to give a brief account of the kinds of research carried out in the days when the headquarters of the institute was located at Lung-ch'üen Cheng.

Tung Tso-pin, assisted by Hu Hou-hsüan, continued his research on the inscriptions of the oracle bone records. The staff members under Tung's direction kept on making ink-squeezes of the inscribed shells from H127, despite interruptions for lack of supplies, especially the thin paper necessary for ink-squeezing, a difficulty that was bound to happen in wartime. Such difficulties were always overcome, however, so the progress of the rubbing was never stopped for long. Hu Hou-hsüan was also assigned to continue the registration of the specimens and to keep a catalogue specially designed for this collection. Tung Tso-pin occupied himself with a more arduous task, namely, tackling the highly technical problem of reconstructing the Yin-Shang calendar system on the basis of the inscribed records. Tung's interest in this particular research was first inspired, as mentioned before, by the Ta-lien-k'eng discovery of the four more or less complete inscribed plastra. During his careful investigation of these pieces, he conceived the idea of expanding the investigation to embrace the whole problem of the Yin-Shang calendar.

Liang Ssŭ-yung, who enjoyed normal health in the first two years of wartime when the institute was in Kunming, completed in this time his first draft of the reports on the royal tombs which he had excavated in 1934–35 at Hsi-pei-kang of Hou-chia-chuang. This enormous labor was almost finished before the institute received the new order to move again to Li-chuang in western Szechwan in 1940. The manuscripts of these important drafts consisted of a number of chapters, the main parts of which were handwritten by the author himself and were deposited with the Archaeological Section. On the basis of Liang's manuscripts Professor Kao Ch'ü-hsün edited, annotated, and amended with many plates and figures the various reports on HPKM 1001, 1002, 1003, 1004, and 1217 published in Taiwan in the Hou-chia-chuang series of the *Archaeologia Sinica* volumes long after Liang's death on April 2, 1954.[1]

Liang's manuscripts preserved in the Archaeological Section were composed of the following important items:

Contents of MSS Reports	Number of Pages of Liang's MSS
HPKM 1001	28
HPKM 1002	12
HPKM 1003	16
HPKM 1004	17
HPKM 1129	1
HPKM 1217	12
HPKM 1400	9
HPKM 1443	9
HPKM 1500	17
HPKM 1550	14
Small tombs (collective)	63
Small tombs (individual)	not written
Location	5
Discovery	4
Excavations	34

This brilliant archaeologist's handwritten draft reports on the royal tombs of Hou-chia-chuang are among the treasures preserved by the Archaeological Section. Without these drafts, which not only provided the basic data but also set a model for scientific reporting in the Chinese language, it would have been impossible for Professor Kao Ch'ü-hsün to carry out the gigantic task of describing the royal tombs at Hsi-pei-kang of Hou-chia-chuang.

Liang's original draft manuscripts also include a list of projected chapter headings, as follows:

Chapter I. Geography, Location, and General Environment of the Hsi-pei-kang Cemetery

Chapter II. The Story of Its Discovery

Chapter III. Excavations

Chapter IV. Cultural Deposits of the Hsi-pei-kang of Hou-chia-chuang and the Position of the Yin Tombs in the Stratified Deposit

Chapter V. Large Tombs: A General Description

Chapter VI. Individual Large Tombs, (1)–(10): HPKM 1001, 1002, 1003, 1004, 1129, 1217, 1400, 1500, 1443, 1550

Chapter VII. General Description of Small Tombs

Chapter VIII. Individual Description of Small Tombs

Chapter IX. Artifacts: Classified Descriptions (not written)

1. Bronzes and Other Metals
2. Stones and Jades, etc.
3. Bones, Ivories, and Tortoise Shells
4. Shells
5. Potteries
6. Traces of Ritual Tools (no MSS)

Chapter X. Analysis of Decorative Potteries (no MSS)

Chapter XI. Human Bones (no MSS)

Chapter XII. Animal Bones (including Birds, no MSS)

Chapter XIII. Later Tombs (no MSS)

Chapter XIV. Analysis of Small Tombs (no MSS)

Chapter XV. Position of Yin-Tombs in the Stratifications:
A Tabular Analysis (8 pages)

Chapter XVI. Registered List of Excavated Objects (no MSS)

So far, Professor Kao Ch'ü-hsün has been able to complete the editorial work on Liang's written materials through those classified above under Chapter VI.

Liang's research on the later chapters which he originally designed was tragically cut short. When he first arrived at Li-chuang, he had immediately started on Chapter IX and pursued in minute detail his research on the bronzes and stone carvings discovered from the royal tombs. Unfortunately, he contracted tuberculosis in Li-chuang, and a sudden attack of pneumonia harmed his health almost beyond recovery and compelled him to stay in his sickbed most of the time. Naturally he could not do any writing according to his original schedule.

The investigation of the ceramic materials under my guidance was pursued on an analytic basis; namely, to study and examine the different aspects of the whole problem one after another. In the Kunming days, I first, with the expert assistance of Dr. Wu Ginding, worked on a general examination of the various sample specimens that we had been able to bring with us and made a careful survey of their textures, outside appearances, and decorative compositions. We started with the help of *A Dictionary of Color* by Aloys John Maerz[2] to reclassify the various outside appearances of all the individual specimens and also experimented on the absorption power of different types of specimens classified on the basis of the color scale: gray, red, black, white, and the hard and glazed wares.

The absorption tests were carried out with only a specific gravity balance (August Sauter, Ebingen), which could give the weight accurate to 1/2,oooth of a gram. With the balance to measure weight, and with steamed, clean water, I was able to measure the absorption power of twenty-two black pottery sherds, twenty-two gray sherds, twenty white sherds, and twenty pieces of the hard ware, including some with glaze. The result of these various tests showed that while the differences among the gray, the black, and the white wares were noticeable, the variation in the amount of water-absorbing power between the above three groups and the hard ware was sharply different. Of all the hard ware specimens tested, almost every piece showed less than 1.00 percent in the test, while the specimens of the other three groups gave an average absorption power between 15.50 and 21.50 percent.

It should be mentioned, however, that in these various series of tests we were unable to measure the true specific gravity, so only apparent specific gravity was measured and used in the calculation. These provisional data, nevertheless, gave me a relatively firm basis for my further investigations of the ceramic materials.

I also made further attempts to carry out more chemical analyses, a work that had been started in Nanking with the cooperation of the Institute of Geology, where there was a chemical laboratory well equipped for analytic purposes. But in wartime Kunming, owing to the lack of certain chemicals, the Institute of Geology was unable to help us even on a small scale in this project, and we had to give up the idea of investigating the clay composition of the Anyang pottery on a chemical basis.

Kunming was a new environment to practically all the members of our institute, for none among us was a native Yünnanese, and the general mode of life in this southwestern province was almost completely different from both north China and the Yangtze Valley from which most of us came. Thus a new opportunity was offered to those of us whose observations and studies had been for years channeled and disciplined in the anthropological and archaeological fields. The attention of the archaeologists was first attracted by the discovery that, in building a new house in Lung-ch'üen-cheng where our temporary headquarters was located, the people still made use of sundried bricks, and of planked earth-pounding for laying foundations and building up walls. The method of earth-pounding seemed to be simpler than that still in common practice in north China at that time, but the use of sun-dried bricks rather thrilled those of us born in the Yangtze and the Yellow River regions, where kiln-firing of bricks had long ago replaced the sun-dried process. Shih Chang-ju realized the opportunity of deepening our archaeological understanding by examining the indigenous industry and art still current in Kunming; he studied the native ceramics, the irrigation system on the farms, and also the bronze industry—all of which were worthy ethnological research topics in themselves. But, since our collective interests were concentrated on the Anyang materials, naturally such side research was also promoted for a better understanding of the archaeological data gathered in the Anyang excavations. Let me give one practical instance.

The irrigation system in the vicinity of Kunming city was well developed. The remarkable fact was that in most of the irrigation canals the banks were strengthened by wooden piles—an observation that immediately reminded the Anyang archaeologists of their findings in the underground ditches discovered in Hsiao-t'un, which were arranged similarly in a network fashion of interrelated channels and also strengthened on both banks apparently by wooden piles.

While in Lung-ch'üen-cheng, some of us actually built temporary living quarters in the village. In watching the erection of these new buildings, many of us observed with both surprised amusement and historical interest how much attention the native architect paid to the accustomed rituals, offering a sacrifice when the soil was first "broken" to lay the foundation, when the first pillar was to be erected, and so forth. The most important ritual seemed to be reserved for the day when the main beam of the roof was to be set and the whole building was completed. On such occasions, celebrations took place marked by killing a cock and a goat and the performance of rituals appropriate for these great events. All the laborers were to be entertained with meat and drink on the day when the new building was completed.

These observations and a number of others, familiar to ethnographers and anthropologists in general, proved especially helpful to the archaeologists who had excavated in north China where certain ancient practices had been replaced by new technology long ago, but were still surviving in southwestern China in the thirties and forties of the present century. So during the two years' sojourn in Yünnan in the early wartime, our archaeologists exploited to the utmost the opportunity to collect materials on these ancient survivals to promote our understanding of the Anyang collections.

When we moved to Li-chuang, Szechwan, in 1940, we were again in a different environment, but not altogether as new to us as the natural and social conditions in Kunming. It took half a year for the institute to complete the mass migration from the southwestern province of Yünnan to Li-chuang on an upper reach of the Yangtze River, at a time when means of transportation were extremely limited and oil was as precious as diamonds. By the time the members of the institute were resettled in Li-chuang, it was near the end of 1940. Beginning with the year 1941, the research work of the institute once more returned to normal.

The new headquarters of the institute were located in a hilly place, where an old family with the surname of Chang possessed extensive farmland. The Changs, over the generations, had built a number of large houses, including a special theatre. When the war started, the old family's fortunes had already declined and the household was divided into a number of subfamilies. The institute succeeded in negotiating with the elders in charge of the family property to use their empty houses for a nominal rent. These houses constituted an isolated hamlet in a hilly region. At the foot of this hilly region, the Yangtze River flows down from I-pin to Lu-chou, where the mighty river is joined by another large stream. There were daily sailings of a small steamer between I-pin and Lu-chou, both of which were well-known prosperous district cities in the western part of Szechwan province. Li-chuang was at that time under the jurisdiction of Nan-ch'i district, the administrative city of which was located just a little distance below Li-chuang, on the northern bank of the Yangtze.

For more than four years during World War II, Li-chuang was a considerable center of learning. The Institute of Social Sciences of Academia Sinica, the Tunchi University from Shanghai, the National Central Museum, and the Society for the Study of Chinese Architecture also found their asylum here. Eminent scholars, both foreign and Chinese, like the British biochemist Joseph Needham, and the logician Professor Chin Yüeh-lin, paid visits to Li-chuang; some of them came quite frequently. Thus, in spite of war fever all over China, Li-chuang was one of the few places in free China where scholars could meet and discuss academic problems. Joseph Needham, for instance, gave a talk at Li-chuang, discussing the historic reasons why science did not develop in China as it had in Europe.

This general atmosphere was at least congenial to the specialists who had some highly technical research topics to pursue, and there was quite a number of such professional men gathered at Li-chuang in the latter part of the Chinese Resistance War against Japanese militarism. A large number of them worked in the Institute of History and Philology. The research done in this period by members of the Archaeological Section and their contributions to the study of the Yin-Shang collection from Anyang deserve special mention.

The best-known and the most distinguished achievement was the completion and publication of *Yin-li-p'u* by Tung Tso-pin, whose hand-written manuscripts were lithographed at Li-chuang in 1945, and published the same year.

Director Fu Ssŭ-nien, writing an introductory note (dated February 15, 1945) for this monumental wartime publication made the following main points regarding Tung's important contributions:

1. Tung's synthesizing power was the main source of the fruitful results in this publication. In the study of oracle bone inscriptions, many eminent scholars have participated. There have been, however, only four pre-eminent stages, each marked by the distinguished contribution of an authority, which have brought scholarship a step forward in this progressive journey. And all these scholarly works have been synthetic in nature. These four milestone works are: (1) Wang Kuo-wei "Yin-pu-tz'ŭ-chung so-chien hsien-kung hsien-wang k'ao"; (2) Tung Tso-pin's "Chia-ku-wen tuan-tai yen-chiu li"; (3) Kuo Mo-jo's *Pu-tz'ŭ tung-ch'uan;* and (4) Tung Tso-pin's *Yin-li-p'u.*[3] Of the four monumental contributions, Tung was the author of two. What above all distinguished his contributions from other writings was the fact that he had at his command the newly discovered archaeological materials to provide a new basis for his research.

2. Tung Tso-pin, according to Fu, was the first Chinese scholar to make extensive use of a new technique in his study of the calendar system by checking it with modern astronomer's records of eclipses of the moon and sun. This checking no doubt helped him to make better use of the related data found in the oracle bone inscriptions.

3. Finally, Fu paid special tribute to Tung's ability to clarify the difficult problem of the total period sequence of the ruling Shang dynasty which had been, owing to many different traditions and confused opinions, in a chaotic state. Fu believed that Tung in this new work had reduced this difficult historical and technical problem to order and had actually solved it.

Fu's laudatory Preface placed *Yin-li-p'u* on an extraordinary level among learned publications. He added finally: "Anyone who wants to pass critical comments on these learned volumes must, first of all, besides carefully reading this publication, qualify himself with both a competent knowledge of the ancient scripts of the Yin-Shang dynasty, and an expert acquaintance with the technology of calendar calculations, ancient and modern."

As a matter of historical truth, Fu's prediction made thirty years ago, has, in the course of these ensuing decades, proved to be almost prophetic in every word. Since the Japanese surrender, there has been almost complete neglect of this important publication in academic circles. It seems to me that this neglect is, however, mainly due to a change of interest on the part of the present generation rather than to a lack of talented successors. It is true that there were a number of questions raised, and comments made, and discussions hotly debated immediately after the publication of *Yin-li-p'u;* but even then, none of these notes or discussions touched the more essential contents of *Yin-li-p'u* as a whole, as Fu had foretold in his Preface. The problem that received the most attention was that of determining the actual ruling period of the Shang and Yin-Shang dynasty; and in particular, the exact year of conquest of Yin-Shang by the succeeding Chou dynasty. This highly technical and important historical problem did arouse some hot debate and passionate discussion which, however, stopped with no decisive conclusion. Before we go further in evaluating Tung's monumental contribution, let me first briefly give the important points set forth in the *Yin-li-p'u.* The following notes are based mainly on certain of Tung's own statements found scattered here and there in the book.

First, Tung said in his own Preface that the plan for this book started in 1934 and it was completed in 1943; the working time required was, then, nearly ten years, mainly during wartime, in both Kunming and Li-chuang. It took another two years to put the drafts into manuscript form for lithographic printing.

Second, the author's interest in the study of the Yin calendar went further back than the first planning of this book. He said that as early as 1930 he had made notes on "Calendric Data in the Oracle Bone Records," and in 1934 he wrote an article on "Some Important Problems of the Yin Calendar." [4] By this time he had already been attracted by this group of important written materials, which obviously had chronological significance. He said: "At that time I knew very little about the astronomical basis needed for a general understanding of the calculation of any old calendar system. When in 1935, I compiled the inscribed records of oracle bones of the fifth period according to my own standard of periodization, I discovered the chronological order of the five basic types of sacrificial offering to early kings and ancestors in the era of King Ti-I and also that of King Ti-Hsin." In these records the year, the month, and the day when the sacrifices were to be made are sometimes registered together; the day of occurrence is usually given by one of the permutated two symbols—characters used in the sexagenary cycle, similar to the ancient Babylonian system. The twin-symbols for the sixty names in the Chinese sexagesimal system are derived from what are commonly known in China as the heavenly stems (*t'ien-kan*) and the earthly branches (*ti-chih*), the former composed of ten characters (Chia, I, Ping, Ting, Wu, Chi, Keng, Hsin, Jen, Kuei), and the latter, twelve characters (Tzŭ, Ch'ou, Yin, Mao, Ch'en, Ssŭ, Wu, Wei, Shen, Yu, Hsü, Hai). By permutating the ten characters of the heavenly stems and the twelve characters of the earthly branches, sixty combined twin-symbols are produced and were used by the ancient Chinese to register the day, at least as early as the time of the oracle bone inscriptions and probably much earlier. It is now well known that almost every complete oracle record includes one of the sexagesimal twin-characters, such as Chia-tzŭ—which only means the name of a particular day when the recorded event took place or occurred. When the deciphered characters in the oracle bone inscriptions became better understood through the accumulated efforts of paleographers, it also became absolutely clear that such was the general way of recording any divinatory event.

When Tung found, in the course of his continued study of newly discovered oracle bone inscriptions, some that could be grouped within a definite period and assigned to a definite king, and bore, in addition, the name of the day occurring together with a definite month, occasionally also with the year, given in a definite number— these discoveries, Tung said, heightened sky-high his enthusiasm to study the Yin calendar system and helped him to concentrate his academic efforts on this promising research project. He started by writing to ask a number of astronomers to tutor him about the basic astrological and astronomical ideas on which past calendar systems had depended for their calculations. Professor Kao P'ing-tsŭ, a well-known authority on the development of Chinese calendars, soon became Tung's intimate friend. These two scholars worked cooperatively to attack the various problems arising from the abundance of calendrical data discovered in the oracle records. All this happened before the Japanese invasion.

Once he had determined to go into the details of this difficult task of investigating of the Yin calendar system, Tung pursued the work for ten years with a steadfastness and concentrated energy that astonished all his friends. He began the work in the Kunming days when he asked Mr. Kao Ch'ü-hsün to assist him in the laborious calculations involved. At the suggestion of his astronomer friends, he made use of Josephus Justus Scaliger's table of day-counting by starting with January 1, of 4713 B.C. as the zero day, and followed it by continuous numerals to number the days which succeed each other indefinitely. It is well known that Scaliger's counting is based on the Gregorian calendar, so Tung, following the terminology of Professor Chu Wen-hsin, named the serial numbers of day-counting as the "Julian day number" (Ju-lüeh-chou-jih).[5] These serial numbers constituted the fundamental basis of Tung's other calculations, which resulted, by checking with the sexagesimal days found in the oracle records, in the final compilations of the thirty-five calendar tables published in Yin-li-p'u.

These thirty-five tables are, according to Tung's original scheme, divided into ten subdivisions, namely:

  I. Annual Calendar Table (Nien-li-p'u)
  II. Calendar Tables of Sacrificial Offerings (Ssŭ-p'u)
 III. Tables of Recorded Eclipses of the Moon and Sun (Chiao-shih-p'u)
 IV. Tables of Recorded Solstices (Jih-chih-p'u)
  V. Tables of Recorded Leap Years (Jun-p'u)
 VI. Tables of Recorded First Days of a Month (Shou-p'u)
 VII. Tables of Recorded Decades (Hsün-p'u)
VIII. Tables of Recorded Months (Yüeh-p'u)
 IX. Tables of Recorded Days (Jih-p'u)
  X. Tables of Recorded Nights (Hsi-p'u)

A number of the ten subdivisions, because of the abundant amount of new inscribed data, were again divided into a number of sections; for instance, in subdivision II, the author found it necessary to treat the accumulated data in three sections: (A) on the records relating to King Tsu Chia, (B) another group relating to King Ti I, and (C) a third group relating to King Ti Hsin—all amply illustrated by hand copies of the original ink-squeezed records.

Tung, in his first edition of *Yin-li-p'u,* said that of the thirty-five calendar tables published in his book, he considered subtables III-4, III-6, IV-2, VI-1, and IX-3 as the most important. On these five groups of tabulated data, one could build a firm foundation for the calculation of dating the ruling period of the Shang dynasty and the various epochs of the ruling kings.

In his early article [6] Tung had divided the oracle bone periods into five successive eras, namely:

Period 1:
    (a) from King P'an KENG to King Hsiao I
    (b) King Wu TING's reign
Period 2: King Tsu KENG and King Tsu CHIA
Period 3: King Lin HSIN and King K'ang TING
Period 4: King Wu I and King Wen-wu TING (also known as T'ai TING)
Period 5: King Ti I, King Ti HSIN

The durations of the various rulers from King P'an KENG onward are given in *Yin-li-p'u* (Vol. 1, p. 8), as follows:

P'an KENG	28 years [7]	1398–71 B.C.?
Hsiao HSIN	21 years	1370–50 B.C.
Hsiao I	10 years	1349–40 B.C.
Wu TING	59 years	1339–1281 B.C.
Tsu KENG	7 years	1280–74 B.C.
Tsu CHIA	33 years	1273–41 B.C.
Ling HSIN	6 years	1240–35 B.C.
K'ang TING	8 years	1234–27 B.C.
Wu I	4 years	1226–23 B.C.
Wen-wu TING	13 years	1222–10 B.C.
Ti I	35 years	1209–1175 B.C.
Ti HSIN	64 years	1174–12 B.C.

The total number of years amounts to 287, from which 14 years should be subtracted for the time when King P'an Keng was still ruling in the old capital; that is, King P'an Keng made his decision to move the capital to Yin in the fourteenth year of his reign and actually accomplished it in the fifteenth year; so the total duration of the Yin-Shang period is 273 years according to Tung's estimate.

What Tung Tso-pin had done was to equate and fix the sexagesimal days found in the oracle bone inscriptions to the exact day numbers of Scaliger's Julian calendar days. For instance, Tung was able to fix through a series of complicated calculations, and conclude definitely that the first day of the first month in the fifteenth year of King P'an Keng's reign, according to the Yin calendar, corresponds with January 14, 1384 B.C., in terms of the Julian calendar; and the numeral of that Julian day in the estimate of Scaliger is: 1215931.[8] Tung also identified the sexagesimal day symbol for that day as Chia-shen. These two calculated reference points provided the basis for the computations of all the other tables. Tung's attempt to link the amazing amount of oracle bone materials with modern dating by means of scientific methodology, and the painstaking efforts he put into it, represented an important phase of Chinese intellectual modernization at its best during the war period.

The classified data from the oracle bone inscriptions in Tung's *Yin-li-p'u*, have, besides their basic contributions to chronology, also provided abundant source materials for other historical investigations. Tables under subdivision II, for instance, which gathered and classified records of sacrificial offerings to ancestors and other spirits on certain days, not only give the reader a bird's-eye-view of deep-rooted superstitions—"belief in the ghost," as Ssŭ-ma Ch'ien put it more than two thousand years ago—but also revealed the nature of the performance of these ceremonial rituals. The five most important types of ceremonial rituals in ancestor worship as set forth in *Yin-li-p'u* are: (1) Yung; (2) I; (3) Chi; (4) Kuan; (5) Hsieh.

Tung's studies concerning the various rituals practiced in the Yin-Shang period were a laborious program. In *Yin-li-p'u* he concluded that the sacrificial rituals in the early days were multifarious, but that in King Tsu Chia's time they were reformed and reduced to an indispensable minimum. Only the five essential types were preserved in chronological order. It would have taken nearly a year's time, according to Tung's calculation, to complete a cycle of the various types of worship. That is the reason, he concluded, that during the reigns of the last two Kings (Ti I, Ti Hsin), a *nien* (year) was also recorded as *ssŭ* (sacrifices to the dead). It is amazing to realize that it took a whole year to perform all the ritualistic offerings to the various ancestors even after Tsu Chia's reform!

As is well known, the names of the ruling sovereigns in the Shang dynasty each included one of the ten symbols of the heavenly stems. And in terms of the Yin calendar, as mentioned above, every day was named by a twin-symbol in the sexagenarian order, each of which also included one of the heavenly stem terms. A traditional and annual court event was devoted to making offerings to an individual ancestor whose name in terms of heavenly stems corresponded with the day's heavenly stem: for instance, on the day Chia-tzŭ all those past sovereigns whose names had a "Chia" stem— such as T'ai Chia, Hsiao Chia, Ho-t'an Chia, Wo Chia, Yang Chia, Tsu Chia—were to receive offerings from the ruling king. It is clear that every dead sovereign on the ancestral roll was to receive some kind of offering every ten days at least. Besides, there were times when all the ancestors were to be worshiped in a united service which was known in oracle bone terminology as "Ho-chi." This festival was evidently a heavily ritualistic occasion; its nature, however, still remains to be clarified.

As *Yin-li-p'u* is packed with data from the original written records, Tung's classified groups, important as they are, could be intelligible only to a few specialists. The data relating to the two well-known war expeditions—Wu Ting's battle in the northwest and Ti Hsin's expedition to fight the Tung-I (eastern barbarian)— are of great historical importance. They have been only briefly mentioned in past records, and may, one hopes, be better studied by more competent scholars in the future. There are other classified data which also deserve more attention, but I believe I have given a sufficient account of the wartime work of this paleographer.

Meanwhile, I myself pursued my investigation of the Anyang ceramic collection. Although like Liang, I also suffered some personal misfortunes in both Kunming and Li-chuang, I could still keep on working when there was time. I say this, because I had other administrative duties to attend to and half a dozen trained persons to take care of as chief of the Archaeological Section, and also as director of the National Central Museum. In these capacities, I organized and sent several small research expeditions to Ta-li, to Cheng-tu, and one as far as Tunhuang in the northwest. I myself even participated in some digging parties. All these of course took time. I was not as fortunate as Tung Tso-pin in being able to concentrate all my energy and time on the study of the precious Anyang collections.

My interest in the Anyang collections was naturally manifold.

But there is one principle which I have always observed, namely, to give my colleagues the first opportunity to study the field data in which they have a special interest. I have found in my past experience that this is a fundamental principle for leaders of scientific research to follow, if such cooperative works are to be successfully accomplished at all. Judging from my personal experience, there are always problems and collected data for one to handle and get busy with, no matter how many participants are in the party.

After our move to Li-chuang, I once more involved myself with the huge mass of Anyang ceramics of which I had with me specimens of all the important types and a complete set of field records. In this new headquarters, I determined to complete a corpus for the total ceramic collection.

My own interest in doing this was by no means accidental. As early as 1924, when I happened to read, in J. G. Andersson's "Early Chinese Culture," his preliminary report on his excavation of Yang-shao Ts'un, the first prehistoric site in north China, I was deeply impressed by his emphasis on the discovery of the *li*-tripod and *ting*-tripod in the course of his digging there. I was also familiar with H. Frankfort's studies in early pottery of the Near East.[9] So when I settled in Li-chuang, with all the field records on hand and sample specimens ready for detailed examination, I decided to work on the shapes first, as other technical studies were almost impossible to carry on in the Li-chuang community, learned as it might be.

In the library of the institute and my own limited supply of books, I could find only a copy of Sir W. M. Flinders Petrie's *Prehistoric Egypt* corpus for my reference. My aim was to complete a corpus of the ceramics collected from our digging in Hsiao-t'un and Hou-chia-chuang, and naturally Petrie's book became important for me. As I found Petrie's principles of classification, however, rather inadequate for my purpose, I started discussing with my colleagues of the Archaeological Section what principles I should follow in the corpus arrangement. This discussion took a long time and, with Tung Tso-pin's oracle bone inscriptions, constituted one of the main topics of our professional talks in the Li-chuang days.

Meanwhile, I decided, with the technical assistance of Mr. P'an Ch'üeh and Li Lien-ch'un, to draw figures of all the sample specimens on a uniform scale and also to photograph all the complete specimens available. It took quite a long time—several years—for

P'an and Li to complete all the drawings on a uniform scale (one-quarter the size of the original), each specimen portrayed half in cross section, the other half according to its external shape. It also took several years to complete the photographic work.

Comparative studies of the shapes of the various sample specimens also led me to investigate the methods of pottery manufacture and of course to speculate on the nature of the clay, and to undertake some serious study of the outside decoration. Though all these problems appeared to me important in themselves, my principal focus of attention did not deviate from study of the evolution of every individual type specimen that possessed a complete shape, whether original or restored.

The related shapes fell into a few groups, among which the tripods attracted my personal interest first and foremost. There was a historical reason for this as I recollected that, in the excavation of the first prehistoric Black Pottery site at Ch'êng-tzŭ-yai, many subtypes of tripods had been found, in contrast to the limited type-forms—*li*-tripod and *ting*-tripod—discovered by J. G. Andersson at Yangshao Ts'un. Among the Anyang ceramics, the field team had been long accustomed to encountering various subtypes of the *li*-tripods. They were so numerous that in fifteen seasons' time the accumulated pot-sherds classified as from *li*-tripods though varying in both size and shape amounted to several ten thousands, making this largest of all the groups.

In these comparative studies, I was finally led to formulate two fundamental ideas regarding the corpus arrangement.

First, I decided to include all the Yin-Shang and pre–Yin-Shang potteries excavated in both Hsiao-t'un and Hou-chia-chuang. This decision was important and for a definite reason. When I studied the field records in detail and examined the contents and history of the underground deposits in all the subterranean caches, pits, and caves, I soon found out that Hsiao-t'un was populated in prehistoric times by the Lung-shan Culture. Consequently it became obvious to me that, with the exception of the post-Yin burials, practically all the pot-sherds and complete pots found from our diggings would have been produced in one or another of three subperiods: (1) prehistoric, (2) early Shang, and (3) Yin-Shang. The last of these three subperiods was of course the most important because it represented the period which we study. At the same time, it was clear to me that it would be impossible to divide these subperiods since they were all continuous and stratigraphically impossible to differentiate, so the best solution was to analyze the collection as a whole.

Second, I decided to give up the fundamental idea of following the Egyptologist's framework of corpus-making, namely, the simple procedure of beginning with the most open (and shallow) and advancing to the most closed. A set of new rules for arranging the pottery shapes was devised and found not only workable but also suitable for the Anyang ceramics, of which more than one thousand restorable complete specimens were on hand. These rules or principles were as follows:

A. To divide the pottery group into ten classes, including one for the covers.

B. To make use of the morphological features of the lowest part of each complete pot as the standard for class-division, namely: (1) round-bottom; (2) flat-base; (3) ring-foot; (4) tripods; (5) tetrapods; (6–9) reserved for new types; and (10) covers. Within each class, I still followed Petrie's practice of arranging the most open and shallow pots first and specimens with tall bodies and small openings at the end.

These class-divisions when put on printed sheets (16 leaves) showed a natural sequence that amazed all the members of the Archaeological Section. Liang Ssŭ-yung, lying in his sickbed at Lichuang, was the first to congratulate me for completing this task, with which he was as satisfied as I myself.

This corpus was published in my study of *Pottery of the Yin and pre-Yin Period* in 1956.[10]

Before the unconditional surrender of Japan in 1945, I also found time to write a few articles with the Anyang data as basic materials. The one on pre-Yin cultural deposits that I contributed to *Hsüeh-Shu Hui-k'an,* a wartime publication of Academia Sinica issued in Szechwan, had provided the basic reference data for all the stratigraphical discussions of the underground cultural sequences of the Waste of Yin Site.[11] This article was published in 1944, very near the end of China's resistance war.

8 Postwar Academic Working Conditions

and Studies of the Anyang Finds

THE IMMEDIATE RESULT of the unconditional surrender of the Japanese was naturally a general feeling of relief among the hard-pressed Chinese. But politically, it was by no means a simple change. It brought forth all sorts of social and international problems that the government found extremely difficult to handle.

So far as our Anyang collections were concerned, we were able to transport them quietly from Szechwan back to our headquarters in Nanking, which the Japanese had turned into an exhibition room during their military occupation. The National Central Museum building, which was not completed when the war started, had been occupied by the invading army as their Nanking command center. Returning to Nanking after the Japanese surrender we found the capital altogether a different city.

Nearly all those who had worked in Li-chuang during the war, but none of those who had left the institute earlier, returned to the institute at Nanking. Postwar conditions changed rapidly in the next few years, and the personnel of the Institute of History and Philology suffered many changes. Tung Tso-pin received an invitation to visit Chicago; I myself was commissioned to oversee postwar conditions in many places in China and Japan. But I was one of those who decided at last to concentrate my efforts on the investigation of the Anyang collections which, on the whole, still remained in a more or less well-preserved state. Other colleagues made their decisions according to their personal needs.

It was at this time that I initiated a series of programs for the detailed investigation of ancient Chinese bronzes, with the Anyang collection naturally as my starting point. In order to lose no time, I gave up all outside engagements, including the directorship of the National Central Museum, which I had held for almost ten years.

Liang Ssŭ-yung, who had never recovered his health since the beginning of the Li-chuang days, did not return to Nanking after the war; he requested a leave of absence so that he could return to Peiping for a number of reasons. The climate is drier there and was considered by friends to suit him better. Also, the fact that he had spent his childhood and adolescence in Peiping and Tientsin led them to favor his recuperation in Peiping.

In Nanking, with the departure of Tung Tso-pin for the United States and Liang Ssŭ-yung for Peiping, only I among the seniors remained, and I made up my mind to continue working on the Anyang collection. I had the good fortune to be assisted by a number of junior workers, including Shih Chang-ju, Kao Ch'ü-hsün, and Hsia Nai, who had joined the institute during wartime when the headquarters was still located at Li-chuang.

I was able to edit and publish the *Chinese Journal of Archaeology* and issue further numbers of the Anyang Series of *Archaeologia Sinica*. Three numbers of the *Journal* were edited, two of which were actually published in Nanking. The first number of the ink-squeezes of oracle bone inscriptions were compiled once more and sent again for publication.[1]

Postwar Nanking, immediately after the Japanese surrender, was busily occupied with all sorts of restoration and reconstruction. Both the Institute of History and Philology and the National Central Museum were repaired and brought back more or less to their prewar condition, becoming in the course of time suitable for carrying on research work. From the collections that we had not taken west during war-time we were able to recover much of the fauna and abundant pot-sherds as well as a number of other duplicates. The "painted earth blocks" collected from the Hou-chia-chuang royal tombs were still well preserved; the Japanese archaeologists had treasured and made detailed studies of them. When I was in Kyoto during my first postwar visit to Japan, Professor Sueji Umehara presented me with a colored print of these "painted earth blocks."

My research work on Anyang had continued in Nanking less than two years when the political and international situation degenerated to the point where it became necessary for the government to move to Taiwan. In the winter of 1948 I was commissioned by the director of the Institute of History and Philology to assist Mr. Hsü Shen-yü, an old scholar renowned for his versatile knowledge of Chinese antiquities and Chinese bibliography, who had been appointed by the government to transport the Palace Museum treasures to Taiwan for safety. Director Fu asked me to act as Hsü's associate and to take special charge of moving the collections of the Institute of History and Philology to Taiwan for the same purpose. A navy transport was assigned. My senior, Hsü Shen-yü, saw me off and told me he would follow with the other boats, a promise which, however, he never fulfilled although a number of other treasure-carrying boats followed.

When we first arrived at Taiwan in the winter of 1948–49, the institute was installed in a place known as Yang-mei Cheng, about half way between Taipei and Hsin-chu. With the help of the provincial government, the institute was loaned some storage buildings near the railway station at Yang-mei. There the Institute of History and Philology established a temporary headquarters and its members and staff found living quarters rented from the local inhabitants. Here those who followed the new migration of the institute worked for five years (1949–54).

Meanwhile, Fu Ssŭ-nien received a new appointment to the important post of president of National Taiwan University, which he fully reorganized. Unfortunately President Fu, who was also still taking care of the Institute of History and Philology, passed away while attending a meeting of the Taiwan Provincial Assembly. This occurred in December 1950, about a year and a half after his appointment. In his capacity as president of the university, he had engaged a number of research fellows of the Academia Sinica to take up teaching positions left vacant by the departure of the Japanese faculty. Through his initiative, I was engaged to take up the post of chairman of the Department of Archaeology and Anthropology in the School of Arts of his university. This new job seemed rather congenial to me, for more reasons than one. I was of course glad to assist my old colleague and, besides, there was the fact that the Department of Anthropology had in the Japanese days been headed by Professor Uturigawa Menozo, who had been trained in the Peabody Museum at Harvard University. When he organized the department in Taiwan, he had followed closely the Harvard model familiar to me. In fact he had studied under Professor Roland B. Dixon, the same professor who had directed my Ph.D. thesis on "The Formation of the Chinese People."

So for a number of years, I spent much of my time in organizing the department, while Tung Tso-pin succeeded as director of the Institute of History and Philology. For the first few years in Taiwan, I actually carried on my Anyang investigations in the department's building at the university. In the early years after the Republic of China established the capital at Taipei, the university progressed slowly but steadily under the new president, Ch'ien Ssŭ-liang, who succeeded Fu Ssŭ-nien after his death. Many of the research fellows of the Institute of History and Philology, at the invitation of the university, taught in several departments in the School of Arts—Chinese, History, Anthropology, Archaeology, Paleography, and so on. So the academic standard of the university was commensurate with the average level of achievement of the national research institute. Nearly all the articles in the first number of the *Journal of Literature, History, and Philosophy* issued by the School of Arts of N.T.U. were contributed by faculty members working in the Institute of History and Philology.

In 1954, owing to economic pressure, Tung Tso-pin decided to give up the directorship of the institute and to accept an invitation from Hong Kong University. He left for Hong Kong without finding a successor and without, in fact, resigning. After Tung Tso-pin's sudden departure, the president of the National Academy, Dr. Chu Chia-hua, sent some friends to negotiate with me about succeeding Tung. It was a difficult and also a delicate situation, difficult since there was only a limited budget for Academia Sinica, and delicate because Tung had departed without resigning the post.

Whatever the difficulties Tung's successor had to face, I myself had to look at the problem from my own angle, namely the absolute necessity of completing the Anyang report as soon as possible; and I had the temerity to believe that I was the only man to carry it out. So I mustered my courage to take up the challenge without any assurance of help from anybody. I accepted the task mainly because I felt it was my academic duty "to fight to the finish" in the completion of a piece of scientific work developed under my guidance.

Soon it became clear that Tung's departure for Hong Kong had been mainly for personal reasons. As far as the Institute of History and Philology was concerned, Tung had been gaining all the support that was available. Dr. Hu Shih, who was residing in New York City at that time, had been the first man to extend a helping hand and, as early as 1951, he had already approached the Rockefeller Foundation for some assistance in erecting a building to house the precious Anyang collection and the library collection of this institute, the only research unit which had up to that time migrated to the island of Taiwan. Dr. Hu succeeded after some delay in gaining the support of the Rockefeller Foundation, which promised to give some financial assistance on condition that the China Foundation would do the same. Dr. Hu proceeded to negotiate with the officials of the China Foundation and accomplished his end in due time. By the time of Tung's sudden departure for Hong Kong, the storehouse built by funds from the two foundations had already been completed in Nankang and the headquarters had actually moved to the new building. As the new headquarters, it was to become the seat of three different functions: storage, research, and administration.

My appointment became effective in August 1955. On my initiative the Academia Sinica invited Professors Shen Kang-po, Li Tsung-t'ung, Liu Ch'ung-hung, and Yao Ts'ung-wu to be corresponding fellows of the academy; all were teaching in the history department of the National Taiwan University. In reorganizing the research work of the Institute, I also made a number of changes. Since Ch'en Yin-ko had been unable to come to Taiwan, and the plan for an Institute of Ethnology had matured, I requested Mr. Ch'en P'an to take up temporarily the position of acting chief of the History Section, and Ruey Yih-fu to be chief of the Anthropological Section, while Dr. Chao Yüan-ren was persuaded to direct the Philological Section as usual.

The new headquarters at Nankang was a quiet place, suitable for the pursuit of academic work. Those who had been working near the noisy railroad station at Yang-mei for years found in the new headquarters a much more peaceful and congenial atmosphere.

Living quarters had been built for those who resided in Yang-mei; but a number of the senior members, who had teaching jobs at

N.T.U. and had enjoyed the privilege of staying in the university living quarters, consequently kept on living there.

My assumption of the directorship of the Institute of History and Philology was soon followed by a number of events that directly or indirectly contributed to the advancement of our research work. The China Foundation, the Rockefeller Foundation, the Harvard-Yenching Institute, and finally the Science Foundation of the Republic of China have, in the course of time, all contributed funds to the institute to help its research program. A quite unexpected event was Dr. Hu Shih's decision to return to Taipei from his long sojourn in New York City. He was soon elected and appointed to succeed Dr. Chu Chia-hua as president of Academia Sinica, a post which he accepted against the advice of a number of his most intimate friends residing in New York.

Dr. Hu's appointment, whatever its political significance, was a fortunate choice in the eyes of those working in the Institute of History and Philology, of which he had been a corresponding member ever since its establishment.

As the essential reason that I accepted the directorship of the institute was to complete the report on the Anyang materials, I had to do the best I could to reapportion the collective labor among the available research members who were qualified and competent in this field. One of the great problems was of course Tung's departure and his subsequent gradual loss of interest in any project of theoretical importance. While in Hong Kong he spent his time in the compilation of a reconstructed historical calendar of ancient China, making use of all available data, regardless of the nature of their sources. His energy seemed to have declined and his synthetic power to have ceased to be creative. After he returned from his Hong Kong sojourn in 1958, Tung requested that the institute add one more research unit—to be devoted to the study of paleography with oracle bone inscriptions as the main source material—a request immediately granted by Academia Sinica in November 1958.

But Tung's health deteriorated rapidly and on November 23, 1963, this talented researcher, pioneer of the Anyang field work, passed away in the University Hospital of Taita; he was later buried right in front of the Nankang compound.

While Tung was still living, the senior members of the institute had agreed on the division of labor on the final report of the Anyang collection. Since his death, the program has been strictly followed at Nankang. Let me give a summary of the general division and a brief account of the progress of this work as well as of the publications.

The collective work was divided among members of the Archaeological Section as follows: Tung Tso-pin, Ch'ü Wan-li, Chang Ping-ch'üan, and Li Hsiao-ting were to study oracle bone inscriptions. Shih Chang-ju was to review the Hsiao-t'un field notes; he was to have a number of junior assistants to help summarize the field data of the Hsiao-t'un excavations. Kao Ch'ü-hsün was to take up the editing of Liang Ssŭ-yung's manuscripts on the Hou-chia-chuang royal cemetery and put them into final form. Li Chi was to serve as editor-in-chief of *Archaeologia Sinica* and to supervise both the research and publications of the final report, in addition to his own research.

Mr. Young Hsi-mei of the Anthropological Section was persuaded to take up the investigation of the human skeletal material which had remained without expert examination ever since Woo Ting-liang had given up the work. This collection had again migrated thousands of miles from Szechwan and overseas to Taiwan after Woo's departure.

The oracle bone collection of the institute naturally remained the one group that more than any other attracted public notice. Let me first give an account of the publications of the ink-squeezes and other related publications. In the early days, before the war started, it had already been agreed by the director and the editor of *Archaeologia Sinica* to publish, in one volume, rubbings of all the registered fragments with inscriptions found in the first nine seasons. Notes, decipherments, and interpretations would follow. The main idea was to publish registered new data as soon as possible so that paleographers everywhere might be able to make use of them.

This basic idea was however interrupted by the Japanese invasion, which made printing of the first volume impossible. So the first volume of rubbings was not published until 1948, when Tung Tso-pin was in Chicago where he wrote an introductory note.[2] This volume contains only the rubbings of the inscribed oracle bones found in the first nine expeditions, which constitute, as mentioned before, only a minor portion of the institute's total collection.

Tung was naturally eager to follow it by publishing all the rest of the rubbings that had been completed before the war terminated. But postwar conditions in Nanking and Shanghai deteriorated so rapidly that publication was not as easy as one might have imagined. Only after another five years, by which time the institute had migrated to Taiwan, could this next group of ink-squeezes of the oracle bone inscriptions be issued.[3]

To publish the ink-squeezes of the inscribed oracle bones was only the first stage of the original plan. It was to be followed by a volume of annotations to accompany each of the ink-squeeze publications. While the migratory upheavals scattered the various experts widely, still, among those who came to Taiwan there were a number of paleographers who wanted to continue work along this line. I was fortunate enough to convince Professor Ch'ü Wan-li to take up the work of annotating Volume 1 of the ink-squeeze publications, which he completed and published in 1961.[4]

Long before Chang Ping-ch'üan succeeded to the post of chief of the oracle bone inscription unit, I convinced him without much difficulty to undertake the systematic work of piecing together the fragments of the broken pieces of oracle bones in our collection. By this time the pioneer paleographers had already developed two distinct criteria for this kind of highly specialized research. The first was to follow the anatomical guide, for if investigators are lucky enough to handle original specimens, it is comparatively easy to recognize to which part of the tortoise shell the inscribed fragment belongs anatomically unless it is too tiny. The second criterion was the one worked out long ago by Professor Wang Kuo-wei, that is, to decipher correctly the contents of the inscriptions. Since Chang Ping-ch'üan had at his command all the original specimens from Hsiao-t'un, he could naturally pursue the piecing together almost routinely. From 1954 Chang worked on the project for more than ten years. The institute also decided to publish a third series in *Archaeologia Sinica,* to print the restored shells. The following volumes have already been published:

Archaeologia Sinica, sub-series C; vol. 2; fasc. 3	DATE OF PUBLICATION	No. OF RESTORED SHELLS WITH INSCRIPTIONS
Pt. 1 (i)	1957	54
Pt. 1 (ii)	1959	56
Pt. 2 (i)	1962	57
Pt. 2 (ii)	1965	60
Pt. 3 (i)	1967	55
Pt. 3 (ii)	1972	67
		349

So, up to the present time, 349 restored shells have been reconstructed; these more or less complete tortoise shells with inscriptions constitute, at present, the majority of documents available which were originally, for some reason or other, written together on the same plate. These restored documents certainly provide the most reliable source materials for researching a number of important historical problems, much more valuable than information extracted or entirely based upon inscriptions of fragmentary oracle bones. It is true that among inscribed records on the same plate there may be a number of independent queries and answers that may or may not be related to each other. Still the very fact that these records are found on the same plate indicates at least the order of occurrence of such events—a sort of time relation of various queries made.

Chang Ping-ch'üan, in one of his articles, mentioned that by studying the records on these specimens which he had pieced together he had discovered the important custom of making a single query a number of times—sometimes as many as ten times.[5] If the query, for example, was about the forecast of the weather in a certain month and the answer was "rain," the same event might be recorded ten times. Anyone who studied weather conditions using fragmentary records as his source materials would probably conclude that these records constituted definite evidence that it rained ten times in a certain month in the Yin-Shang period, but Chang's discovery indicates that he would have been very much misguided. We know that a number of scholars in the past did attempt to study climatic conditions on the basis of the oracle bone records before these specimens were restored. Chang has himself written an article on "Agriculture and Climate," in which, of course, he paid considerable attention to the repeated records of the same event.[6]

A great deal more may be said about the work of restoration, but the above reference is sufficient to show the importance of this somewhat time-consuming task, whose results will benefit future epigraphists.

Before I stop this narrative about publications concerning oracle bone studies, I must mention one more book, published in 1965, which is widely used and much appreciated: Li Hsiao-ting's *Chia-ku wen-tzŭ chi-shih*. This dictionary of oracle bone characters in the style of the *Shuo-wen* dictionary was one of the few publications of the institute which soon had to be reprinted by popular demand. In compiling it, Li made a systematic effort to include all the studies and decipherments of every individual character. The book therefore provides the source materials for any scholar who would like to get acquainted with the views of past masters, besides serving as a handbook to introduce the uninitiated to the earliest Chinese writing discovered so far.

The project to publish the royal tombs excavated at Hou-chia-chuang under the leadership of Liang Ssŭ-yung was placed in the hands of Professor Kao Ch'ü-hsün as soon as we had settled at Nankang. Although Liang's original manuscripts had already examined and presented the principal tomb contents, they were not illustrated. What Kao had to do was in fact more laborious than was at first thought. He had to proceed in accordance with the following steps: (1) to go carefully over Liang's manuscript as well as the original field notes; (2) to check all the field photographs and take pictures of every individual find from the different tombs; (3) to draw accurate figures of all the finds to demonstrate both (a) tomb structure and structures of important finds, and (b) the relative position of every individual tomb in the group; (4) to describe the structure of every tomb and the important finds from it in concise and technical terms; (5) to check the registered field numbers of all tomb contents against field records, and also against Liang's manuscripts and the sketches made in the field; and (6) to pay attention to records of early plunderings and diggings and illustrate the amount of damage done to the original tombs through such early plunderings as well as through recent pilferages.

Kao was one of those who had been privileged to follow Liang in the field and had learned from him the technology of his field operations. He had also learned to respect the master and worked on his manuscripts with dedication. He has been able to annotate and illustrate the manuscripts in a truly professional way; HPKM 1001 was published in 1962 in two volumes: one being text, the other composed of 270 plates, with an extra appending volume of colored plates printed specially in Japan to present the extraordinary records of Yin-Shang painted designs preserved in the "colored clay blocks," which Professor Umehara had worked out and printed in Japan during wartime.

Since we came to Taiwan, Professor Umehara has paid the Institute of History and Philology frequent visits, and thus become better acquainted not only with the Anyang finds, but also with the archaeologists of the Archaeological Section personally. His devotion to and genuine interest in the study of Anyang artifacts really touched most of us; so when the HPKM 1001 report was ready for publication, I approached Professor Umehara for some help to have the "colored clay" illustrations printed in Japan and issued together with the two volumes which had already taken Kao Ch'ü-hsün many years to complete. This request was soon complied with. I mention this cooperation between the learned men of China and Japan just to show how in academic work cooperation can find expression in a number of ways.

The Hou-chia-chuang series of publications is still going on. Up to 1973, reports on HPKM 1002, 1003, 1004, and 1217 have all been published. Kao has practically completed the reports of all the other huge tombs: these are to be issued like the first five volumes already in print. Only the necessary illustrations in plates and figures remain to be done and, also, the necessary publication funds to be found. It is expected that Professor Kao will be able to complete this work in due time.[7]

The task of reporting Hsiao-t'un differs from the Hou-chia-chuang series in two important respects: in the first place, the diggings at Hsiao-t'un, in twelve seasons which lasted nine years (1928–37), underwent a great many changes—changes in command and personalities, in fundamental ideas, and in methodology. Consequently the field records are more mixed in nature than the Hou-chia-chuang field data, which were collected under one leader and are therefore of a much more uniform standard. The field records, the field photographs, and the field sketches of Hsiao-t'un differed as seasons changed and as needs arose. When Shih Chang-ju took charge of the Hsiao-t'un field report after the Archaeological Section settled in Nankang, he found the task initially much more arduous than reporting the royal cemetery of Hsi-pei-kang at Hou-chia-chuang.

In the second respect the Hsiao-t'un data, being concerned mainly with dwelling sites, are much more complicated in nature; they are composed of all sorts of materials requiring architectural, social, political, religious, ornamental, etc., interpretation. The purpose and significance of some finds are revealed in the materials themselves; others have to be deduced from the mutual relationship among the discovered art-objects. Thus the deposits found in those underground caves and caches may have been formed for purposes quite different from each other, while in the case of tomb finds, the archaeologists are at least sure of what the buried goods were meant for.

Still, when Shih took up the work he also had certain advantages, including his own field experience and his wartime efforts in various related investigations. One of the most useful of these preliminary works, initiated during the Kunming days, was the project to piece together all the detailed sketch maps surveyed and drawn in the twelve seasons, and match all of them on one sheet of drawing paper, thus integrating them into one complete map to show the location of every trenching, underground pit, dwelling cave, burial, foundation unit—all the structural remains ever disclosed during the excavations. This consolidated map was designed on a scale of one to five hundred, a scale large enough for the smallest structural remains to find a place. It was intended to serve as a sort of index-map, and also a historical atlas of the Hsiao-t'un diggings from 1928 to 1937.

This elaborate project was accomplished by collective efforts in the space of a year. All the field men who were in Kunming provided the data, but the man in charge of this task was Shih Chang-ju; the actual map was made by P'an Ch'üeh who, in the field, had also done much surveying in addition to other duties. This huge atlas was completed in color, to indicate different types of underground structures, such as dwelling foundations, altars, pits or burials, and so on.

It should be noted in this connection that all the surveying work done in the field, from the fourth season on, started from a point about fifty meters southwest of Hsiao-t'un village, where a block of reinforced concrete was buried to mark a permanent reference point.

This atlas guide was occasionally referred to in Li-chuang days. By the time the Archaeological Section settled in Nankang, the line drawings made more than a decade earlier had already become faint, and the color pigments had decayed. So we decided to repair and redraw the map.

It was repaired by P'an Ch'üeh, who had originally drawn it in Kunming, and now copied it again on the same scale. This guidance map served hereafter, as before, many different research programs. It served as a geographical guide for all reports concerning Hsiao-t'un excavations and was particularly useful for Shih's final report; in addition, for example, my own final report on the pottery could not have been completed without frequent reference to this map, for, in my description of different types of ceramics and their distributions as well as their depository sequences, I had to take into consideration their locations.

Shih Chang-ju's first work after settling at Nankang was a report on the architectural remains of Hsiao-t'un, published in 1959.[8] This important publication was the result of nearly twenty-two years' hard labor; the work clarified the confused data about pounded earth, the "pisé" method of building, accumulated in nine years of field operation. Turning to the principal contents of this monographic report, I shall in the following account use the term "pisé" as a technical term for all the structural remains of pounded earth discovered and described in Shih's account.

In this report Shih divided the architectural remains found at Hsiao-t'un into three geographical groups, designated *Chia, I, Pin* (which I intend to render in the first three letters of the Greek alphabet: α, β, γ), and located on the site as the northern group, the main group, and the southwestern group (Fig. 21). The *alpha* group was found mainly in the northern portion of the farmland, right beside the bend of the Huan River, corresponding to Subareas E and D of the early seasons' excavations. Within this area of nine thousand square meters (N.S. 100m. × E.W. 90m.), nearly fifteen units of pisé foundations were traced. Most of these pisé foundation units are rectangular in shape (Fig. 22). The larger ones apparently were oriented E.W., while the smaller units may have been oriented southward. It is difficult to say whether these units were related to one another in any way.

The *beta* group (β), which seems to have been the main portion of the Yin-Shang architectural remains recovered by our excavations, is located directly south of the *alpha* group, corresponding closely to our Subareas B and C. Shih estimated the size of this area as it still survived during the time of our excavation to be nearly two hundred meters from north to south, and more than one hundred meters in the E.W. dimension. But as the Huan River had eroded much of the eastern bank (Fig. 23) and destroyed an extensive part of the pisé foundations of this portion, it is impossible to say how far eastward the pisé area may originally have reached. Judging by general observation, Shih characterized the peculiarities of the pisé remains here as (1) all large-sized foundation units oriented southward; (2) some foundation surfaces covered by white lime powder; (3) indications of regular arrangements with terrace (nearly square) of purely yellow earth on the north (β_1), and

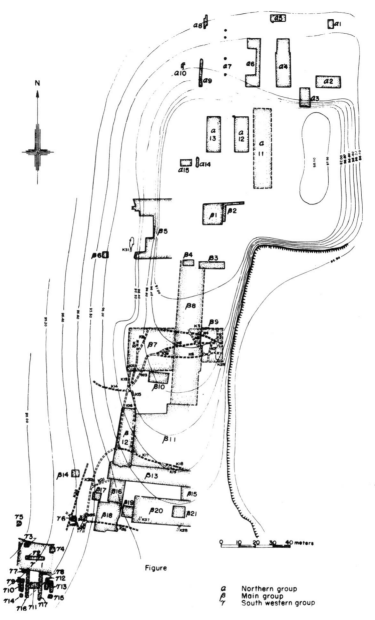

Figure 21. Pisé foundation units recovered from Hsiao-t'un

α   Northern group
β   Main group
γ   South western group

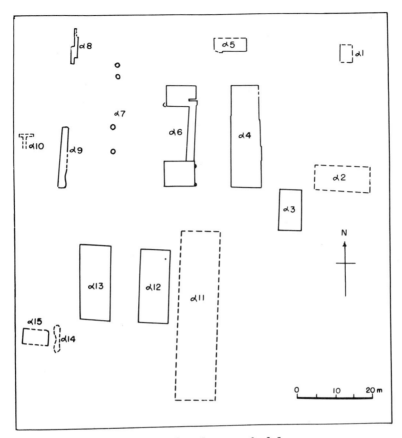

Figure 22. The fifteen pisé foundations of *alpha* area

remnants of three relatively large-sized foundations apparently in
front of the altar, that is, south of the terrace. These three pisé units
(β7–9) of large size may have been the foundations of some large
halls which were attached to five gates. The arrangement of these
rooms was probably somewhat symmetrical but unfortunately this
portion of the foundation is located right beside the present Huan
River bank, so it had been more than half eroded away and submerged by flood long ago. Two-thirds of the twenty-one units of
pisé foundations recovered in this portion still preserve the pillar
foundation stones in order, which of course helped greatly in Shih's
attempt to reconstruct these remains. The most essential feature in
this group is the fact that all the twenty-one units of pisé remains

153

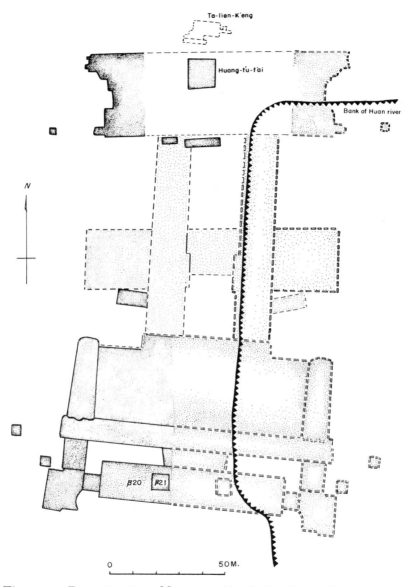

Figure 23. Reconstruction of *beta* area (fine broken lines indicate traced boundaries of pounded earth; heavy broken lines indicate reconstructed boundaries of pounded earth)

were apparently linked in one way or another; they seem to have originally constituted a planned and unified building.

Since the Huan River cuts into the farm here most intrusively, it is quite possible that in the past, for some reason or other, this part of the Waste of Yin may have suffered some kind of catastrophe, natural or human, which damaged the foundations of the main buildings in particular, so that in later times the Huan River was easily able to undermine them.

The *gamma* group is comparatively small in size, and located at the southwestern corner of the *beta* group. Shih described this group of pisé remains in the following terms.

1. The area occupied by the *gamma* group measures (N.S. 50 × E.W. 35m.), a little less than 2,000 square meters (1,750 m.²).

2. Fifteen units of pisé remains were found, apparently related to one another; the orientation is southward.

3. There is one large square pisé foundation, surrounded by other smaller squares.

4. Pillar foundations are not well preserved.

5. Burials discovered in and near this area were found in regular arrangements; human burials on the left side according to southern orientation, beasts on the right side. The burials included cremated remains.

As to the date of construction of the pisé buildings, Shih's main conclusion is that this new method of building was introduced in the reign of King Wu Ting and followed afterwards. Shih's report gives an estimate of the approximate construction periods of the three groups of architectural remains.

I shall have occasion to refer to Shih's reconstruction in some detail later.

Following this important publication, Shih has in recent years brought forth three more volumes in the Hsiao-t'un series of *Archaeologia Sinica:* two more volumes on the burials of the northern section (*alpha* group) and one on the main section (*beta* group).[9] These reports include detailed descriptions about burials both natural and sacrificial, of both human beings and beasts. I am confident that in the course of time he will be able to complete his Hsiao-t'un report, as he is still working on it actively in spite of his advanced age.

Finally I wish to mention briefly another series of research under my direct guidance. Through the generosity of the Harvard-Yenching Institute, the Archaeological Section has received substantial help in financing a laboratory for the study of our bronze collection from Anyang. I was able to secure the services of Wan Chia-pao, trained and graduated in the School of Engineering, N.T.U., and with experience in industrial molding of plastics. A man full of curiosity, he became interested in the technology of Anyang bronzes after examining our collection of molds as well as the bronzes in Nankang. He joined the Archaeological Section in 1962 to cooperate with me in investigating the various problems from both a technical and an historical viewpoint.

Many clay molds in our collection could be easily identified as the negatives for the bronze *ku*-beaker, so we started with detailed studies of examples of this particular type of bronze, which is represented by more specimens than most other bronzes from the Anyang excavations. The results of these cooperative studies were published in the new series of *Archaeologia Sinica;* up to 1972 five volumes of this new series have been published. They are respectively: New Series no. 1, *Studies of the Bronze Ku-Beaker,* 1964; no. 2, *Studies of the Bronze Chüeh-Cup,* 1966; no. 3, *Studies of the Bronze Chia-Vessel,* 1968; no. 4, *Studies of the Bronze Ting-Cauldron,* 1970; no. 5, *Studies of Fifty-three Ritual Bronzes,* 1972.[10] These five volumes in the new series cover all the ritual bronzes excavated by our archaeologists in the fifteen seasons in Hsiao-t'un and Hou-chia-chuang. In these studies Wan studied the detailed processes of casting by means of piece-molds and, testing the process in the laboratory, succeeded in producing duplicate bronzes exactly like the original. My main task was to study all the other aspects of the bronzes—shape, ornament, function, inscriptions, and so on. The completion of this series still leaves two groups of bronze artifacts untouched, namely, the weapons and the decorative pieces, mainly from chariots. I have written in my early investigations several times on both the halbert *ko* and the spearhead *mao* and am convinced that the spearhead probably was imported into China together with chariots and at the same time. As for the chariot, it is a topic which has already been covered by Mr. Shih for Anyang and also by several non-Chinese scholars on a comparative basis. So there is little left for me to add.

Up to now, the mid-seventies, we have not done all we should. I feel particularly sad at the loss of my charcoal collection, which would be particularly valuable now in view of recent developments in scientific analysis for acquiring new archaeological data. The skeletal materials, to which I have paid so much attention in collecting and studying, are still fruitless. Let me hope that in addition to our hard work over the long years to date miracles may yet happen.

9 Prehistoric Remains

and Traditional Accounts of Ancient China

THE REMAINING CHAPTERS of this book will give a brief summary of the various special studies of the Anyang finds up to the present time. It may be useful here to start with some account of Chinese prehistory as it has been discovered mainly in the last sixty years or so. To refer briefly to the earliest human traces, *Sinanthropus Pekinensis* and *Lantienensis*, certain scholars still persist in tracing the origin of the Mongoloid race of Homo sapiens to Peking Man. This theory is based principally on the morphological characteristics, especially the shovel-shaped incisors, which are shared by the majority of the present-day Mongoloid people and also by Peking Man in Chou-k'ou-tien, who lived nearly a million years ago and whose teeth have been studied by experts. It does not matter whether these fossil finds constitute a new genus, a subgenus, or a species; these solid physical characteristics seem to have impressed the anthropologists most deeply. And recent discoveries of

Hominidae in many places in southern and southwestern China, fragmentary as they are, on the whole tend to confirm the idea that the Mongoloid branch of modern humanity has been evolved in Eastern Asia. Personally the author is not yet convinced that the evidence gathered so far has proved the case. Determining these origins is not only in itself a problem of great magnitude but is definitely related to the formation of the Chinese people, whose racial history undoubtedly bears the most intimate relation to the early history of the migration of the Mongoloid race as a whole.

As far as Chinese civilization is concerned, recent investigations have revealed that its early foundations do not appear much earlier than the neolithic age culture, whose remains have been found to spread all over China. It is true that pre-dating neolithic times, mesolithic relics and also paleolithic sites have been occasionally found; but their cultural relationship to Chinese history is still obscure. So it is perhaps more profitable to examine the historical background of the Yin-Shang civilization beginning with neolithic culture.

If we confine our efforts first to the region of the Huan River Valley, archaeological diggings there have revealed ancient remains from mesolithic times onward successively, in seemingly close progression. But since the discoveries of those remains have been made in a reverse sequence—historic, neolithic, mesolithic—there is a possibility that even earlier remains may yet be discovered in this region in the future.

For our present purpose, however, even the mesolithic remains discovered a few years ago on the upper course of the Huan River seem to be only remotely related to historical events. There is hardly any doubt that as soon as agriculture began, Chinese cultural development made a leap forward. Whether the domestication of animals and plants in China was due to foreign contact or was an autonomous development is still a moot point. By the time of the Yangshao Culture, agriculture was no longer in a primitive stage. It is quite definite that by then millet of several varieties was the common staple food in the Yellow River Valley; and rice may have been occasionally cultivated. Some have suggested that even kaoliang and soya beans were common in Yangshao times. This is by no means impossible. The list of domesticated animals, besides dogs and pigs, consisted of cattle, chickens, and sheep, and possibly also horses. Bone-made tools and pottery constituted the main handicrafts. Ceramic industry was already highly developed and the products are divisible into at least two classes: those for ordinary use and those made probably for decorative or religious purposes only. The latter class was what has been described as "Painted Pottery." This class of pottery has been widely collected and, in a number of cases, intensively studied. The author, as a young archaeologist, had the good fortune to do his first digging at a painted pottery site known as Hsi-yin Ts'un, as already described. One thing impressed me deeply when I studied specimens of the painted ceramics: it immediately occurred to me that the painting must have been done with a pen-brush, not much different from what every Chinese schoolboy learns to use when he starts writing characters. It was particularly noticeable that the ends of the various strokes on the Hsi-yin painted pottery still retained the hairline ink-traces of the brush. Though this observation was made in 1926 when I was preparing a report for the Ts'ing-hua Research Institute and the Freer Gallery of Art, it was not mentioned in the report, which was limited to the description of artifacts only.[1]

Dr. G. D. Wu, in his *Prehistoric Pottery in China,* pointed out that incision as a technique of pottery decoration was first found in the Black Pottery Culture, which he discovered at Ch'êng-tzǔ-yai in Shantung.[2] In the earlier prehistoric sites when painted pottery was the fashion, incised pottery did not seem to have existed although technically speaking it should be easier to mark soft clay by incision than by painting. Nevertheless, archaeological research has established that as far as the surface decoration of Chinese prehistoric potteries are concerned the technique of painting appeared earlier than that of incision. While painting dominated the Yangshao pottery and constituted its most conspicuous feature, in the case of the Lungshan Culture, commonly known as the Black Pottery Culture, cultural elements other than ceramic decoration seem to have been more important, for instance, scapulimancy. But the fact that incision gradually took the place of painting as a technique of ceramic decoration seems to be more significant than was at first thought. We shall come back to this point for more detailed discussion in the latter part of this chapter.

In terms of scientific archaeology, Lungshan seems to be the last phase of China's prehistoric culture. The Anyang field archaeologists in fact found a stratum of Black Pottery Culture just below the Yin-Shang remains, although it is still a matter of interpretation whether the time span between these two stratified cultures was long or short.

According to traditional accounts, however, before the Shang dynasty there was only the Hsia dynasty, but, preceding it, were the early legendary rulers who made all the cultural contributions to the formative stage of early Chinese civilization. When modern archaeologists testify to the existence of several different paleolithic and neolithic cultures in north China as well as other Chinese areas, is it possible to correlate some of these early traditions with these new archaeological finds?

Let us turn to some of the traditional accounts about the predynastic legendary figures to whom past historians attributed the origin of the more important elements of Chinese culture. Among these legendary figures there are at least four who deserve brief mention here:

1. Huang-ti (the Yellow Emperor), according to tradition, fought two famous battles at Pan-ch'üan and Cho-lu, one located to the northwest of Peking, in Chahar, and the other near Pao-ting in Hopei, in order to unify his kingdom. His territory was estimated by Ssŭ-ma Ch'ien to have extended toward the sea in the east, the Yangtze River in the south, and on the west as far as modern Kansu. In the north he drove away the barbarian Hun-chu, presumably one of the ancestral tribes of the Hsiung-nu of the Han dynasty. He is traditionally important not only because he heads the list of emperors in the *Shih-chi* account, but also because up to the present the Chinese people have considered themselves to be the descendants of the Yellow Emperor.

2. To Huang-ti's first wife, Lei-chu, the invention of sericulture is usually attributed.

3. Ch'i, the ancestor of the royal house of the Chou, served as an agricultural specialist in the court of Emperor Shun, one of two emperors in the Chinese golden age. He has been traditionally considered the man who first taught the Chinese people how to plough the soil and cultivate grain and hemp. His descendants are supposed to have founded the famous Chou dynasty.

4. The Great Yü, the founder of the Hsia dynasty, has been regarded as the first Chinese hydraulic engineer; he is supposed to have succeeded in bringing under control the Yellow River and also other rivers in ancient Chinese territory.

In connection with the legends, it is remarkable to note that modern archaeology has confirmed that both sericulture and agriculture were carried on in north China far back in the neolithic age. As for prehistoric hydraulic engineering, it was closely related to the development of agriculture and the need for farmland as domesticated plants promoted the growth of population. If we accept the tradition that the cradle of agriculture is near southern Shensi, as assumed by some modern archaeologists, then agriculture must have spread first toward the east along the lower course of the Yellow River. So the reclamation of land flooded by the lower course of the Yellow River no doubt needed a great deal of engineering skill. That at this stage there should have emerged a giant figure of Great Yü's stature would be no surprise.

Yü, according to legendary accounts and also according to Ssŭ-ma Ch'ien, was not only a great engineer but also the founder of dynastic China. His accession to the royal throne and the way he passed the royal power to his own son almost constituted a revolution. It is interesting to note how Mencius defended him during the period of the Warring States:

Wan Chang asked Mencius, saying, "People say, 'When the disposal of the kingdom came to Yu, his virtue was inferior to that of Yao and Shun, and he transmitted not to the worthiest but to his son.' Was it so?" Mencius replied, "No, it was not so. When Heaven gave the kingdom to the worthiest, it was given to the worthiest. When Heaven gave it to the son of the preceding sovereign, it was given to him. . . ." [3]

Then Mencius proceeded to give the details of the events, whatever their source, to prove his points. Although it is evident that the true story, from a modern viewpoint, can never be recovered unless there are still hidden documents not yet discovered by archaeologists, the existence of the Hsia dynasty as a historical fact was recognized by both Mencius and Confucius.

In the traditional edition of the *Book of Documents* (*Shu-ching*), there are about half a dozen chapters classified as "Hsia-Book"; but, after later critical examination, it has been proved definitely that the majority of these so-called Hsia documents were later forgeries with the possible exception of "Yü-kung," which was transmitted by Fu Shen in early Western Han. Even this chapter was considered to be a later Chou compilation, but that it was a pre-Han text seems to be beyond question. While this chapter gives a great many details about the hydraulic works of the Great Yü, it teaches us nothing about the founding of the Hsia dynasty, not to mention the subsequent dynastic history. So during the May 4th movement, when there was a great revival of study of ancient Chinese history, the more liberal school denied the existence of Yü and the Hsia dynasty altogether. At that time even a well-known moderate scholar like Dr. Hu Shih agreed that the whole period of the Shang (Yin) should be probably assigned to prehistory. All this happened of course before modern archaeological field work was started.

Ssŭ-ma Ch'ien's chapter on the Hsia, though brief, agreed on the whole with what Mencius said. On the other hand, according to the genuine texts of the *Bamboo Annals* as edited by Wang Kuo-wei,[4] the dynasty lasted 471 years. Further, contrary to the common traditional account, when Yü's successor Ch'i ascended his father's throne, he was interfered with by Yi, to whom the Great Yü was said to have intended to pass the throne and who, Mencius said, had been presented to Heaven by the Great Yü originally. According to the *Bamboo Annals,* however, King Ch'i finally punished Yi with the death penalty. This anecdote contradicts directly the saying of Mencius and the record of Ssŭ-ma Ch'ien. Traditional historians in the past paid scant attention to these particular items of the *Bamboo Annals,* which in later editions were omitted altogether.

The *Bamboo Annals,* like the *Shih-chi* of Ssŭ-ma Ch'ien, listed the ruling sovereigns of the Hsia and recorded briefly the disturbances and revolutions that took place while the dynasty ruled. The last of the kings of the Hsia dynasty was the notorious Chieh, who has been ranked with Tsou, the last ruler of the Yin dynasty, in both cruelty and maladministration, from the time of Confucius. Historians have usually equally regarded these two rulers to be among the worst sovereigns who ever ascended the throne. In their extreme cruelties, their love of luxury, women, and wine, their fondness for listening to the small talk of small men, and their dislike of righteous ministers, they were exactly the same. That is why, according to the teaching of the Confucian school, their dynasties fell to more worthy rulers, like the founders of the Shang and Chou dynasties.

At this juncture, a crucial point of this chapter is reached. The gist of the problem to be faced is how to draw the line of demarcation between prehistory and history—a subject which, since the discovery of the oracle bone inscriptions at the end of the nineteenth century, has been hotly debated. More than seventy years' accumulation of scholarly labors has at least clarified certain paleographic and historical aspects. The most important of these has been to establish the ancestral roll of the house of Shang considerably earlier than T'ang, the founder of the dynasty; it is, however, still not quite definite whether the name of the founder of the house, namely the traditional Ch'i, can be identified in the oracle bone scripts, although some scholars have made such an effort.

Wang Kuo-wei in two essays has tried to trace the migrations of the royal house of Shang—eight times from Ch'i to T'ang and five removals of the capitals after the dynasty was established.[5] Wang even identified the capital sites on the basis of classical materials and historical references. All this has been done since the oracle bone inscriptions were first made known to the learned world by Liu T'ieh-yün and Lo Chên-yü.

It was no doubt a step forward in the history of Chinese archaeology. But it is obvious that some of the problems could not be solved even on this basis. As for determining the line of demarcation between prehistory and history, this involves a fundamental knowledge of modern archaeology.

Even at the present time, this problem still remains in a debatable stage for a number of reasons:

1. Inscriptions on oracle bones are by no means primitive, so there was undoubtedly a long history before this stage of development was reached.

2. The records cannot all be read; the contents of some are still obscure.

3. The readable oracle records confirm a great deal of traditional history, which compels a number of scholars to reconsider the traditional accounts.

Let us therefore turn to a significant traditional account of Shang history, a long quotation from the chapter entitled "Pwan-kang [P'an Keng]" in the *Book of Documents:*

Pwan-kang wished to remove to Yin, but the people would not go to dwell there. He therefore appealed to all the discontented, and made the following protestations.

He said, "Our king came, and fixed on this settlement. He did so from a deep concern for our people, and not because he would have them all die, where they can not now help each other to preserve their lives. I have examined the matter by divination, and obtained the reply—'This is no place for us.' When the former kings had any business, they reverently obeyed the commands of Heaven. In a case like this especially they did not indulge a constant repose,—they did not abide ever in the same city. Up to this time, the capital has been in five regions. If we do not now follow the practice of the ancients, we shall be refusing to acknowledge that Heaven is making an end of our dynasty here. . . .[6]

The above quotations, composed probably near the end of the second millennium B.C., constitute some of the few sections in the

Book of Documents which have been considered genuine after the most critical examination of such an annotator as Yen Jo-chü. Modern researchers who have gone into more detail concerning the textual content, its grammar, and vocabulary, have, on the whole, confirmed Yen's opinions. But even so, these documents would hardly be taken to be contemporaneous with King P'an Keng. The author's colleague, Ch'ü Wan-li, and a few others are inclined to consider that the text of these particular documents of P'an Keng date from the latter part of the Yin or even as late as the early part of the Western Chou dynasty.

The chapter on P'an Keng is usually divided into three sections, only the last of which deals with what happened after the removal of the capital. The first two sections were persuasions or warnings issued by King P'an Keng to the general public, who were unwilling to follow his commands and created trouble and even disobedience.

P'an Keng made it abundantly clear that the old capital was no longer inhabitable, and without removal the people could no longer make a living. The definite reasons why the old capital had to be abandoned for living purposes were, however, not given in the text; the record simply indicated that "they cannot help each other to preserve their lives."

Legge's nineteenth-century English translation, while comprehensible to most English-speaking readers, was hardly adequate for an exact translation of authentic documents handed down from ancient China over three thousand years. So, like most Chinese commentators of the seventeenth and eighteenth centuries, he decided for the sake of clarity to insert words of his own. For instance, in the first sentence of section I of the passage, "Pwan-Kang [P'an Keng] wished to remove to Yin," the words "wished to" were added by the translator in order to make the document readable and logical. The Chinese original as transcribed even in the modern version does not include "wished to" in any expressed form. But as most annotators agree that the first section deals with P'an Keng's attempt to persuade the public, who were discontented and unwilling to move the capital to Yin, it is only fair to Legge to say that in adding "wished to," words not found in the original text, he was doing so on the basis of Chinese commentary.

Such an addition is understandable. There are many obscure passages and vocabularies, including mistranscriptions, which Chinese scholars have worked over for many hundred years without reaching any definite conclusions, yet Legge has had the courage to render them into readable English. It was certainly a daring attempt but it does not mean that he solved all the paleographic problems that have confused and puzzled Chinese scholars from the Han dynasty down to the present.

It may be useful to quote what James Legge, during the time of his translation, considered the main contents of this important document to be. He wrote:

> The whole Book centres round the removal of the capital from the north of the Ho to Yin on the south of it. The emperor saw that the removal was necessary, but he was met by the unwillingness of the people and the opposition of the great families. The first Part relates how he endeavoured to justify the measure. It contains two addresses, to the people and to those in high places respectively, designed to secure their cordial cooperation. The second Part brings before us the removal in progress. They have crossed the river, but there continues to be dissatisfaction, which the emperor endeavours to remove by a long and earnest vindication of his policy.
>
> The third Part opens with the removal accomplished. The new city has been founded, and the plan of it laid out. The emperor makes a third appeal to the people and chiefs to forget all their heart-burnings and cooperate with him in building up in the new capital a great destiny for the dynasty.[7]

The above summary shows the shortcomings in geographical knowledge that Legge shared with contemporary Chinese classicists. For instance, they were unable to locate Yin in a modern district; and they were ignorant of whether the locality was north or south of Ho (the Yellow River).

However, there were certain historical facts which the translator was able to make clear to Western readers. These are important for a number of reasons, because they not only are based on a legendary account other than the *Book of Documents,* but also are of great modern archaeological value.

More than eighty years later, Professor Bernhard Karlgren published his "Glosses on the Book of Documents." [8] These glosses covered merely the up-to-date research results in Chinese phonology and other branches of paleography which the author, as one of the foremost linguists studying the Chinese language, had thoroughly researched from his own point of view. But, like his predecessor, he did not touch on certain fundamental problems related to the important classics as a whole. For instance, how early might these classical documents be? How many were later forgeries mixed with pre-Ch'in texts? It is understandable that Karlgren did not wish to bring up subjects that might arouse historical debates. Still, in the text of P'an Keng, the main theme was concerned with the fact that he wanted to move from an old capital to a new capital known as Yin. This gives rise to at least three problems of geographical importance.

1. Where was the old capital from which P'an Keng wished to move and where was the new capital located?

2. The text mentions: "Up to this time, the capital has been in five locations," and the names of these "five capitals" were identified by serious classicists. Are their locations identifiable?

3. A further geographical problem is presented by the statement that P'an Keng "arose, and crossed the river with the people, moving them to the new capital"; the document does not indicate the direction. It has usually been taken for granted that the "river" crossed was the Yellow River; perhaps so, but in what direction? It could have been crossed from either side to the other, since the locations of these two capital cities are uncertain.

Commentators in the past have devoted a great deal of time to these questions. One of the most notable scholars who participated in this discussion was Professor Wang Kuo-wei. After the discovery of the oracle bone inscriptions, he was able to clarify both the terms "Yin" and "Shang" according to ancient usage and, as mentioned previously, he successfully re-established the ancestral roll of the ruling dynasty far further back than the founder of the dynasty. But there is an important gap in the documents discovered from Anyang—namely, the earliest written materials seem to be limited to the period of King Wu Ting. As there were three kings in the new capital—including P'an Keng—earlier than Wu Ting's time, the question is why, if it was an old practice to keep records on oracle bones, should the inscribed oracles have started long after P'an Keng's time at the new capital?

Recent research carried on in Nankang and other places has taken a new approach to the old problem, namely, by studying the evolution of the method of scapulimancy—the firing marks, the shapes of drilled cavities and of the carvings left by the diviners. It is a well-known fact that scapulimancy was already practiced in the time of the Lungshan Culture—the late neolithic age of north China—and bones used for this purpose were discovered at Ch'êng-tzŭ-yai by the author himself. But, for decades, the older generation of archaeologists have confined their attention to written documents, neglecting almost entirely the method of scapulimancy itself. Only a few years ago, one of the oldest assistants in the Oracle Section of the institute, Mr. Liu Yüan-lin, who has ink-rubbed the oracle bone inscriptions for nearly twenty years, began to propose a systematic study of this group of neglected data. Already several points are obvious:

1. The method of firing changed greatly in the course of time.

2. The method of carving and drilling cavities varied considerably.

3. Scapulae were apparently used earlier than tortoise shells even at Hsiao-t'un.

Mr. Liu in his preliminary study [9] has been able to demonstrate all the above points and, further, he has been able to link certain types of drilled cavities of oracle bones with those first discovered at Ch'êng-tzŭ-yai which were made by a similar method of drilling, before the application of fire. Liu has been able to find one scapula with a definitely early type of carved cavities and also inscribed with one character. This character, strange to say, is readable as "P'an," inscribed with two vertical strokes and linked by two horizontal bars in between (like the letter H in the English alphabet with an extra horizontal bar); it is exactly the oracle bone character for the first word of P'an Keng's name.

Where this research will lead, it is difficult to say; the recent discovery of an early Shang site at Chêng-chou, which has been identified by some authorities as Ao or Hsiao, with its center located at Erh-li-kang, has provided rich comparative materials. But among the relics recovered from the Chêng-chou site inscribed oracle bones are comparatively scarce; so far only three pieces are said to have been discovered. Nobody seems to have made a comparative study of these pieces from a technological viewpoint.

Recent archaeological discoveries, which have been extensive, have frequently referred to sites as those of early Shang capitals, especially when large areas of pounded earth were discovered in southern and western Honan, Shantung, and southern Hopei; in all these regions it is said that more than ten localities could be dated to the time of the Shang dynasty. But with the exception of those in Chêng-chou and a few sites near Yen-shih like Erh-li-t'ou in western Honan, none has been much studied. So the exact locations of the five capitals of early Shang remain for the most part still unidentified. Even the identification of the sites in Chêng-chou as Ao or Hsiao, seems to be somewhat inconclusive. If this identification were to be accepted, the obscure passages in P'an Keng, such as "this settlement" and "crossed the river with the people," would also become clear, and the reason which impelled King P'an Keng to move the capital could also be conjectured. One would suppose that it was the overflooding Yellow River, which invaded Chêng-chou and its neighborhood almost every year, that would have induced P'an Keng to choose another place as the center of administration.

It seems probable that soon Chinese archaeologists will be able to clarify such geographical questions and other problems related to the ethnology of ancient China which led to the stage of Yin-Shang civilization. But there still remain certain problems related to legendary history.

Traditional history gives great weight to the "three dynasties" (San-tai), which start with the Hsia dynasty and include the Shang and Chou. Modern archaeology has confirmed both Shang and Chou as historic facts. According to tradition, the Hsia, which started the hereditary monarchy, was also the first of the trio in the ancient golden age to create a dynasty. Up to the present time, however, archaeology has still been unable to identify definitely its locality.

From the writings of Ssŭ-ma Ch'ien, the *Bamboo Annals*, and the *Book of Documents*, the list of kings of the Hsia dynasty is almost entirely known, although only the last and the first kings are invested with rich biographic accounts. About the other rulers very little is told.

Nearly half a century ago, when modern archaeological knowledge was first attracting the attention of Chinese historians, there was an attempt to identify the Yangshao Culture, discovered by J. G. Andersson, with the traditional Hsia dynasty. The discussion was induced by the author's announcement of a piece of painted pottery discovered at Hsiao-t'un. In a 1931 article on the relationship between Hsiao-t'un and Yangshao, Professor Hsü Chung-shu went into detail about the locations of the Hsia dynasty as given in past records and recognized that the distribution of the newly discovered Painted Pottery Culture corresponded with what had been traditionally considered the center of the Hsia dynasty.[10] According to Hsü, the *I-chou-shu* recorded that the ancient capital of the Great Yü, founder of the Hsia dynasty, was near the River I and the River Lo, both well known near modern Loyang.

When I took a reconnaissance trip in southern Shansi for archaeological purposes in 1926, I passed through a district known as Hsia Hsien, exactly the same name as the "Hsia" dynasty. There I discovered not only the painted pottery site of Hsi-yin Ts'un, but also a group of tombs known by local tradition as those of the kings of Hsia. While the excavation of the painted pottery site followed one year later, there has been no opportunity since for me to revisit Hsia Hsien to have another look at those tombs. I mention these facts here in the belief that they may offer some archaeological possibilities for future investigation of the problems concerning this important period.

In sum, it seems to me that although a historical basis for the tradition of the Hsia dynasty has not been verified substantially as in the case of the Shang dynasty, yet to negate its existence would be premature. There are several reasons for this.

In the first place, although many sections of the *Book of Documents*, especially those attributed to what Karlgren called Pk'ung (i.e., Pseudo-k'ung), the so-called *Ku-wen* documents, have been proved to be post-Han fabrications, there still remain the chapter of "Yü-kung" and a few others that may have been based on some historical events of the Hsia dynasty. More tangible evidence than the traditional accounts has been proposed in the recent attempts by Professor Hsü Chung-shu and others to identify the Yangshao Culture with the Hsia dynasty. While these are still deficient in documentary proofs, they nevertheless suggest possibilities that may help in the solution of other problems of the ancient history of China.

It has been mentioned quite frequently in early reports that, among the thousands of literary documents discovered from the Anyang excavations, occasionally there have appeared inscriptions written in black ink—on bones, and even on pottery and stone. In other words, we have found in the Waste of Yin remains of brush writings just like those found on the wooden or bamboo slips in the Han dynasty.

Ink-writing on wood and bamboo and on paper can be preserved for a long time in suitable conditions, especially when the climate is dry, as in a desert. But ink-writings on other substances—like stone or bone or ivory—do not last long. Most of the surviving specimens of ink-writing on bone, even those which still keep the characters clear, show serious fading of the ink. This is an important consideration, and reminds us how fortunate the archaeologists were to find the oracle bone records which were legible mainly because the bones and tortoise shells were incised. If they had been merely inscribed with an ink-brush without incision, it would be quite uncertain whether these records could have survived in the soil in such great abundance.

Our discovery of documents written in black ink on bone, stone, and even pottery immediately suggested to the field archaeologists that possibly we could find, if we were lucky, other documents unrelated to scapulimancy in ink-writings on other such substances. But in this direction, our field workers were not as successful as in the case of oracle bone hunting.

This failure, however, does not mean that documents of the ink-writing type did not exist. They may be hidden elsewhere, or they may have entirely disintegrated or been destroyed. Whatever the possibilities, the problem remains that the Chinese written characters which appear in the oracle bone writings of the Yin-Shang period must have had a long previous evolution. It seems to me that to account for this long background, there is a possible new approach.

Both archaeologists and paleographers are reported to have paid a great deal of attention to the discovery, at the painted pottery site of Pan-p'o, of what are claimed to be primitive symbolic characters incised on the rims of pot-sherds in a number of cases. Some, it is said, could be identified as primitive Chinese characters, among which are symbols for numerals incised almost like the oracle bone records. It is noteworthy that both the archaeologists and the paleographers limited their attention to incised marks even on the painted pottery.

A re-reading of Professor Hsü's article on the relationship between Hsiao-t'un and Yangshao (see note 10, above) inspired me with the idea that if ink-writing survived in Yin-Shang, it may ultimately have dated back to the time of painted pottery. The fundamental ideas that germinated in my mind are these:

1. Obviously, the pieces of painted pottery were all painted; this has been taken for granted in the past half century. But how were they painted? A careful examination would show that the artist who painted the pottery must have used a sort of brush—somewhat like a Chinese pen for writing Chinese characters.

2. The artists who painted pottery were also able to draw or paint other figures, such as animals, fish, and birds, as already demonstrated by specimens from Pan-p'o and Miao-ti-kou and other sites.

3. The discovery of oracle bones bearing characters written in ink definitely shows that the art of writing by a brush-pen was current in the Yin-Shang dynasty.

4. Even more interesting is the fact that quite a number of the incised characters of the oracle bone records show evidence that the incised lines may have originated from copying the outlines of painted strokes: the examples in Figure 24 are sufficient to prove the case.

The early epigraphists considered these differences to be accidental variations; the examples in Figure 24 seem to indicate that the changing shapes were necessitated by a change of technique. Writing with a brush and ink, whether black or red, it is simply a matter of individual style whether to render the individual strokes fine or "fat"; but once the characters were to be incised on bones or other substances, the cutting edge of the fine tool would naturally make the fat stroke much more difficult or almost impossible, with the result that all the strokes would be cut in fine lines. Thus in

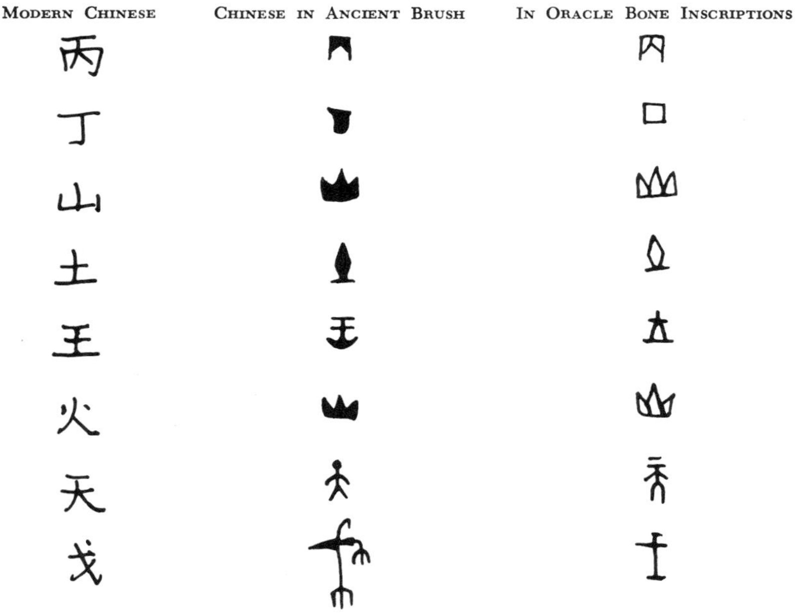

MODERN CHINESE	CHINESE IN ANCIENT BRUSH	IN ORACLE BONE INSCRIPTIONS
丙		
丁		
山		
土		
王		
火		
天		
戈		

Figure 24. Some Chinese characters, ancient and modern. Characters, from top to bottom, signify "Ping" (third *t'ien-kan*); "Ting" (fourth *t'ien-kan*); "mountain"; "soil"; "king"; "fire"; "heaven"; and "halbert"

order to copy characters developed with fat strokes, such as the vertical strokes of *shan* (mountain) and the lower part of *wang* (king), the masters of the new technique found it necessary either to trace with fine lines the outlines of the fat strokes, or, in other cases, just to substitute the fine incised line for the various strokes developed originally by the brush.

If there is anything in this idea, it may account for the early evolution of Chinese writing preceding the incised oracle bone records. It could also explain why there existed some brush-written documents in Yin times; and why from the reigns of the first three ruling kings of Yin, no incised records are preserved. Most important of all, it would account for the changes of shapes of certain characters. Still it could not explain adequately how it happens that, up to the present, earlier brush-written documents have never been found! Maybe they were written on more perishable materials —wooden slips, shells, or even stones. Ink characters written on these, unlike the incised ones, could be easily rubbed off, or the materials themselves may have disappeared altogether!

What has puzzled paleographers for almost half a century is the fact, already mentioned, that though "Yin" was presumably built as a capital at the time of P'an Keng, no written inscriptions earlier than Wu Ting's time have been found there. So far there seems to have been no successful attempt to explain this.

But if we accept the theory that early Chinese records were brush-written, the above puzzle may also be solved. It is possible that incising inscriptions as an official method was adopted only in Wu Ting's time. Before this period, probably the major portion of written records were in ink-writings made by means of the ink-brush. Since we have been able to recover examples of such documents from the Waste of Yin and since painted pottery was commonly found in the pre–Yin-Shang period, this hypothesis may be said to have a substantial basis.

10 Architecture

Structural Remains and Suggested Reconstructions of Surface Buildings

ALTHOUGH SOME of the structural remains found at Anyang—the "royal tombs" of Hou-chia-chuang and the pisé foundation units of Hsiao-t'un—have been described in previous chapters according to the order of their discovery, no attempt has been made to discuss this group of data as a whole. Here, in order to give the reader a general idea of what a Chinese capital might have been like in the last quarter of the second millennium B.C., I would like to bring together and analyze these various discoveries, scattered through a period of nearly a decade.

Pisé, a basic foundation and wall-building technique, was not an architectural invention of the Yin-Shang period. Recent archaeological excavations on the Mainland have shown that construction by earth-pounding existed long before the Shang dynasty moved its capital to Anyang. It was found to have been used both in the Shang sites at Cheng-chou and in earlier sites in western Honan and elsewhere.

The structural remains exposed at the Hsiao-t'un site can easily be grouped into two main divisions: the underground structures and the surface buildings. The underground structures are again divisible into a number of minor categories, some for dwellings, some for storage, and others for burying sacrificial victims or for regular burials. Ditches and water-storage ponds were also found. All these, no doubt, were planned and probably administered by some responsible unit of the government.

Let us examine the undergroup group first.

Underground Structures

Shih Chang-ju divides the underground structures into two subdivisions, one group for dwelling purposes, the other for storage. According to him, underground dwellings disclosed by excavation are much less numerous than pits for storage purposes. Most of the examples of subterranean habitats which have survived are comparatively large and shallow; the depth is usually smaller in dimension than the horizontal cross-section. The extant underground houses usually include stepped passages for ascending and descending. In this connection, it is interesting that in the common vocabulary of the Shang and Chou period, as noted by some specialists, the everyday term for "come and go" is "ascend and descend." The usage of this particular term is no doubt closely connected with the habit of living in underground habitations.

Shih Chang-ju in his 1955 paper describes no less than six of these underground dwelling caves, half of which were overlaid by one or more layers of pounded earth.[1] It is obvious that when a later pisé foundation was laid, if subterranean pits, whether for dwelling or storage, were in the way, they had to be wiped out or filled in before the surface buildings could be erected. Several questions immediately arose when these striking stratifications were first noticed: (1) Were these underground habitats built in the Yin-Shang time? (2) If they were, what is the evidence? (3) If they were not, when were they built?

These questions could only be satisfactorily answered by a detailed examination of the dwelling remains. There are various types of surviving examples, indicating that there was by no means a uniform style for the underground dwellings. The following examples are those given by Professor Shih.

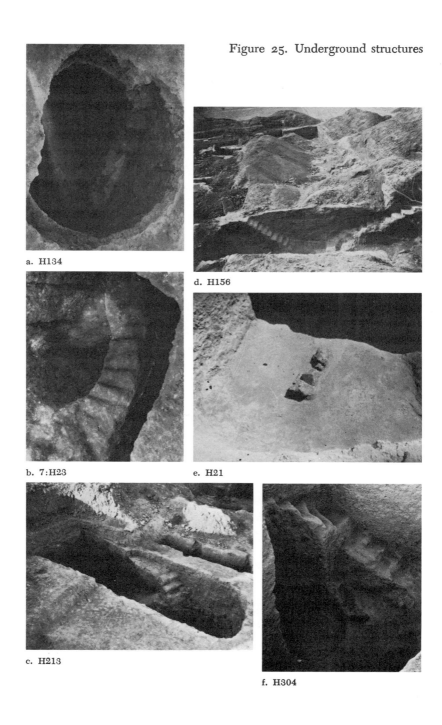

Figure 25. Underground structures

a. H134

b. 7:H23

c. H213

d. H156

e. H21

f. H304

Type I, Circular

A good example for this type is H134, located underneath *beta* 12 on its western margin. The upper entrance began to appear at 1.14m. below the present surface, overlaid by nearly 5cm. of pounded earth. Steps were found along the circular wall; the diameters of the upper entrance were between 2.00 and 2.27m. The depth of this cave was only 2 meters, with a flat bottom. The flight of the ascending and descending passage consisted of seven steps unequal in height and terminated at its lower part in a slope. Potsherds, animal bones and copper rust accumulated on the floor were the principal contents of this cave; near the middle of the floor lay a boulder, relatively large in size (40 cm. × 20 cm.), which had apparently served as a pillar base (Fig. 25a).

Another example of this type given by Shih was 7H23 located underneath *beta* 7, which though classified as circular looks somewhat irregular at the entrance. The upper entrance seemed to be regular, only 7 meters in diameter, but the internal structure was quite complicated. The uppermost entrance began to appear at 40cm. below the present pisé foundation, but the cave itself reached a depth of 5.85m. with seventeen steps in between. The flight of steps was built in the middle of the cave, thus dividing the interior into two parts. The western portion was much shallower, only 4.70m. in depth, while the eastern portion was 1 meter deeper. One piece of inscribed oracle bone was found in the cave, which according to our paleographers belonged to the fourth period (Fig. 25b).

Type II, Oval

Examples of this type were also located in the *beta* area. Shih gives H213 as the first instance of this type. The uppermost part appeared at the depth of 58cm. below the modern surface; it was overlaid by the pisé unit, *beta* 18. The underground cave itself measured 7.02m. in length by a width of 2.28m.; from top to bottom it measured a little over 2 meters (2.02–2.32m.). The northern portion was narrower and also shallower; traces of a stepped passage started at the north, and, as it sloped down along the western side, it measured 80cm. wide. As it descended to the depth of 1.50m., there appeared a sort of wall from the bottom that partitioned the southern part of the cave from the northern part. The floor of the southern part was smooth and could be entered only by first descending to the northern portion, then turning to the south along the smooth separating wall (Fig. 25c).

The cave was filled with pounded earth, obviously preparatory to laying the *beta* 18 unit foundation.

The second example given by Shih to illustrate the oval-shaped underground dwelling cave is H156, the most spacious dwelling cave which has survived. This underground cave measured 12.40m. × 3.80m. in cross dimensions, whereas the depth of the cave reached a dimension of only 2.25m. Its upper entrance began to appear at the depth of 1 meter below the present surface. Like the others, it was overlaid by pounded earth which constituted the foundation unit of *beta* 11. This particular cave had two flights of stepped slopes for ascending and descending, reaching all along the western wall; the southern flight descended from south to north and the northern flight descended from north to south, both of these meeting at the bottom in the middle of the western side. The southern flight was composed of nine steps, and the northern of ten steps (Fig. 25d).

A third example given by Shih is H21 which measured 7.30m. × 2.30m. in cross diameter. It was discovered underneath *beta* 5 within the area of B133. The cave began to appear at a depth of 1.30m., partly under *beta* 5. The depth of the cave was only 2.30m., but it was divided by a stepped passage in the middle which ran from south to north about 60cm. wide and the last step was located at 1.80m. from the entrance. Since many bronze fragments and pieces of molds for bronze-casting were discovered in this cave, it may very possibly have been used as a bronze-casting workshop (Fig. 25e).

Type III, Rectangular

There is only one illustration of an example of this type, located in the *gamma* area. The exact location was on the northern side of *gamma* 1, which was itself a huge unit of pounded earth. According to Shih's account (see note 1, above), this dwelling cave had already been partly destroyed by a Yin tomb (M334) and further disturbed by a modern well. The entrance cave appeared at 37cm. below the present surface. It measured 4.05 × 3.05m. in cross dimensions, and in depth 3.55m., with a flat smooth floor surface. Its flight of steps started at the eastern end of the southern wall and ran down to its western end, and then turned northward along the western wall, but stopped in the middle of this wall without again turning. The whole flight measured 3.60m. with eleven steps, six along the southern wall and five along the western wall. Although a number of these steps were partly damaged by later burial and well-digging, enough remnants were preserved at the time of discovery for a study of the original structure (Fig. 25f).

Each of the above six examples of spacious underground dwelling caves provides one kind of evidence or another indicating that they were used in the Yin-Shang period. But some of them were abandoned when the surface buildings with pisé foundations were planned. The important question is, when did this revolution take place? At the time when King P'an Keng first moved his capital here or later? It is also abundantly clear that in the Yin-Shang period, that is, after King P'an Keng made this place a capital, underground caves and pits were still extensively used at least for storage purposes—for examples, H127, H251, E16, which stored thousands of inscribed tortoise shells. Might this indicate that some of the underground dwelling caves may still have been inhabited in the Yin-Shang era? This problem needs further study.

Turning to underground caves or pits which were definitely and exclusively devoted to storage purposes, there are more than six hundred of these recorded. Some of them may have been survivals of the Black Pottery Culture when Hsiao-t'un was still inhabited by the Lungshan folk. During the wartime the author, in a paper discussing such remains, mentioned H131, H93, and H340 as three examples from Hsiao-t'un that definitely preserved cultural remains of the Black Pottery people.[2] Each of these three underground pits was covered by later pits containing Yin-Shang cultural deposits. Here we are more concerned of course with the culture of the Shang and Yin-Shang periods, so examples in this category have to be chosen from those in which the artifacts indicate some serial development of dynastic Shang. Those immediately beneath the pisé foundation may be taken as prime examples, as many of them were filled in just when the surface building on a large scale was planned.

In a 1970 paper Shih Chang-ju provided further examples of reconstructions.[3] The general rule he observed in these reconstructive efforts was this: "The heavier the structure, the thicker the foundation." It can be definitely shown that the pounded earth at Hsiao-t'un varied considerably in thickness—from 20cm. to 600cm.

in different localities; and, in fact, each unit of these pisé foundations, while not exactly uniform in its horizontal dimensions, actually showed a great variation in the thickness of the pounded
earth.

Shih described one pisé unit of particular interest: namely, *beta*
21, which is located right on *beta* 20. The surface of the larger unit,
beta 20, is nearly 1 meter below the modern surface. Shih calculated
that its eastern side had been eroded away and disappeared long
ago. The original size of the foundation surface of *beta* 20, he
estimated, must have been nearly 80 meters (E.W.), and its width
(N.S.), according to what has survived on the western portion, over
15 meters (Fig. 26).

On this elongated platform, there seem to have been built two
square buildings, one of which, the foundation of *beta* 21, was still
preserved at the time of excavation. For reasons given by Shih, the
superstructure for which this particular foundation was designed
must have been a heavy and probably a tall unit intended for
storage. The pisé foundation of *beta* 21 itself measures 3 meters
thick, deep down into the earth; and its composition, according to
Shih's description, was the most compact and hardest to break in
the experience of the most muscular diggers in the labor gang.
Shih inferred, from this unique quality alone, that it could be
reasonably deduced that the foundation must have supported an
extraordinarily heavy and complicated superstructure on the surface. Before we go into the architectural nature of the superstructure, it is interesting to examine to some extent what underlay this
unit of pisé foundation, in which structural remains were still preserved.

Shih describes no less than four deep-sunken storage pits underneath *beta* 21, which measures approximately 7 meters on each
side with an area of nearly 50 square meters. Within the bounds
of this area, our archaeologists disclosed H361, H462, H463, and
H443—the first three rectangular, and the last one more or less
circular. Each of these storage pits had an upper entrance under
the pisé foundation (β 21) and was more than 2.50 meters in depth.
There is no question about the depository nature of these pits,
since they were all comparatively small-sized and deep, with their
entrances far below the surface. The contents of the pits were
composed mainly of pot-sherds of the Yin-Shang period, articles of
bone, and fragments of piece-molds for bronze-casting. Almost

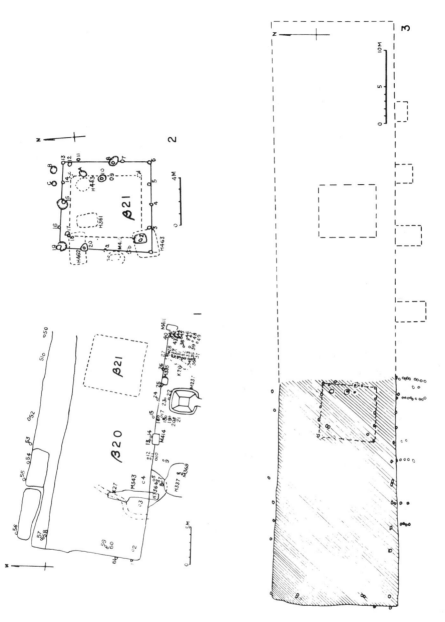

Figure 26. Possible original plan of *beta* 20 and *beta* 21

every pit contained among the ceramic fragments some remains of typical *li*-tripods of the Yin-Shang era.

Summarizing the description of these underground depository pits, Shih says:

These underground deep-sunken pits bear no direct relationship with the strongly built pisé unit. Their existence here serves as evidence indicating that before this place was chosen for foundation building, it was already pitted with storage units. Although their contents as disclosed in the excavation were not the original storage, they represented typical trash of the middle Yin-Shang era. Among the potsherds one can easily identify the *Li*-tripod, the *Tou*-dish, the *Yü*-basin, the *Hu*-pot and the *Pan*-pot— all typical potteries of this period, and in H361, even piece moulds have made their appearance. Taking into consideration the pisé building foundation of *beta* 20 as a whole, I should say that this part of the *beta* area, was built comparatively late.[4]

The underground pits beneath β 21 show evidence that they were probably used till a later Yin-Shang period.

Reconstruction of Surface Buildings

Shih Chang-ju has published four important papers on his studies of the architectural remains of the Hsiao-t'un site, besides his monumental work in *Archaeologia Sinica* (1959).[5] These papers are: (1) "One Example of Restored Yin Surface Building" (1954);[6] (2) "Architectural Remains of the Yin Period" (1955) (see note 1, above); (3) "Hong-t'u [Earth pounding], Pan-chu [Pisé], and Building in General" (1969);[7] and (4) "Further Example of the Reconstruction of Architectures of the Shang Dynasty" (1970) (see note 3, above). The first two papers were published before the monographic report, the third and the fourth were written later. In the first two papers, the author details the bases of reconstructions, which are of some interest to the general reader. For instance, in the second paper he states that the restoration is based on the foundation units built of pounded earth and the boulders, found resting on the surfaces of the various units which were obviously used to support the columns, pillars, or rails. The superstructures, however, had all vanished, so Shih had to depend for these on other resources, namely (1) the pictorial characters in the oracle bone scripts related to houses; (2) classic records like *Ta-tai-li* and *K'ao-kung-chi;*[8] and (3) survivals of simple structural forms and meth-

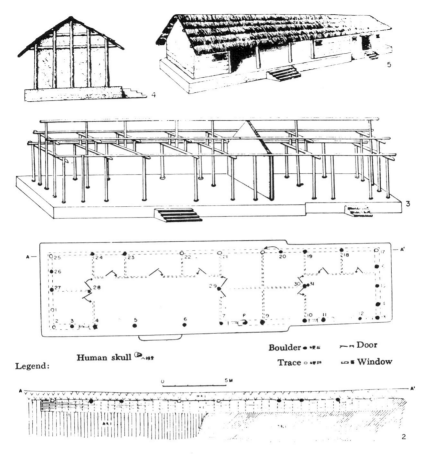

Figure 27. Reconstruction of *alpha* 4

ods still current in Yünnan and Szechwan where Shih had the opportunity to see them during wartime.

On the above bases Shih had been able to reconstruct several buildings which, with his permission, the author is reproducing in this chapter to illustrate the types of houses that might have been built during the time when the Yin-Shang kings were ruling in the capital. Let us follow the reconstructions of Shih according to the geographical distribution of the pisé units given in Chapter 6.

Those on the north (*alpha* area) were discovered earliest in accordance with the archaeological calendar of the institute. It has been noted that in this area fifteen pisé units were uncovered. Of these fifteen units *alpha* 11 is the largest, *alpha* 4 next in size. Shih, for various reasons, chose *alpha* 4 for his experiment in reconstruction. The result is shown in Figure 27.

Shih summarized the general features of *alpha* area building in a recent paper in these terms:

Although the fifteen pisé units in their distribution appear loose and unorganized [see Fig. 22] they are still separable into two sections: the northern and southern. The southern section is composed of five units (*alpha* 11–15), while the northern section is composed of ten units (*alpha* 1–10). The majority of those in the southern section—three units—are large-sized, while in the northern section, the pisé units are in most cases small-sized and center on $\alpha 4$, $\alpha 6$. Whether they were linked with each other, it is still difficult to say. But $\alpha 4$ provides us a complete base, and also all the pillar boulders in their original positions so I have chosen it for an experimental restoration. As this is a rectangular-shaped unit, the starting point of my reconstruction is that the roof follows this shape likewise, and that we have here the prototype of the typical rectangular house so common in China. Like the modern Chinese house, it is to be constructed with a ridgepole along the middle supporting two roof slopes to facilitate the flow of rain water. As for the materials of the roof, sufficient evidence was recovered to show that it was composed of a mixture of grass, thatch, rushes, bamboo and wooden-splits strengthened by some plaster. The art of plastering seems to have been highly developed in the Yin-Shang time, as the good appearance of many deep-sunken pits testify. Shell-lime was definitely used also for building purposes. I should add that in the case of pisé *alpha* 4 there was found a row of boulders along the middle of the foundation unit, arranged just like those found along the borders. This row of boulders along the middle evidently served the purpose of supporting the ridgepole.[9]

The above statement is not an exact translation of *alpha* 4 of Shih's text, but since the author has had the privilege of talking with Shih almost weekly, he has tried to note Shih's most recent ideas in addition to presenting his written opinions.

One might say that the reconstructed house of *alpha* 4 is almost the kind of farm village house still to be found in modern China in an old-fashioned village. Compared with the underground dwelling caves, however, it was undoubtedly an improvement. But this type of surface building, according to recent archaeological discoveries, was alrealy in existence in the neolithic period as the finds in Pan-p'o and Miao-ti-kou, where both round and rectangular huts were found and restored, may testify. So the thatched rectangular surface building not only agrees with traditional accounts, but also is confirmable by neolithic discoveries (Fig. 28).

One may perhaps feel disappointed from this example that the

Figure 28. House #301 of Miao-ti-kou, a vertical cross-section

capital of a kingdom with an extensive territory should have left behind no more impressive ruins in architecture. But let us see what Shih has accomplished in his further restoration of a far more imposing complex situated in the *beta* area.

As pointed out before, the *beta* area is located south of the *alpha* area and its eastern side follows the brink of the Huan River which, as mentioned several times in early chapters, has eroded much of the pisé foundations during the past more than three thousand years. Shih's estimate is that the eroded area of *beta* is at least half of the original foundation area, maybe as large as two-thirds.

The existing remaining portion of the pisé foundation of β 20 measured 31 meters from the western end to the very brink of the river and 15 meters from north to south. On the border of this surviving area were found groups of small boulders—sixty-one in number—the arrangements of which appeared quite distinct from those serving as bases for pillars. Shih interprets them as foundation stones for the short columns of some balustrades, especially those found along the edges of *beta* 20; there are seven of these stones on the northern border edge, nine on the southern border edge, and four on the western border edge. On both the south and north, the balustrade pillars were evidently arranged regularly about 2.50 meters apart. On the western side, the arrangement is somewhat different. The four stones here are found in two pairs, separated by a distance of 8 meters.

Another group of boulders, found mainly south of the marginal area of the pisé foundation of β 20, are what Shih has named "door foundation stones"; Shih gives the boulders the following classifications and lists the numbers in each category thus:

1. Southwestern door: 2 boulders
2. Southern door (no. 1): 8 boulders
3. Southern door (no. 2): 9 boulders
4. Southern door (no. 3): 22 boulders

Shih noted further that these door foundation stones were buried at an average depth of 0.70m. beneath the soil surface, shallower by about 15 cm. than the foundation stones of the railings of the balustrades on the south and north of the pisé unit β 20.

Shih's reconstruction of the whole area of this pisé unit (β 20) measures more than 80 meters long (E.W.) and more than 15 meters wide (N.S.), so the oblong-shaped size of this large unit of pounded earth covers at least 1,200 square meters with a firm foundation more than 2 meters deep sunken in the soil. And on top of it, if we are to be guided by the distribution of the regularly arranged boulders, this big unit seems to have been an open platform fenced by railings that may have constituted balustrades on both the north and the south. On this huge platform, there are reasons to believe that a pair of storied buildings were constructed as shown in the complete reconstruction published by Shih Chang-ju in 1970 (see note 3, above), one of the latest efforts of this aging archaeologist.

Of the two storied buildings reconstructed on the platform β 20, the one of which material evidence survives is what has been referred to as β 21, an extra pisé unit built on top of β 20, with a foundation as hard and solid as rock, as has been mentioned previously. This unit measures about 7 meters on each side and is oriented almost to the magnetic north, just like the more or less square terraced platform on the northernmost side of the *beta* area, namely, the Huang-t'u-t'ai (β 1) (see Fig. 23). It is Shih's belief that on this square foundation of the hard pisé unit, there must have been a heavy structure, as the boulders found on the top of β 21 *in situ* show apparently two parallel rows (each with five stones) on the external margin, while for the inner square, according to Shih's reconstruction, only one boulder stone at each corner was originally laid, some of which were mislocated due to later disturbance and burials. Working from these arrangements of the pillar base stones, Shih experimented to arrive at a possible restoration of the originals, for which he tried various plans. At his fourth attempt, he felt satisfied. In 1970, after a long period of experimental restoration, he settled on a two storied construction which he published in the article cited in note 3. Shih believes that there were a pair of these storied buildings, standing symmetrically on the platform of β 20. As restored, they look very much like a pair of drum and bell towers of the sort built everywhere since the Han dynasty (Fig. 29).

Shih assumes that these restored buildings functioned as watch towers and also probably to house guards, for the following reasons:

1. These two buildings were the southernmost buildings of the β area, and since their orientation was toward the south, they occupied the frontal, entrance position.

2. Along the south front of β 20, there are remains indicating the original existence of seven flights of stairs, the longest and main one being in the middle, flanked by three minor staircases on each side. This presents a magnificent frontage and reminds the reader not only of the drum and bell towers in historical times, but even of a prototype of the altar for the most sacred worship dedicated to the supreme deity: Heaven or Tien. We shall come back to this subject in a later chapter.

3. Finally, Shih said the door of the second story of this storied building opened toward the north, for the reason that all the main buildings are located on the north as the restored sketch of the geographical distributions of the β area shows. But the door of the first floor opened eastward so that the guards might watch the entrance directly.

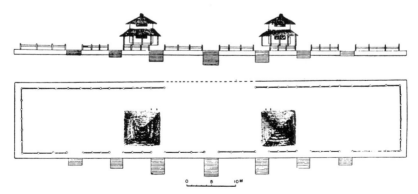

Figure 29. Reconstruction of surface buildings on *beta* 21

I must say that I am inclined to agree with most of Shih's opinions, especially the parts dealing with the reconstruction based mainly on the distribution of the pillar-supporting boulders. However, as to some of the interpretations which Professor Shih has taken so many pains to make plain, I still entertain some different opinions, particularly as to his interpretation of the post-pisé sacrificial burials, which he believes to have been all closely related to different stages of the surface construction—foundation laying, pillar erection, gate or door building, completion of the structures, and so on. No doubt some of the sacrificial burials are related to these architectural works but one has to keep in mind, as Ssŭ-ma Ch'ien wrote nearly two thousand years ago, that the Yin-Shang people were noted for their belief in ghosts, and the oracle bone records are full of evidences of sacrifices both to ancestors and to other spirits. If the reconstructed section of the surface building was a temple or an altar, it would have been a matter of religious duty for the kings to make sacrificial offerings there at regular intervals.

When we examine the restored surface buildings as a whole, the foundation units in the *beta* area definitely give the imposing appearance of an ancestral temple, especially the square altars, the northern-most of which, composed of clean yellow soil (*huang-t'u*), was discovered by the author personally in the fourth season. This platform, so to speak, was impressive and distinguished from the very beginning by its appearance. As its soil composition was pure yellow, the workmen as well as the archaeologist in charge called it in the field "Huang-t'u-t'ai." Its dimensions were 11.30m. (N.S.) × 11.80m. (E.W.). No boulders were found on the top surface. The southern, eastern, and western sides were all bounded by pounded earth somewhat different in color.

The top of the pure yellow earth appeared about 30 centimeters below the present surface; this soil distinguished by its yellow color measured nearly 1 meter deep. So, taking Huang-t'u-t'ai as an independent unit, its total dimensions were 11.30 × 11.80 × 1.00m.

This unique platform or altar was not only damaged by later burials of the Sui-T'ang period, but before it was built this very spot was occupied by many underground caves, mainly for depository purposes.

Although along the northern side of the *beta* area there exists no pisé foundation, it was here that the well-known "Ta-lien-k'eng" was located, where we found a large number of oracle bones and the unique piece of painted pottery.

To return to the Huang-t'u-t'ai itself, what surprised the field archaeologists in the beginning was not only its soil composition but also the orientation of this nearly square altar exactly to the magnetic south.[10] In later excavations we uncovered a large part of the *beta* area and traced out most of the building units; at the southern end of the surface buildings were found to be also oriented toward the south but not necessarily in the magnetic direction— their position seemed to be guided simply by the sun. This difference made the yellow earth platform appear even more unique.

In conclusion, the evidence indicated that all the buildings of the *beta* area were intended for a sacred purpose. To perform rituals to Heaven and other spirits, and to offer sacrifices to various ancestors, were the most sacred duties of the reigning sovereigns. The excavated architectural remains, when reconstructed, seemed to be suited for this supreme duty.

It is regrettable that nothing more on this subject can be said on the basis of our field records. These proposed reconstructions, fragmentary though they be, may nevertheless serve as a starting point for other discussions.

11 The Economy

Agriculture and Artifacts

Agriculture and Other Natural Resources of the Yin-Shang Dynasty

WHEN KING P'AN KENG moved the capital to Yin, the district of modern Anyang, from Ao (or Hsiao), presumably an earlier Shang capital discovered near modern Chêng-chou, there seems to be no question that most of the populace over whom this dynasty ruled were already farmers accustomed to cultivation of the soil for thousands of years. So, naturally, agriculture was the fundamental resource for the wealth of the kingdom. Several important papers, dealing with the development of agriculture and based chiefly on the oracle bone records, have been published since the Anyang excavation. The authors of these papers are all well-known paleographers specializing in the study of these early Chinese scripts. The following three papers may be cited as examples to show successive stages of improvement in understanding Yin-Shang agriculture with the advancement of paleographic research and increased knowledge of the science of agriculture.

Stage 1 can be represented by Woo Ch'i-ch'ang's paper published in 1937 in the *festschrift* volume honoring the well-known chief editor of the Commercial Press, Mr. Chang Chü-sheng, on his seventieth birthday.[1] The paper is full of opinionated interpretations of the day, and is incapable of standing a more severe test.

Stage 2 is represented by a significant paper written by Mr. Hu Hou-hsüan, who was originally an assistant to Tung Tso-pin. Just after the Sino-Japanese War, in 1945, he joined Cheeloo University, which had moved during the wartime to Ch'eng-tu and had invited the well-known historian Ku Chieh-kang to take charge of the Department of Chinese Studies. Hu, unable to bear the hardship which the members of Academia Sinica suffered during the wartime days in Kunming, gave up his work at the institute. After he moved to Ch'eng-tu he made use of his firsthand knowledge of the excavated oracle bone inscriptions, which he had copied and studied during his apprenticeship under Tung Tso-pin, to write an important paper on agricultural problems.[2] This paper marked the beginning of some real understanding and unprejudiced interpretations of the genuine oracle bone records from the Waste of Yin.

More recently, in what can be considered Stage 3, agriculture of the Yin-Shang period has been studied from several different angles, especially as prehistoric remains have provided abundant comparative materials. Mr. Chang Ping-ch'üan's paper on agriculture and climate, published in 1970 in *festschrift* dedicated to Dr. Wang Shih-chieh, ex-president of Academia Sinica, can be considered representative of the present stage.[3]

It is still difficult to make a definite statement about the approximate size of the territory of the Yin-Shang kingdom. But since modern Anyang was the last capital of this ruling dynasty, it can be considered as the definite locus to start with. Whether the dynasty actually stayed there 273 years may remain debatable, but that the locality and its adjacent region (Yin, namely Anyang) served as an important cultural and political center of the kingdom for nearly three hundred years seems to be almost certain.

If we take a look at the Anyang district in modern times, what kind of environment do we find? To examine its agricultural products first: those of us who have worked in the field there for a number of years naturally know that wheat and cotton are the two main cultivated farm crops. But the most important cultivated plant is still millet, which remains the staple food of north China, although rice and wheat are also considered food for general consumption. In Honan province, while wheat is generally raised on the farms, rice is not. Potatoes and Indian corn, which are comparatively rare, are also cultivated by farmers of this region.

Of the above-mentioned agricultural products, everybody knows that cotton, potatoes, and Indian corn were imported to China in later historical times, within the last millennium. Among those that can be traced to the Yin-Shang period are wheat, rice, and millet. As far as food plants are concerned, millet (*hsiao-mi*) has been discovered in quantity in neolithic sites where specialists have identified two distinct varieties, *Panicum milliaceum* and *Setarise italica*. In Chinese terminology there are also several different terms, the connotations of which, however, cannot be defined on a scientific basis. For instances, the term *shu* is generally translated as "glutinous panicled millet," or simply as "varieties of millet," while the term *chi* is translated as "panicled millet." Among the northern Chinese, *shu*-millet has provided the daily food of the agricultural community up to the middle of the twentieth century.

Wheat and rice were evidently generally cultivated in the Yin-Shang period and all the evidence indicates that both were among the common crops although it is not known to what degree they were consumed by the people at large. Some specialists would perhaps insist on raising some technical problems concerning both the cultivation of rice and the spread of wheat. This is hardly the place to go into details, but in so far as they relate to the economic foundations of the kingdom of this period, a few lines may be devoted to the nature of these problems.

One frequent inquiry concerns the water supply of the Anyang region and its immediate neighborhood. At present, Anyang does not grow rice because there is not a sufficient supply of water. Was the water supply more abundant three thousand years ago? The answer, in the opinion of many archaeologists, is "Yes," for two reasons. There is much evidence indicating that the climate of Anyang in the time of Yin-Shang was wetter and warmer, because not only did elephants and rhinoceroses exist in the neighborhood, but also quantitative analyses of the Anyang fauna by Dr. C. C. Young show that buffaloes were among the most numerous domesticated animals, almost equal in number to domesticated pigs.[4] A more direct evidence, although somewhat inferential in nature, is of primary importance. This relates to the lower course of the Yellow River, which, according to the historic geographers, took a northern course and flowed into the sea at the Gulf of Pohai near Ta-ku. According to the research work of the classicist Hu Wei, the Yellow River followed this course to the sea until 602 B.C., which is the fifth year of Chou Ting Wang.[5] In the opinion of this well-known scholar, whose *Yü-kung chuei-chih* has been considered a model of Ching scholarship for nearly three centuries, the lower reaches of the Yellow River followed this northern course over one thousand years from the time of the Great Yü to the fifth year of Chou Ting Wang. Since 602 B.C. historical documents have recorded major changes in the lower course of the Yellow River five more times. They occurred:

1. The second year of the usurper Wang Mang   A.D. 10
2. The first year of Chia-yu of the Sung dynasty   A.D. 1056
3. The fifth year of the Ching Chang-tsung   A.D. 1194
4. The twenty-sixth year of Kublai Khun   A.D. 1289
5. The third year of Hsiao-Tsung of the Ming dynasty   A.D. 1502

The author has cited these various changes of the lower course of the Yellow River—they are all well known from historical records —just to show that the research of Hu Wei, made before accurate modern geographic knowledge, may not be far from what did really take place.

Among the Anyang fauna, what surprised the field archaeologists most was a huge piece of the whale's scapula, measuring more than one meter in its upper margin, and also a number of vertebra from this same sea monster. These finds obviously indicate that three thousand years ago Anyang must at least have had some easy means of communication with the seacoast. They also lend support to the conjectural route of the lower course of the Yellow River as reconstructed by Hu Wei for the period before 602 B.C. These geographic reconstructions also seem to have received support from most map makers of historical atlases such as the *Herrmann Atlas* published by the Harvard-Yenching Institute in 1935.

Before entering into a more detailed discussion of agriculture of the Yin period as revealed in oracle bone records, I would like to say something about the economic resources of the Yin-Shang kingdom in general, especially the natural environment and the climatic conditions of north China during this period at least three millennia ago.

Climate and Natural Environment
of the Yin-Shang Period

According to both modern geological research and the studies of the oracle bone records, there are at least two different opinions about the climate of Anyang three millennia ago. One school of opinion is that the weather of Anyang in the Yin-Shang time was about the same as the present day. This opinion was sponsored especially by the leading paleographer Tung Tso-pin, who reviewed all the oracle bone materials to support his thesis.[6] Tung's own pupil, Hu Hou-hsüan, thought differently. He hypothesizes that the Anyang of three thousand years ago was warmer and wetter.[7] In addition to data from the oracle bone records, he cites other archaeological evidence such as the presence of rhinoceroses and so on. On the whole, Hu Hou-hsüan's opinion is quite defensible although a number of scholars still follow Tung Tso-pin. At any rate one set of evidence that has not received much attention is the quantitative analysis of the Anyang fauna by C. C. Young and his colleagues.[8] As already noted, Young found to his great surprise that among the fauna of Anyang, buffalo was one of the three animals that have left more skeletons than other groups. According to his estimate, buffalo bones numbered more than one thousand, at least three times as many as ox bones. These unique finds could point to the fact that the weather of Anyang was quite suitable to buffalo life, namely, much damper than at present.

These occurrences, together with the fact that the Yellow River was at this time taking a course that could provide plenty of water, seem to indicate that Anyang and its neighborhood did not lack a water supply. This does not necessarily mean that, as Hu Hou-hsüan argued, the climate at that time was wetter and warmer. But geologists have provided some evidence to show that the north China coast was probably frequently flooded during the Pleistocene and the early part of Holocene, mainly by the lower course of the Yellow River which was not yet well channeled. The result of this was, of course, that all of southern Hopei, northern Shantung, and eastern Honan, that is, the general area east of the Taihang Mountains, was filled with great numbers of lakes and pools and small rivers directly or indirectly related to the Yellow River. The geologists have developed a theory that, since the main sources of the water of the Yellow River were from the melting of glaciers in the Himalayan Mountains which had accumulated during the Pleistocene Age, summer flooding was an almost annual event regardless of whether or not there was rain, even in historical times. This may have been the case in northern China ever since the end of the Pleistocene. If this geological interpretation is accepted, the fact that big herds of buffaloes were kept by the Yin-Shang people is adequately explained. Here we probably can go a step further by a discussion of rice as a domesticated plant in this region.

It should be recalled that, in the early days of oracle bone studies, even the most eminent paleographers such as Lo Chên-yü and Wang Kuo-wei were unable to decipher in the oracle bone texts the character *tao*, which means rice. It was not until 1934 that the brilliant T'ang Lan, who followed the suggestion of a number of some others, first gave a coherent interpretation of this character in the oracle bone record.[9] T'ang Lan's decipherment was accepted by a number of others, except for Ch'en Meng-chia who thought that *tao* represented some other kind of grain quite different from rice.

Recent archaeology has more than once identified the cultivation of rice in ancient times all along the Yangtze River from Chekiang to Hupei, and, of course, traces of rice were also found in the fabrics of the Yangshao pot-sherds which the archaeologists recognized as the earliest indications of rice cultivation in north China. As far as the Anyang region is concerned, however, no such detailed examination has been undertaken. But since 1934, paleographers have given the closest attention to the newly recognized character *tao*, which appears quite frequently in the oracle bones. The Japanese paleographer Kunio Shima took great pains to classify the data from the oracle bone records and published his classification in 1970.[10] According to his estimate, there were 111 items about the crop year for the plant *shu* (glutinous millet), and, according to his statistical count, at least 19 entries of the crop year for rice. But there seems to have been no record for "wheat." These comparative figures must be judged with the understanding that millet had not only a longer history of cultivation, but also a wider distribution than rice, whose origin is not yet clear to modern archaeology. Rice was first cultivated in south China as shown by recent archaeological discoveries, while wheat was presumably a foreign import. Thus, even in the provinces of Hopei, Shantung, and Honan, the domain of the Yin-Shang dynasty, where rice was grown it must have been more limited in geographical area than millet, glutinous or not. But when we find in the oracle bone records that the crop yield for rice was nearly one-fifth as much as recorded for the crop yield of millet, it seems to indicate that with regard to wheat and rice the Yin-Shang people must have exerted greater efforts in promoting the latter, a relatively more recently cultivated grain from the Yangtze region.

It is possible that the early ancestors of the Shang were in intimate contact with the native inhabitants of the Yangtze area where rice was first cultivated. This theory may be further supported by the fact that the pre-dynastic Shang people were apparently intimately related to folk of the Lungshan Culture. In our excavation of Anyang, we found that the underground ditches were among the most remarkable of the underground structures that have puzzled archaeologists for several generations. Parallels for these structures have recently been found in an earlier site at Chêng-chou. Our careful workers have never put forth any systematic interpretation of these ditches found in Anyang. It seems to the author now that, since rice cultivation in Yin-Shang times has been established on the basis of various studies, we have a safe basis for identifying the network of underground ditches as traces of irrigation canals developed in the Yin-Shang dynasty. This interpretation would harmonize with the geographical distribution of the various rivers and ponds in this area. Furthermore, the ditches found in Anyang were probably the work of early Shang people in this area before King P'an Keng moved there (Fig. 30).

If we take rice cultivation as one of the main progressive steps in the agricultural development of this area during this dynasty, it provides a link between the early ancestors of the Yin-Shang people and the inhabitants of southeastern China, especially of the Huai River and the Yangtze River areas. This important link, as we shall see later, will also help us interpret a number of other archaeological features found in Anyang and hitherto not made clear. One of these, for instance, is glazed pottery, which originally appeared in the Anyang ceramic collection as altogether unique and strange in regard to both its technique and its shape. Recent archaeology, however, has made it quite clear that the earliest glazed pottery was probably related to the Ts'ing-lien-kang culture located to the southeast in the northern part of Kiangsu.

Another instance is the problem of sericulture. Although silk itself as found on the remains of Anyang bronzes and other articles has not yet received scientific examination, the term "silkworm" does appear in one of the oracle bone records and was given some

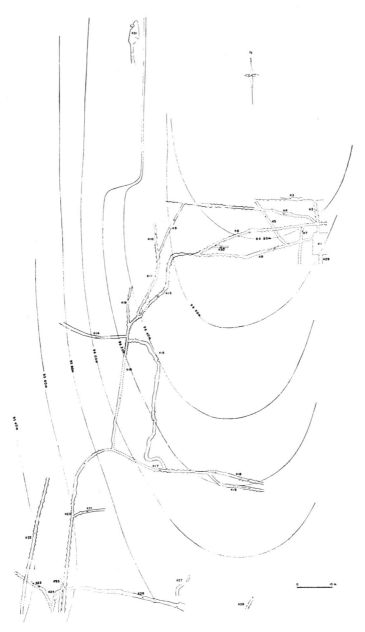

Figure 30. Underground ditches discovered at Hsiao-t'un, probably for irrigation purposes

kind of sacrifice, mulberry trees seem to have been well cultivated, and recently definite traces of silk were found by archaeologists at the site Ch'ien-shan-yang on the Yangtze River. So, taking together all the fragmentary evidence of the findings of sericultural remains, it is possible that although the earliest appearance of silk is datable to the Yangshao age, it is nevertheless more reasonable to deduce that it was a part of early Yangtze culture. From a place like Ch'ien-shan-yang, silk may have been transported together with rice and glazed pottery northward during early protohistorical times and developed a step further in the Yin-Shang period.

Before we turn our attention from agricultural resources, something must be said about wheat, which was evidently also one of the main grain products in the Yin-Shang period. Certain paleographers long ago concluded that wheat was an imported crop; their reasoning, however, was mainly epigraphical. The earliest character for "wheat" (麥) found in the oracle bone records was also deciphered as meaning "coming" (來); from this they deduced that this double meaning for the same character must be due to the fact that wheat in north China was a crop that came from other places. This deduction seems to the author to be far-fetched and hardly conclusive. Still, no archaeological evidence has been found either to support or to refute this deduction.

At any rate, the fact that wheat was first cultivated in Mesopotamia as early as the third millennium B.C. or possibly even earlier seems to be an established fact. If the wheat in north China mentioned in the oracle bone records had been imported from the west or other quarters, it would not be surprising. According to Professor Chang Ping-ch'üan's study, wheat was cultivated in China at least before its earliest record on the oracle bones.[11] Whether wheat was as commonly cultivated as millet, it is difficult to say. Judging by the mention of these various grains in the agricultural rituals, including those praying for rain, for crops, for harvest, and a number of others, wheat no doubt constituted one of the important crops of the time.

To sum up, as a result of various research works of scholars of the last fifty years, we have a very substantial account of the agricultural resources of the Yin-Shang dynasty. There is hardly any question that the grain for the common folk was millet, which could be used for wine-making and for staple food. Both wheat and rice were probably the food of the more privileged classes.

Chang Ping-ch'üan has, in his study, estimated the distribution of agricultural land in this period by identifying the various geographical names mentioned in the oracle bone records in connection with agricultural produce. According to his estimates, it spread to the north as far as southern Shansi, to the west to the eastern border of Shensi, to the east as far as Lintze in Shantung, to the south covering the land of both Kiangsu and Anhui; but the northeast border he could not define. This farming territory may be said to have covered the major portion of what later historians have called the central plain, which no doubt constituted also the heartland of the Yin-Shang kingdom.

It has always been a great historical problem whether the people of the Shang dynasty were 100 percent sedentary. Many have thought that some of the Yin-Shang folk remained pastoral or even in the hunting stage. Judging by the fact that sheep and oxen were so frequently used for sacrificial offerings, part of the Yin-Shang people were still nomads who lived in the steppes within the territorial limit of the kingdom.

Let us speculate further on natural resources. Archaeological finds bear strong witness to the high craftsmanship attained by fishermen and hunters of the Yin-Shang time. The Shang people seem to have been fond of making amulets by carving small fish on stones, shells, and bones. Also, the deer was found to be one of the three most numerous of the Anyang fauna. This, together with the hunting records in the oracle bones, is sufficient to show that the pursuit of wild animals was at least one of the royal sports. So we have sufficient reason to believe that near and around Anyang, perhaps in the west near the foot of the Taihang Range, there were heavy forests plentifully inhabited by wild animals, and that along the lower course of the Yellow River there were numerous lakes and streams teeming with fish.

Handicrafts, Industry, and Trade

Although the crafts of the Yin-Shang era will be discussed in another context in the following chapter on decorative arts, a bird's-eye view here will enhance our understanding of the economic basis of this civilization. Our knowledge of these matters was greatly increased by the artifacts discovered during the archaeological excavations at Anyang. In view of their abundance, it seems easier for general understanding to divide these artifacts on the basis of their material. Consequently, the author has found it convenient to classify them into the following major groups: (1) lithic industry, including all the artifacts made of stone whether for ornament or for actual use; (2) clay industry, including all ceramics; (3) bone industry; (4) bronze industry; (5) other important industries, including textiles, architectural engineering, transportation, and so on. It is necessary to realize that certain artifacts discovered at Anyang cannot be classified in any of these groups, for instance, the perforated cowrie shells which were probably imported. But, on the whole, the industries classified above cover the most essential aspects of the material civilization of this period. The following briefly summarizes the main results of the investigations regarding each of the four major industries.

Lithic Industry

Of all man-made tools, those of stone probably have the oldest tradition, at least as far as archaeologists can testify. In the twentieth century, of course, stone is still used for a variety of purposes. In the case of the Anyang finds, the author has paid special attention to this lithic group, for a very simple reason. During the May 4th movement many of the new historians thought that Yin-Shang was still in the Stone Age. So, when in 1928 the Academia Sinica started excavating this historical site, Tung Tso-pin particularly noticed, besides the inscribed oracle bones, a number of stone objects,[12] and in 1952 the author made a systematic study of all the edged stone tools collected from Anyang—about 444 specimens.[13] This number is insignificant compared with the number of bronze tools from the same site, indicating that such tools served only limited purposes and that most of them were probably survivals of an earlier culture. But the fact must be recognized that the Yin-Shang people in the Bronze Age were still using stone tools, especially stone axes and stone knives as my studies have shown.

Products of the lithic industry found at Anyang are generally classifiable into the following categories: (1) weapons, (2) tools, (3) decorative pieces, and (4) ritual objects. Of the four groups, most of the stone weapons, especially arrowheads, had already been replaced by bronze, so whatever stone arrowheads we collected from Anyang were with a few exceptions survivals of an earlier age. But stone tools were much used at that time. Edged tools such as axes, knives, shovels and digging tools, and so on, were evidently still in common use in the Yin-Shang period as testified by hundreds of specimens found in the excavation. At the same time, stone receptacles such as bowls, dishes, mortars, and other artifacts such as hammer stones, grinding stones, and so on, were commonly found in the Waste of Yin. Among the decorative pieces we found a most unique development in the stone industry: a series of sculptures. Some of these were for architectural attachment, including several marble figures of owls and tiger-headed monsters. There were also comparatively small carvings of birds, pigs, and turtles. Some of the larger sculptures have a vertical trough on the back indicating that they were originally fitted into angular protrusions, presumably from the wall of a house. Besides decorative pieces, there was also a group of stone objects that were used probably only on ceremonial occasions, such as the well-known *pi*-discs and *tsung*-square tubes. In later periods these ritual objects were mostly made of jade, but in the Yin-Shang time very few were actually made of this precious stone. In this connection, it may also be mentioned that a number of Shang halbert blades were made of precious stones with the appearance of jade but, when the substance was carefully examined, very few proved to be genuine jade in the technical sense. They were either onyx, opal, or chalcedony, or other stones of similar quality. Occasionally true jade was found, but only very rarely.

If we grade these lithic objects according to their method of preparation, we find that the Yin-Shang artifacts range from the most crude and primitive way of attacking stone to the most refined and technologically advanced stage of preparatory work. For instance, stone boulders were used to support pillars for building purposes without any preliminary trimming or flaking. Stone weapons such as arrowheads were made by pressure flaking or even simple chipping. For larger tools like hammers, axes, or shovels, the method of preparation depended on the nature of the stone. In the case of soft material, simple chipping or trimming were sufficient, but for hard materials, the general methods used were either hammering or pecking. For the more precious stones with great hardness, polishing was usually employed at least for finishing. The technology of stone-polishing, as judged by the objects we found in Anyang, is divisible into several grades. In the case of genuine jade, the finished article certainly required a very high skill, but most of the "precious stones" which appeared in Anyang were highly polished whether they were jades or not.

Clay Industry

The main features in this category are divisible into three groups: (1) clay figures, (2) pottery, and (3) miscellaneous articles. The clay figures found were relatively few, but of great importance. Two of these clay figures have attracted a great deal of attention from the learned world because they were fully clad, and they evidently represented prisoners as their hands are bound (see Figs. 36–37 and further description in Chap. 12). It is curious that in our fifteen seasons of excavations such figures were never found in great number.

Pottery constituted the bulk of the clay work of this period.[14] In Chapter 6 I have already given a brief account of the main groups that made up this important collection, but here I would like to go into more detail about the significant characteristics of this industry. The typical Yin-Shang ceramics were divisible into the following five classes:

Class 1   Gray pottery, nearly 90% of the total collection
Class 2   Red pottery, about 6.86% of the total collection
Class 3   White pottery, about 0.27% of the total collection
Class 4   Hard wares, about 1.73% of the total collection
Class 5   Black pottery, about 1.07% of the total collection

The number of pot-sherds classified as "black ware" amounted to 2,655, much more than Class 3, the white pottery. In addition to these there was one piece of painted pottery.

Some characteristics of the major pottery group, namely Class 1, the gray wares, deserve special notice. As mentioned above they constitute nearly 90 percent of the quarter million sherds registered and catalogued in the fifteen seasons of field work. This majority group is, however, not uniform in nature. Although most of the pieces were corded, the cord marks were by no means evenly distributed on the surfaces, and they varied not only in their impressions but also in their structures. Firing of the work was also not even; some of the light gray wares appeared to be fired quite uniformly, but others not.

The term *gray* is given to this group mainly because for years it was the common field terminology with which every digger was familiar. When the collection was assembled on various occasions for more careful analysis and comparison, it was soon discovered that the gray wares not only varied considerably in texture, hardness, and outside decoration, but the specimens were also different in the depth of their color tone, which I finally differentiated into four grades: (1) light gray, (2) normal gray, (3) deep gray, and (4) dark gray. What is remarkable about these four grades of gray color is that the deeper the tone, the more it varied in the appearances of a single ware, while the light gray was a much more uniform color evenly distributed over the whole body of a complete article, no matter how complicated the shape might be. Wu Ginding, who had devoted much time to the study of the prehistoric pottery of North China, considered that the light gray wares represented a subsequent advance in technology. They were probably a development made at Hsiao-t'un in the Yin-Shang time.

The other groups seem to be much more uniform in their appearance, but they also are not quite homogeneous. The white wares, for example, which have attracted more attention than any of the other groups, are obviously of two different shades: some are snow white, others are tinged with a yellowish color. This ware has been analyzed a number of times both in Japan and in China and its chemical composition shows amazing similarities to kaolin clay, which is normally used to manufacture modern porcelain. One characteristic that marks the white pottery of Anyang is that these wares are usually elaborately decorated, very much like the bronzes of the same locality. But typologically most of the white wares belong to a special kind of *tou*-dish group—the high pedestal dish. There are also tripods and ring-footed wares made of white pottery; apparently most of them are decorated like bronzes. It should be noted, however, that besides these decorated white wares, there is another group of white sherds which appear softer and are left plain. These plain and soft pot-sherds are important in the study of Anyang ceramics for tracing the origin of the white vase to its ultimate sources, as they seem to be more primitive in shape and design as well as in clay mixture.

Besides the white wares, something must be said of the extraordinary group of glazed hard wares. Most of the glazed wares were jarlike bottles, each with a band of incised decoration. The cover was large and bowl-like, covering the entire shoulder.

As already stated (see p. 138) in the author's monographic study of pottery the complete corpus is divided into the ten following classes: (1) round bottomed; (2) flat-based; (3) ring-footed; (4) tripods; (5) tetrapods; (6–9) reserved for new types; (10) covers. This corpus has served a useful purpose, especially when the shapes of other vessels, such as bronzes or stoneware or pottery of different localities and ages are brought together for comparative purposes. The Anyang corpus has served as a standard for such comparative investigations.

The third group—miscellaneous—includes a great number of minor articles of clay, such as marble clay rings, net-sinkers, spindle-whorls, and other objects of unknown use.

Bone Industry

Bone tools may be as old, traditionally speaking, as stone implements. We know definitely that in Chou-kou-tien, Peking Man used bone extensively for scraping, digging, and so on. In the Yin-Shang time, this industry reached a very high stage of development, almost as refined as the stone industry. In the course of the Anyang excavations, many of the storage pits were found to be half-filled with raw materials of bone, collected evidently for workshop purposes. In the archaeological collection of Anyang, it is possible to subdivide this industry into two subgroups. First and foremost I should mention the scapula bones collected for divinatory purposes. In this period, bones used for divination seem to have been limited to the scapulae of oxen and to tortoise shells. These must have been collected by special agents and also prepared by specialists with the required amount of technical knowledge and skill. It can almost be safely assumed that those who participated in this type of work must have belonged to a privileged class.

There are also other works of bone that required a considerable amount of training. First of all, we should mention bone arrowheads, which show a variety of shapes. Most of the arrowheads were used for hunting. Remains of bone arrowheads are quite abundant in the Anyang collection. For ordinary use, there were such tools as pins, awls, scrapers, and so on.

Two articles will receive further attention in the following chapter. One of these is the *ssŭ* (spatula), which appeared in the Anyang collection in several shapes. Antiquarians have usually considered that this group of implements was intended for food purposes, but exactly how they were used remains to be investigated. The other article is the hairpin. The Shang ladies seem to have been particularly fond of elaborate hair dressing, ornamented mainly by bone or jade hairpins with carved tops. In times of abundance, some hairpins were carved of ivory and precious stones, but those that have survived are comparatively rare.

Bronze Industry

Bronzes excavated from Anyang are divisible into four groups: ritual bronzes, weapons, tools, and miniature objects specially made for the dead. Of these, the ritual bronzes and weapons have from an early period attracted the most attention from the archaeologists. Very few ordinary tools, such as knives, cutting implements, axes, and so on, have survived. What amazed the field archaeologists were those miniature objects that were apparently made to accompany the dead who could not afford anything better for their burial. Perhaps we should add a fifth group, which consisted of the decorative pieces that may have been parts of, or belonged to, a composite instrument such as a chariot or other means of transportation, or wooden furniture. The various bronzes recovered from Anyang total a great number; they have been recently studied jointly by the author and Mr. Wan Chia-pao, each investigating a specific group of problems. As Wan had had some metallurgical and engineering training, he went into the problem of casting and tried a series of casting experiments to discover the production methods of Shang bronzes according to the materials collected by the field workers. The author, on the other hand, was specially engaged in the investigation of the various shapes of the different bronzes and their evolution, as well as the method of decoration and the motifs. As a result of continuous labor by both for a number of years, five volumes on ritual bronzes have already been published in a new series of *Archaeologia Sinica*, each devoted to a specific group of these ritual bronzes.[15]

Some of the results from these studies are of general interest and deserve summary here. First of all, technically speaking, the authors have proved both by actual finds and by experiment that the Shang bronze workers cast the bronzes by means of the piece-mold method. In Anyang, the field archaeologists collected several thousand fragments of these molds. These included a few fragments that could be pieced together and their original shape restored. With these findings as a basis, the Institute of History and Philology, with a special fund from the Harvard-Yenching Institute, built a small laboratory to experiment on the technique of the Anyang bronzes. The experiment started with the making of piece-molds based on the Shang prototypes, which were actually the negatives of a model to be cast. The clay molds were imprinted on the model and then baked somewhat like pottery. When these piece-molds were assembled together, the inner face of the assemblage would serve as a negative of the outside appearance of the bronze article to be cast. The technical details are much more intricate than can be described here; those who are interested can be referred to the original article in the new series of *Archaeologia Sinica*.[16] The second stage of the experiment involved studying how to pour liquid bronze into the assembled molds; the detailed description of the procedures has been given in both English and Chinese in the original report. It is sufficient to say that the bronze articles cast by means of this process bear the special marks of the Shang articles. This proves that this experiment has accomplished its original purpose, to determine that Shang ritual bronzes were all cast by the piece-mold method. The laboratory experiment has so far been limited to the study of ritual bronzes. Since the other groups have not been subjected to experiment in the laboratory, it is still too early to say whether the weapons, tools, and other bronze articles were all cast by the piece-mold method. We must not omit to mention the important proof we are able to provide that the cire-perdu method never existed in Shang times as far as our experiments could show. This statement is important because many students before our time have thought that such a method did exist in that period.

The shapes of various bronze articles collected from Anyang excavations indicate quite diverse origins. Many of these were doubtless indigenous and their origins could be traced to prehistoric times, such as the halbert group among the weapons and the *ku* (beakers) among the ritual bronzes as well as some of the bronze knives among the tools. At the same time, quite a number of the objects of this group originated through outside contact and some in fact could definitely be identified with foreign origins, for example, the spearhead among the weapons and socketed axes among the tools.

The author has devoted a great deal of attention to the evolution of the ritual bronzes represented in the Anyang collections. The origins and evolutionary changes of the *ku* and the *chüeh,* the two ritual bronze vessels most commonly found in the tombs of the Yin-Shang Dynasty, have been definitely traced and show the most genuine native Chinese development. Other specifically indigenous Chinese types include the tripod and tetrapod *tings,* the *hsien* (tripod steamer) and also the *chia* (tripod vessel), all of which also occur frequently among the bronze objects found in the various Yin-Shang tombs. Still other types of bronze ritual vessels are the *lei*-urn, the *hu*-pot, the *kuei*-bowl, the *pien*-jug, the *chih*-goblet, the *yu*-flask, and so on. For those whose shapes have been traced, all indications are that they were evolved from the neolithic type of pottery vessels in north China. The same cannot be said about the various tools and weapons. In the case of tools, the socketed celts or axes, for instance, can hardly find a Chinese ancestral origin, so these have been taken as definite evidence of Western influence on China in the Bronze Age, long before the Anyang period. Recent investigations by the members of the Institute of History and Philology lead one to believe that the appearance of certain types of tools and weapons and probably the wheeled carriages resulted from external contact. But the fact remains impressive that practically all the ritual bronzes have shown a completely indigenous character. So there remains the important question, as far as the bronze culture as a whole is concerned, whether the weapons and tools were developed before the ritual vessels or vice versa.

Other Industries

In addition to the four Shang-Yin industries mentioned above, one should note that there are others which are perhaps equally important, but because of the paucity of archaeological remains our understanding of them is quite limited. Nevertheless, something should be said about them here. First of all, there is no doubt that a wood industry existed in view of the high development of cutting implements such as hatchets, axes, celts, and so on. Some of the wood carving was probably even of high artistic value. Shih Chang-ju found at Hsiao-t'un evidence of a wooden lacquered *tou* that had almost completely disintegrated. Many of the remains in the huge Hou-chia-chuang tombs strongly reminded us of disintegrated parts of elaborate wooden furniture. The horse chariots, of course, whose bronze elements were found in such great number, must have been made of wood. Above all, the houses, whether underground or on the surface, could hardly have been made without some use of timber. Unfortunately, details of these are all lost to us.

In addition to the wood industry, textiles should be mentioned. Remains of woven cloth probably originally used for wrapping have occasionally been found on bronzes and other materials. So far, no detailed examination has been done. It is possible that the fibers were silk. Shang people perhaps made use of fur and hemp as well as silk for clothing, but the archaeologists have not been able to find any tools related to the weaving industry, except the spinning whorls.

12 Decorative Art

of the Yin-Shang Dynasty

MORE THAN TWENTY years ago, in 1953, I prepared a paper for the Eighth Pacific Science Congress held in Manila on "Diverse Backgrounds of the Decorative Art of the Yin Dynasty." [1] In it, I made use of the Anyang material only to a limited extent as I had not yet started my intensive research on bronzes and other works of art such as the sculptures discovered from Hou-chia-chuang. Nevertheless, several important ideas which I had already developed were presented in this paper.

Two works of art discovered at Anyang were immediately suggestive: a human torso in marble decorated with designs which resembled tattoo marks, and a bone handle carved with *t'ao-t'ieh* masks, ranged vertically one above another. In these two objects I found evidence of the ancient practice of tattooing and of the existence of totemism. Another group of artifacts convinced me that an extensive and advanced wood-carving art must have existed in ancient China. The wooden prototypes must have been fully decorated if, as I concluded, the bronzes were copied from them. The field archaeologists did find vestiges of numerous wooden vessels such as the *tou* and of wooden drums, but these were totally disintegrated. Of the bronze vessels, all those of square- and rectangular-bodied type are usually fully decorated while the vessels with round or oval shape are not. My assumption at that time was that the square-bodied vessels copied their shapes from the wooden prototypes and the round-bodied inherited their form from the ceramics.

With this paper as a starting point, I have continued for nearly twenty years my research on the Anyang materials with special attention to the bronzes. Most of the important results have been published in a new series of *Archaeologia Sinica* in five volumes which cover all the ritual bronzes found in Hsiao-t'un and Hou-chia-chuang. Up to the present, most of the preliminary ideas first set forth in the 1953 paper seem still to hold good. In this chapter, I will endeavor to cover the important aspects of the art work found in the Anyang collection. As in the previous chapter, the materials will be discussed in four groups: pottery, bone, stone sculpture, and bronze.

Pottery

The pottery excavated from Anyang has been carefully recorded and studied and the results were published in 1956.[2] I found as a result of my research that very few of the major group, namely, the gray pottery, are decorated, and these are either open-mouthed basins or covered jars. On the outer surface of the decorated vessels are incised circumferential zigzag lines, single or double (Fig. 31). But on most of the gray pottery the surface has been treated by beating, or marked by either coarse or fine strings or networks, or by simple incised horizontal lines. Whether these markings are regarded as primitive beginnings of decoration depends upon one's point of view. Dr. G. D. Wu, one of the earliest students of China's prehistory, considered them to be simply traces of manufacturing. The incised belt of zigzag lines was, however, a definite artistic attempt that seems to have been inherited from the Lungshan Culture.

The white pottery found at Anyang presents an altogether dif-

Figure 31. Incised gray pottery

ferent case. Pottery in this group is divisible into three subdivisions: soft; semisoft; and hard and highly polished. With the exception of the highly polished subgroup, examples of the other two subgroups are all luxuriously covered by incised patterns (Figs. 32, 33). These patterns seem to be copied from bronze with, however, one exception, namely the *tou*-dish, a form of ritual vessel that has no bronze counterpart in the Yin-Shang time. The outside of the *tou* is also decorated somewhat differently from the other patterns of white pottery. The designs are mainly square spirals arranged in a

Figure 32. Carved designs of white pottery

Figure 33. Carved designs of white pottery

checkered pattern. I am of the opinion that white pottery of this carved subgroup was a later development. I have reason to believe that the Shang people valued white pottery much higher than the bronzes, a theme that I fully expanded in my paper on the "Evolution of the White Pottery of the Yin Dynasty" published in 1957.[3]

The so-called glazed group of pottery has very simple ornamentation; almost without exception, every jar has near its shoulder a band composed of simple wavy lines or short slanted strokes between circumferential lines. Occasionally, there are even designs that cover the whole body in a checkered pattern (Fig. 34). The surface treatment of the red pottery is almost the same as that of the gray, with string impressions. To close the discussion of pottery decoration, I would like to mention certain other fired clay objects we have found. Among these are some specimens very similar in shape to a shovel, with a handle on the back whose top is molded in the shape of an animal head, a dog, or a horned beast. These may be tools of some kind, but, if so, their function is unknown

Figure 34. Glazed pottery with incised or imprinted decor

(Fig. 35). Two clay figurines almost completely dressed in long gowns that concealed their lower limbs constituted another puzzling find. Both are evidently prisoners, and each has his hands fettered, one in front and one in back. Both also have their necks banded by some kind of shackles and their heads shaved clean (Figs. 36, 37). This pair of human figures appeared very early in our diggings, and from a disturbed area. Nothing similar was ever found afterwards.

Figure 35. Pottery article of unknown use with animal-head handle

Carved Bone

Of the several subgroups of carved bone, the most numerous are hairpins. In Hou-chia-chuang the field archaeologists once discovered a tomb in which nearly one hundred hairpins were found at the top of the head of a female skeleton, indicating how elaborately the Shang ladies dressed their hair. The ornamental tops of the pins have attracted special attention. They are carved into different shapes, divisible, according to my preliminary study, into eight main groups.[4] In the early period the tops of the hairpins were comparatively simple and were carved in a flat shape expanding into a flat piece of platform. At the other extreme are those carved into elaborate animal or bird shapes (Fig. 38). These shapes were further changed into geometric shapes of various patterns.

Next in number to the hairpins are the *ssŭ*, a spatula used in food handling, found in great abundance in both Hou-chia-chuang and Hsiao-t'un. One subgroup of *ssŭ* was comparatively long and slender, usually made from the rib bones of oxen. The whole instrument was usually somewhat curved, following the original shape of the material. The handle bore a decorative carving, but the functional

Figure 36. Clay human figure   Figure 37. Clay human figure

part was flat and rounded at the end. Another subgroup was stouter and shorter, with the same width at both ends but somewhat slenderer in the middle. These spatulas were usually made from the leg bones of oxen. If we divide these tools according to their actual length, we find the surprising result that very few measure the same. But on the whole, it is possible to subdivide the *ssŭ* into three categories. Those made of ribs constitute the longest, usually the least decorated or trimmed, measuring somewhat over 40cm. long. The middle group, usually less than 30cm. long, had an angular handle at one end and a carved spade at the other. The average length of this subdivision was usually shorter than that of the first group and the handle was usually considerably carved. The third group was the shortest and also the broadest, but also included some spoon-shaped articles made of foot bones. This group seems

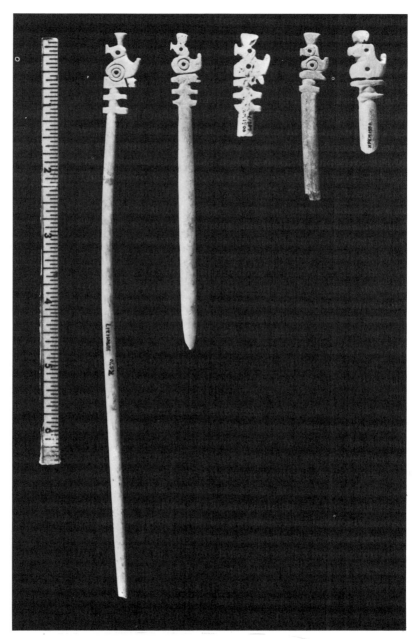

Figure 38. Hairpins with bird-shaped heads

Figure 39. *Ssŭ* handle
with carving of dragon

Figure 40. *Ssŭ* handle with
carvings of three birds
on top of each other

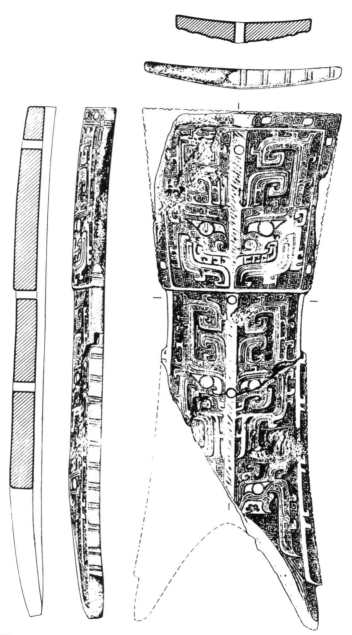

Figure 41. Carved bone plates

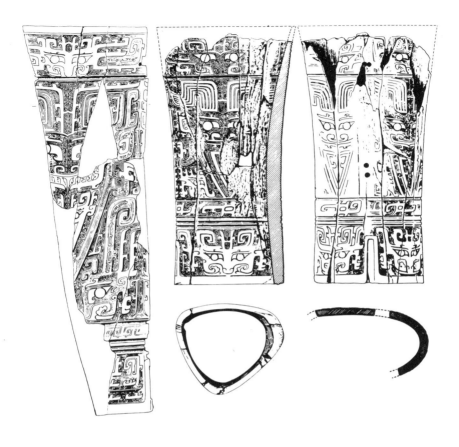

Figure 42. Carved bone tubes

usually to have been made of the leg bones of oxen; the handle was
angular while the other end was often sharpened at the edges. The
handle of the *ssŭ* was usually decorated with incised animals, either
realistic or mythical, such as dragons (Fig. 39), *t'ao-t'ieh* heads, and
birds (Fig. 40).

Other bone objects are flat plates (Fig. 41) or tubes (Fig. 42),
ocarinas (Fig. 43), and handles (Fig. 44). The carvings of the
ocarina almost duplicate those found on an ocarina made of white
pottery.

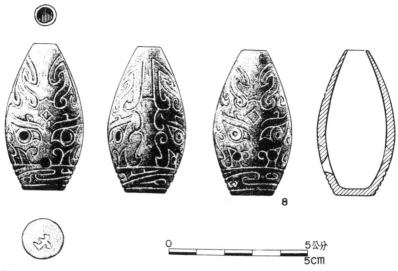

Figure 43. Carved bone ocarina, three faces

Stone Sculpture

J. G. Andersson, as early as 1923, claimed that he had found a carved animal figure from the prehistoric remains of Sha-kuo-t'un on the Liao-tung peninsula, which he had discovered that year.[5] This seems to have been not only the first mention but also the earliest example of stone carving in China.

The stone carvings turned up in the course of the Anyang excavations were an unexpected and exciting discovery.

It was in the third season of the expedition to Anyang that the field archaeologists came upon the fragments of a stone-carved human torso. In the field excavations, these fragments had appeared merely as fragments; when they were brought to Peking in the fall of 1929, the archaeologists on further study discovered that some of the fragments could be pieced together. One restored piece was found to be the lower part of a human figure in a squatting posture, but unfortunately the more important upper half was not recovered. The recovered part weighs more than 15.4kg. (Figs. 45, 46). How do we account for this carved torso discovered at Hsiao-t'un? According to Ssŭ-ma Ch'ien's account, in the early Chou dynasty the natives of Kiangsu still practiced tattooing. So it is possible that the

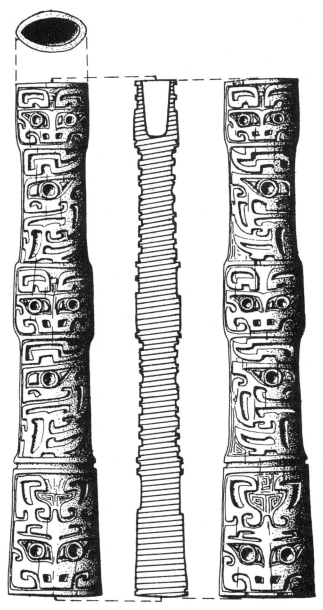

Figure 44. Carved bone handle with five animal masks on top of each other

Figure 45. Stone torso from Hsiao-t'un: front view

coastal people of north China in Shangtung might have kept up the same habit. If this could be assumed, it is quite probable that among the subjects the Yin-Shang dynasty ruled there were still tattooing people, which naturally would provide another example of decorative art for this period.[6]

This remarkable discovery, which immediately attracted world-wide attention, marked the beginning of our knowledge of the art of stone carving in the late Shang dynasty. Following this discovery, a series of other artistic stone sculptures appeared, mostly in animal forms—turtles, tigers (Fig. 47), and so on.

It was not until the thirteenth season, when we started excavating at Hou-chia-chuang, that more complete specimens began to appear. Here in these royal tombs, the sculptures were somewhat different. Most were in the shape of mythical animals, half beast, half human: a tiger-headed monster with a human body (see Plate 5); or a double-faced monster with an elephantine nose (Figs. 48, 49) or the t'ao-t'ieh mask (Fig. 50). The majority were carved in the round, but some only in high or low relief. Unfortunately, as most of these were not found in situ but were excavated from the debris in the plundered tunnels, it is not possible to know in exactly what part of the tombs they originally lay. Among them, there was one

Figure 46. Stone torso from Hsiao-t'un: side views

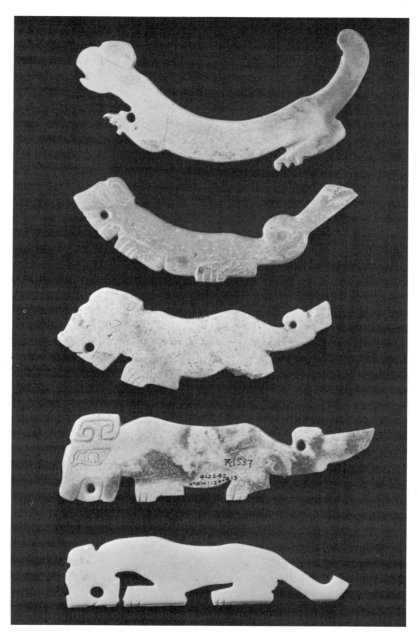

Figure 47. Carved stone tigers

small group of broken fragments, which, when pieced together, proved to be a portion of the body of another human figure (see Fig. 13 and discussion in Chap. 5), well dressed, again without a head, but fortunately his costume remained quite visible.

This figure was in a kneeling-sitting posture almost exactly the same as that of a modern Japanese sitting on the *tatami* floor at home. This discovery soon aroused intense interest. Comparing this figure with the torso discovered at Hsiao-t'un in the third season, the author discovered for the first time that the Japanese *seiza* was actually the regular sitting posture among the Chinese as early as the Yin-Shang dynasty. To judge by the costume, this figure may have represented the well-dressed Yin-Shang ruling class.

The robe has two sleeves, an open front, and a waist band. There are pennants below the knee which might represent a skirt. The borders of the robe are embroidered with geometric designs. Whether this figure is a male or a female, it is difficult to say. At any rate, this represents the earliest well-dressed human figure of China based on archaeological remains; the only regret is, of course, that the head was not recovered. These two stone figures—this one and the squatting figure from Hsiao-t'un—have attracted special interest because they happen to be human.

Another stone figure recovered from the Hou-chia-chuang royal tombs, although miniature in size, represents a complete figure in silhouette. Cut from a flat piece of hard stone, it depicts a figure in squatting posture with the hand curved underneath the chin. The lateral view of the human body is complete, the eye is wide open in a horizontal position, and there seems to be no trace of the epicanthus fold that so conspicuously marked the bronze mask (see Plate 20). The ear, the nose, the mouth, and the chin are all in good proportion, but there is no foot. The top of the head is elaborately dressed; whether it represents a hairdo or a fashionable headdress cannot be definitely said (see Plate 8e).

Paired with the Hou-chia-chuang miniature figure is a carved human figure in jade from Hsiao-t'un, which the artist decorated with positive lines in relief, representing the head of a human figure. The eye, the ear, the lower jaw and the prominent chin, the flattened nose, and so on, are all rendered by positive and graceful lines. On the top of the forehead, there is a distinct horizontal band, surrounding the roots of the hair, and from it a cockerel crest rises straight upward at first and then bends backward above the occipital region. Here, again, it is difficult to say whether it represents

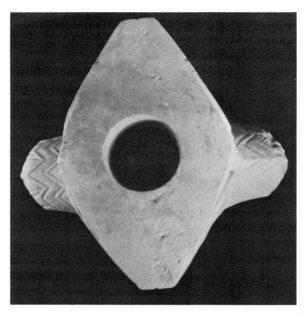

Figure 48. Double-faced monster with elephantine nose: top and lateral views

Figure 49. Double-faced monster with elephantine nose: frontal view

a hairdo or an elaborate headdress of the Yin-Shang fashion (Fig. 51).

Stone carvings of this period cover a very wide range of animal figures, including both the real and the mythical. The raw materials also cover a great range, from semiprecious stones like serpentine to common marble. In certain cases, we noticed definite differences of style among the stone carvings. Although most of these were found in fragmentary condition and scattered so that it is impossible to determine the exact positions that they originally occupied, the variations of style and wrokmanship in the finished products are important archaeological features that need further investigation. Nearly every one of the larger stone animals has a deep, vertical trough cut in its back, like the torso first discovered at Hsiao-t'un. For instance, this vertical back trough was found not only on the tiger-headed monster, but also on the marble owl (see Plate 4). It seems obvious that these vertical channels were cut to fit into a projection, perhaps on a wall.

Figure 50. The so-called *t'ao-t'ieh* mask carved in stone

Bronze

The bronze objects collected from the Anyang excavation are classified in the following categories: (1) ritual bronzes, (2) weapons and tools, (3) functional or decorative metalwork for use on chariots, or other wooden structures, and so on, and (4) the *ming-chi* group made purely to accompany the dead.

In our own collections, the total number of the ritual bronzes, the most abundant group, was 171, including a number of incomplete pieces. Within this class, the *ku*-beaker and the *chüeh*-cup are not only the most numerous specimens—forty *ku* and thirty-nine *chüeh*

Figure 51. Carved human figure in jade

Figure 52. Animal masks found on *ku*-beaker

—they are also typical of the bronzes of the Yin-Shang period as they seem to have disappeared rather early in the Chou dynasty.

Among the other ritual bronzes, the *chia*-vessel, although fewer in number than the two just mentioned, appeared at least sixteen times in Anyang, whereas the *ting*, in both the tripod and tetrapod forms, appeared altogether twenty-three times. There are also fifty or so other types, of which the most important are the *ts'un*-vessel, the *fang-i* casket, the *p'an*-plate, the *yü*-basin, the *chih*-goblet, the *hu*-pot, the *kuei*-bowl, the *hsien*-steamer, the *yu*-flask, and in addition there is a bird-shaped *ts'un* and another horn-shaped vessel.

Although most of these bronzes are ornamented, some of them heavily, there are also exceptions. For instance, some of the *ku*-beakers are undecorated. The decorated *ku* can be divided into three subgroups: (1) those with the middle section ornamented only, (2) those with both the middle and lower sections decorated, and (3) those which are fully decorated. The same holds true for the *chüeh*-cups, except that there are more plain ones. Of the thirty-nine *chüeh*, twelve are without any elaborate ornament. Of the other twenty-seven, sixteen are ornamented by a single horizontal band, while the other eleven specimens show more complicated designs.

The main decorative band in both the *ku* (Fig. 52) and the *chüeh* (Fig. 53) groups is composed of a centrally divided animal mask. The most typical of such designs is found on the middle section of the *ku*. The decorative band surrounding the *chüeh* is sometimes interrupted by the cup's handle. This handle usually straddles vertically so that it just interrupts the decorative field.

The methods employed for executing the ornamental designs on the various bronzes have been very carefully studied by Wan Chia-pao on the basis of laboratory experiments. He has concluded that, in the technique of casting, five methods of mold preparation can be distinguished, each of which gives rise to a different result in the ornamental designs. These five methods are: (1) simple incised mold design, (2) composite model-mold design, (3) engraving and appliqué on model, (4) relief on model, and (5) deep incision in the mold.[7]

As to the contents of the décor, we may consider the middle section of the *ku*-beaker as an instance and examine its decorative design. Of the thirty-five examples of *ku* from both Hou-chia-chuang and Hsiao-t'un, thirty-four have a pair of animal masks arranged diametrically opposite each other on the same horizontal

Figure 53. Animal masks found on *chüeh*-cup

belt surrounding the waist of the vessel. Whatever discrepancies there are will be found in the filling-in with what the Chinese antiquarians call *yün-lei-wen,* namely, the square and circular spirals.

The ornamentation of the *ting*-cauldron seems to be more complicated than that of the first two groups. Typologically, the twenty-three *ting* specimens are obviously subdivisible into three types. I have named the first group *li-ting;* these are the lightest in weight and only three specimens were found. The middle group includes most of the specimens, eighteen, whose average weight is 3845.2gms. The largest are the two giant rectangular specimens—the *lu-ting* (see Plate 9) and the *niu-ting* (see Plate 10), weighing 60,400 and 110,400gms. respectively. The *lu-ting*, whose decorations I would like to describe in some detail, resembles a rectangular wooden box with a flat bottom and four side walls flaring slightly outward. There are two standing lugs at the narrower sides on the rim of the body for lifting. The four legs are cylindrical in shape and hollow; their unsealed tops are holes in the four corners of the interior. The external surfaces of the walls, the lugs, and the legs are covered with luxuriously well-designed ornament, most probably symbolizing ideas of profound social and historical significance. The center of each of the four external walls is decorated with a complete deer head with a pair of prominent horns rendered in high relief and a sectional flange occupying the middle line. The antlers on the upper portion of the deer's head have prongs branching upward and ears underneath. The face seen in front view is most compactly and very realistically composed with a vertical flange as the nose line. Between the horns a pair of dragons confront each other in lower relief. The upper two-thirds of the deer head is flanked on each side by a pair of composite birds also rendered in high relief.

Origin and Some Characteristics of Decorative Art

The main characteristics of this decorative art was partly inherited from prehistoric times and partly developed in the Yin-Shang period. Many of the spirals that later developed extensively into the *yün-lei-wen* originated in the painted pottery and black pottery times. As far as the definite geometric patterns are concerned, I have compiled in Figure 54 a comparison to illustrate this point. Even the biological figures such as fish, human faces, and some plants or horned animals may trace their origin to the period of Pan-p'o and other painted pottery sites. There is another element of which I have made a special study—the bow-string lines which were first developed in the Lungshan Culture and which the bronze makers of the Yin-Shang period seem to have copied extensively, especially in their making of the plain *chüeh* and *ku* and even the *ting*-tripod. As for the more elaborate designs of the Shang dynasty,

Figure 54. Decorative elements evolving through the Painted Pottery, Black Pottery, and Yin-Shang cultures. (*Left:* 1–3, from Ma-ch'ang, 4, from Hsin-tien, all taken from Andersson, "Researches into the Prehistory of the Chinese"; 5, after Black Pottery specimen from Jih-chao; 6, bone carving from Hsiao-t'un; 7, stone carving from Hsiao-t'un. *Right:* 1, 2, 4, after incised pottery from Ch'eng-tzu-yai and Hsiao-t'un; 3, from Andersson, "Researches"; 5, bone carving from Hsiao-t'un)

particularly as shown in the bronze vessels, some traits which set them apart from the work of contemporary artists in the Mediterranean are: the special concept of symmetry—for instance, the confronting pairs of animals or snakes; the decoration of a vessel with a horizontal belt usually divided into a number of partitions; and the piling up of these horizontal bands vertically to total as many as seven or eight belts in some cases.

13 Genealogy, Chên-jên

and Some Aspects of Kinship

THE GENEALOGICAL CHART reproduced in Figure 55 is translated from Tung Tso-pin's 1952 compilation, with some omissions of attached details.[1] It is divided into four parts: Early Ancestors, Late Ancestors, Early Kings, and Late Kings; the first two parts belong to the predynastic ancestors and the latter two to the dynastic period. If we count from the founder of the house, we find a list of fourteen names on the predynastic ancestral roll. The great T'ien I, the founder of the dynasty, belongs to the fifteenth generation. Although ancient accounts do not always agree, the succession is clearly given in Ssŭ-ma Ch'ien's biographical account beginning with T'ien I. It is extraordinary that when the oracle bone records were discovered near the end of the nineteenth century, after having been buried deep in the soil over three millennia and totally unknown to the scholarly world, they proved that he was amazingly accurate so far as the list of the ancestors and kings of the Shang dynasty is concerned. Not that there is absolutely no difference between the oracle records and the early historian writing over two thousand years ago, but whatever difference there is seems insignificant in view of the major confirmations not only of the actual names of most ancestors and kings, but also of the order of their succession. Reference has already been made more than once to this important historical confirmation; I am repeating this point here for another purpose.

A number of scholars in the past have pointed out a unique and significant fact regarding the names of the kings of the Shang dynasty. Beginning with the predynastic ancestor Shang Chia Wei, the first of the Late Ancestors, each of the descendants who ascended the throne bears a name related to what is known in Chinese as the ten celestial stems (see earlier discussion in Chap. 7), consisting of Chia, I, Ping, Ting, Wu, Chi, Keng, Hsin, Jen, and Kuei. This feature which characterized the nomenclature of Shang kings has recently received a great deal of academic attention. One theory is that since the Yin-Shang calendar had early adopted the sexagenarian system of recording days, the royal house of Shang perhaps had the habit of naming the newly born baby for his birthday of which the first character would be one of the celestial stem characters. Another theory, which seems to prevail today, is that it was the day of death that was used as a posthumous title of the sovereign, the reason being that as far as available historical records go no living being seems to have borne a name with a celestial stem in the Yin-Shang days. The second theory is definitely based on a more compelling reason, namely, that the custom of giving a posthumous honorific title continued to the last days of the Chinese Empire. There are of course other theories that we shall consider later.

This genealogical tree also reveals some other social practices of great significance. From the founder T'ien I down to the last ruler, there were eighteen generations during which thirty kings succeeded each other and ruled the kingdom. So, in many generations brothers succeeded each other; as shown in the tree, in nine generations out of the eighteen, the throne passed from brother to brother. It is also remarkable that it is usually the youngest brother who passed his throne to his own son. Yet it is important to note that in the last four generations, none of the ruling kings seems to have had a brother. Whether this corresponded with historical facts or not is open to question. And if not, why this change?

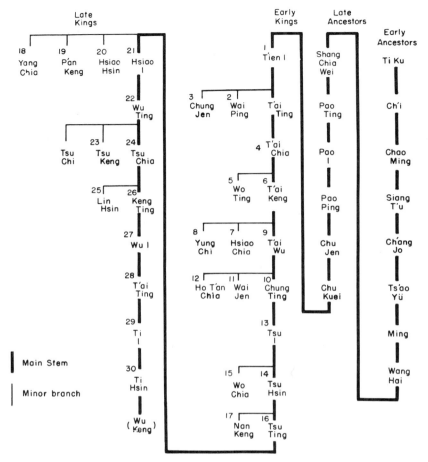

Figure 55. Genealogical table of the royal house of the Shang dynasty (according to Tung Tso-pin's 1952 reconstructions)

One of the most distinguished classicists, Wang Kuo-wei, advanced the theory that the founders of the Chou dynasty achieved a great political and social revolution in two respects.[2] One of these was the establishment of primogeniture and the abolition of fraternal succession to the throne, in order to avoid one of the obvious sources of family troubles. The institution of primogeniture, in Wang's opinion, also helped to stabilize the political system of ancient China by reducing to a certain order the confused social conditions created by clan and family troubles. The second achievement was the differentiation of social status according to that of the baby's mother's rank, depending on whether she was the first wife or a concubine. This social stratification led to a further classification of the family structure. Wang Kuo-wei's comments on these various changes, unlike his epigraphical contributions, have not received universal support. Professor Ch'en Yin-k'o, for example, one of Wang's most intimate friends, entertained a different opinion, and for good historical reasons.[3] Ch'en believed that the institution of primogeniture had probably already started in the latter part of the Yin-Shang period, and, as to the different social status of those born to the first wife and to the concubines, he was somewhat dubious about its ultimate social significance.

Professor Ch'en's view leads the reader to re-examine the genealogical table of the Yin-Shang dynasty, especially the last five kings: King Keng Ting, the twenty-sixth ruler of the dynasty, inherited his throne from his elder brother Lin Hsing (twenty-fifth ruler), but from that time onward for five generations or four successive rulers, to the last king of the dynasty, Ti Hsin, the throne was always passed from father to son, according to both Ssǔ-ma Ch'ien and other sources. To trace the actual passage, when King Keng Ting died, Wu I succeeded as the twenty-seventh ruler of the dynasty; when Wu I died, T'ai Ting succeeded as the twenty-eighth ruler; when T'ai Ting died, Ti I succeeded as the twenty-ninth ruler; and finally when Ti I died, Ti Hsin succeeded as the thirtieth ruler of the dynasty—all were father-son successions.

Naturally, the interesting question is: did the last four kings of the Yin-Shang dynasty have only one male descendant, or did a change of rule of succession take place in the time of King Keng Ting? Historical documents, however, do tell us that, as far as King Ti I (twenty-ninth ruler) is concerned, he had at least two sons. Ssǔ-ma Ch'ien definitely states that Ti Hsin was not the eldest son of Ti I, but since he was born to the first wife, he had the prior right as the crown prince. That is the reason why Wei-tze, though an elder son of the king and possessing talent and virtue, was disqualified to succeed his father. In other words, the mother's high status was evidently, in the later days of throne succession, a prerequisite. This rule obviously could not have existed in the early days. If it had, in a number of early generations brothers born of different mothers could not have succeeded one another.

Whatever opinions later historians may express about those rules of succession, scholars have to face some of the distinguishing characteristics of the Shang royal family. First, they each adopted one of the celestial stems as a posthumous title. Second, in the early part of the dynasty, probably following a native custom, they passed their royal throne to either a brother or a son, but not to a daughter. Third, whoever had been chosen to the throne was to be worshipped in the ancestral hall, including a wife or wives whose sons had later ascended the throne. As to the fortunes of the other children born to the sovereigns, history has given us no hint whether they were allowed special titles or political privileges. Ssŭ-ma Ch'ien has said that the brothers of the last king of the Shang dynasty who were born to the concubines of Ti I, although they were highly respected because of their personal virtues, did not seem to have any political title, though some of them were older than the last king.

This leads to the question of whether anything like the institution of feudalism was established in the Shang dynasty. It would be strange if the members of the royal family enjoyed no special political privilege at the time.

Professor Ting Shan was one of the most learned epigraphists who had in his early days not only received a basic training in the ancient classics but also was just of an age to have benefitted by the new ideas which flooded China in the May 4th movement. He joined the Institute of History and Philology when it was first organized, and stayed in the institute for a few years before leaving for a teaching position. He continued his epigraphical studies, however, without much interruption. After the war he stayed on the Mainland continuing his academic work and became specially interested in the social institutions of the Yin-Shang time. Two of his studies constituted very important contributions to an understanding of the social organization of the period.[4] In the first essay, Ting was able to identify each of more than two hundred of these clans with a definite name, and in the following essay, he went further by trying to trace the exact location of most of the identified clans. According to Ting, each clan had a definite territory and clans were distinguishable by definite totemic symbols. He cited the ancient Manchurian custom of offering sacrifice to Heaven by Nurharchi himself with a pine pole more than thirty feet long representing the symbolic Heaven. Professor Ting considered the pole to be the survival of the ancient totemic symbol. To what extent this is accepted as true depends on the reader's own historical background. But there are at least two points which Ting Shan's essays seem to have made clear. First, there is no question that clan organization, which in Chinese is called *shih-ts'u,* existed extensively in the Yin-Shang period and must have had a totemic attachment, and, second, those clans were politically under the control of the royal house, but they also had their private farms to cultivate. It is possible that some of the powerful clans later evolved into feudalistic states. The records clearly indicate that while it was the king's duty to keep the various clans safe and peaceful, the clans, large or small, also had the duty on the other hand to pay toll or tribute and to send draft soldiers for the defense of the dynasty. The Shang dynasty presumably monopolized the secret of bronze-casting and was able to produce the most effective weapons through this power, while the various feudal clans in northeastern China, including present Shantung, Hopei, a part of Honan and Shansi, and the northern part of Kiangsu and Anhwei, were under her tutelage. In addition to this powerful material weapon, there was another power with which the royal house of Shang seemed to exercise great influence, namely the expert manipulation of the art of scapulimancy together with the ability to keep written records.

It is difficult to say how early the art of scapulimancy started. But the fact that it was associated with the earliest written records could not have been merely accidental. One must admit that in whatever ways the professional experts manipulated scapulimancy, there was always an element of mystery associated with it. Whether this element of mystery was intentionally deceitful or not, when it became generally accepted and commanded the common belief of the masses, it became itself a power. To understand the practice of Shang politics it is important to acquire some knowledge of the psychological background of those men in charge of divination who, as the records show, actually played a very significant part in decisions of importance regarding such matters as war-making and the removal of the capital.

One of the greatest contributions by Tung Tso-pin in his early study of the oracle bones—and one of the most important contributions he made in his life's research in paleography—was his discovery of what he named "diviners." It was important in many respects but here let us take up its relation to practical politics.

The original Chinese term for diviner was *chên-jên.* Tung first discovered the existence of this important office and its group of officers when he studied the first four more or less complete tortoise shells discovered in the well-known pit, the Ta-lien-k'eng, in 1929, in the third season of Anyang digging. This discovery not only led Tung gradually to a concentrated interest in oracle bone inscriptions from the paleographic angle, but also widened his historical interest in the detailed contents of these records. By means of studying the inscriptions alone, he eventually succeeded in periodizing the records into at least five periods (see also discussion on p. 133):

1. The Wu Ting epoch, including the period from King P'an Keng (19) to Wu Ting (22).

2. The Tsu Chia (24) period, probably including the reign of King Tsu Keng (23).

3. The Lin Hsin epoch, including King Lin Hsin (25) and King Keng Ting (26).

4. The Wu I (27) period, including also T'ai Ting (28).

5. The last period, including the last two kings: Ti I (29) and Ti Hsin (30).

Tung in his 1955 publication on oracle bone records recorded that there were twenty-five *chên-jên* in the first period, eighteen in the second period, thirteen in the third period, seventeen in the fourth period, and four in the last period.[5] Tung Tso-pin noticed with particular attention that in the last two reigns, Ti I and Ti Hsin both took the unusual step of performing the divinations personally. It seemed to indicate that these two monarchs could not trust anyone else to carry out this sacred duty of obtaining readings of divine order which bore such a close relationship to the exercise of royal power. The exact duties of this *chên-jên* might here be looked into.

Here something should be said of the technical procedures of scapulimancy or plastromancy. It is now well known that in prehistoric times the inhabitants of north China, especially the black pottery people, had already acquired a superstitious belief in scapulimancy. They would pick up the scapulae of deer, cows, sheep, or other herbivorous animals and drill a series of cavities on one face of the scapula, then scorch that face to cause a crack to appear on the other side. It is of course an interesting question whether all these technical procedures were done by one trained person alone and whether the ability to read the significance of the crack was a technician's business or a sacred profession. These same questions would apply to the historical time of the Shang dynasty when scapulimancy had already developed to a more precise stage and the materials used included tortoise shells. In the traditional accounts recorded in Chou dynasty writings, tortoises were already given a special position in the animal kingdom as possessing the ability to foretell human events. We know at present that the plastron of the tortoise was used for divination in place of the scapula, perhaps because it presented a bigger flat surface and was therefore capable of more frequent usage for divination purposes. But whether interpreting the cracks was the business of a technician or a witch doctor (or, if we want to be more respectful, a sort of religious person) is still a puzzle. We are aware of the fact that there were many special monographs devoted to their arts as late as the Han dynasty. Tung Tso-pin's discovery of the *chên-jên* does not seem to help solve this problem. In the first place one cannot be sure what the exact duty of such a person was except perhaps that he was in charge of reading the crack signs. But did he pass judgment on the crack's significance, and have the final say whether it was auspicious or not? According to circumstantial evidence, the *chên-jên* was probably the man to do this and was not the man who performed the technical duties preliminary to the application of heat to the cavity. If this assumption is accepted, then the *chên-jên* would certainly be an important political counselor who would be in a position to help the king decide state events of both political and religious importance. It is noteworthy in this connection that in Wu Ting's time, one of the most prosperous periods, there were at least twenty-five *chên-jên* whose names are known, but in later period there were far fewer.

The matters that were decided by the oracle and recorded on the bones can be grouped into the following categories: (1) sacrifices, (2) war, (3) hunting, (4) royal trips, (5) fortune of the coming ten days, (6) fortune of the day and of the night, (7) weather, (8) harvest of the coming years, (9) disease, (10) life and death, (11) birth, (12) dreams, (13) construction, and (14) others. Lo Chên-yü, on the basis of his own collection, recognized that among the readable records which he rendered into modern Chinese the first category, consultation about sacrifices, was the most numerous.[6] There are 538 items on his list. On the other hand, the number concerned with military expeditions was quite limited. Those comparative figures are interesting but by no means conclusive. They do signify that as far as consultations on the oracle bones are concerned, sacrificial performances to ancestors counted first and foremost, at least in Wu Ting's time. Whether his successor actually obeyed this rule or not may be open to question.

Lo's groups are by no means complete, but they may be taken as representative of the major events of great importance about which the king had to consult the oracle bones for final decision. Tung Tso-pin believed that in addition to the *chên-jên,* there was an official who recorded all the events and was probably responsible for the writing, and he called these officials the historians of the court. What is not clear, however, is the procedure by which the final decision was made. We do not know definitely whether it was the *chên-jên* who, by reading the oracle bone signs, told the king the results of the cracks, or whether the king could read the symbols himself. But according to the practice of scapulimancy, the crack signs were presumably definite symbols that could foretell whatever might happen in the particular event about which the divination was made. The real problem is: was the *chên-jên* as a professional man and trained expert in reading the crack signs in the position to have the last word about their ultimate meaning in consultation with the king? Whether the king agreed with him or not was of course another matter. It was perhaps by no means accidental that the last two kings of the Yin-Shang dynasty, notorious for their misrule, consulted the oracle bones personally most of the time. Judging by what happened in their time, one in inclined to believe that each king consulted the oracle bones personally for one reason—so that he might be able to make his own decisions.

Another important question concerning the kinship and social organization of the royal house of the Yin-Shang dynasty is the ultimate origin of this house. There is of course quite a coherent account according to traditional documents about the genealogy and descendency of this dynasty. The oracle bone records have confirmed the major points of this historical account as has already been noted. There is, however, one basic point which only a few scholars seem to have paid much attention to. This concerns the sudden appearance of a calendar system in the Yin-Shang period and the related posthumous names of the kings of the royal family and their immediate ancestors. In the oracle bone records, the sexagenarian system was already used and seems to have been inherited from an earlier tradition (see earlier discussion in Chap. 7). Epigraphists claim that they have found regular tables for the sexagenarian system of sixty names of double characters, each name combining one character from the celestial stems and another from the earthly branches. This system brings to mind the history of the early Babylonian sexagenarian system.

Turning to the ancestral roll of the royal house of the Shang dynasty, the king who first made use of the stem and branch terms was Wang Hai, whose name appeared frequently in the oracle bone records. In 1913, Lo Chên-yü first noticed this name, to which no scholar of ancient Chinese history had previously paid much attention.[7] Lo brought this discovery to the attention of Wang Kuo-wei, whose subsequent investigation of Wang Hai contributed substantially not only to the study of oracle bones but especially to clarifying the lineage of the predynastic ancestral figures. Wang Kuo-wei coordinated much scattered information which earlier scholars had been unable to understand, as will be discussed in more detail in the following chapter.[8]

While Wang Kuo-wei's contributions were much appreciated by early scholars, there is one aspect of the queries raised by these new data which very few people carried further. From a purely paleographic viewpoint, one finds that these twenty-two stem and branch terms are found at the very end of Hsü Shen's *Shuo-wen* dictionary; and what surprises a great number of paleographers most is that, ever since Chu Chün-shen's time (nineteenth century), paleographers have found Hsü Shen's original interpretation of these twenty-two characters inconsistent with his own basic idea. As for the reason why these twenty-two characters were grouped into two categories, there seems no philological basis. Recently, Professor Chang Ping-ch'üan, who has made a systematic inquiry in this investigation, concludes with the remark that this body of characters did not originally constitute a consistent system.[9] None of them seems to keep the original primitive meaning and practically every character is used in a borrowed sense. Before archaeological excavation started at Hsiao-t'un, some Japanese scholars had labored a great deal on the Yin-Shang sexagenarian dating system. Professor Shinjô Shinzô, whose contribution is probably well known to a number of Western scholars, is one of those who contributed most. He was one of the earliest scholars who tried to compare the Hindu, the Babylonian, and the Chinese dating systems. In China, Kuo Mo-jo was the first to propose a definite link of these three systems scattered in China, India, and Babylonia.[10]

It may take a long time to go a step further. But from the Chinese angle, there seems to be one point that can be clarified. It concerns Wang Hai, the first among the predynastic ancestors of the Shang to make use of the stem branch (*kan-chih*) term as a personal name. Since the publication by Prof. Wang Kuo-wei, Wang Hai has been identified in scattered materals. He presumably lived in King

Hsieh's time (1996–1980 B.C.) in the Hsia dynasty, about two centuries before the Babylonian King Hammurabi. According to the *Bamboo Annals*, he was supposed to have been the man who domesticated bulls, and this contribution to their welfare was well remembered among the ordinary people. However, the fact that he was given the word Hai, the last of the branch characters, as his personal name never seems to have aroused any curiosity among historians. But if we take the sexagenarian cycle as a whole, this query is obviously important since, according to historical accounts, after his time his descendants down to the founding of the Shang dynasty all assumed stem characters as their names. Was he the man who originated the sexagenarian system of dating? Or did he in a moment of inspiration adopt a Western system of names? [11]

In addition to the initiation of the new system of nomenclature by Wang Hai, we also read in the oracle bone records that enormously heavy sacrifices were offered to the founder of the new system. Very frequently thirty or forty oxen were killed and sometimes as many as three hundred were offered on one sacrificial occasion to this Wang Hai. While the story that he was the man who domesticated wild bulls remains to be authenticated, the heavy tribute paid by his descendants in these offerings could not have taken place without a reason. From the time of Wang Hai onward to the last king of the dynasty, this unique system of naming each generation in power by a celestial stem name was used consistently. This is certainly historically significant. But what makes it extraordinary is that this system was never followed afterwards. A number of theories have been created to interpret this particular feature of the Yin-Shang dynasty, but since we know the historical facts of the Yin-Shang dynasty so little and its social organization even less, none of the theories seems to be sufficiently comprehensive.

Social anthropologists, basing their study on relationship terms, claim to have discovered that while there are indeed definite terms for *father, mother, elder brother, grandfather,* and *grandmother* in the oracle bone inscriptions, there are no such terms as *uncle, aunt, nephew, niece,* or *younger brother.* From these discoveries they have deduced a great number of interesting theories. One of these is that while the royal family does have a family name, which according to Ssŭ-ma Ch'ien is Tzu, the royal Tzu family could pass the throne either to the younger brothers or to the second generation, usually to the ruler's own son. Modern ethnologists who have given some consideration to the above facts would like to interpret the royal family tree in a new light. They argue that since in the oracle bone vocabulary the younger generation would call all members of the older male generation *father,* the heir to the throne, if he was of the younger generation, would not necessarily be the son of the ruler. He might be any of the sons of the ruler's sisters or brothers, since all of them called him *father* whether he actually was or not. The author, however, does agree with some of the theoreticians that totemism played an important role in regulating social functions, and there may have been complicated rules governing exogamy and endogamy. But our paleographic research has not yet reached the stage to read oracle bone characters maturely. There are so many characters whose meanings are obscure. We know in fact very little about family, clan, or totemism of this period. There is no question that very soon there might be fruitful research along this line.

14 Worship of Ancestors

and Other Spirits

ONE CHINESE CUSTOM that has always impressed foreigners is ancestor worship, a custom which originated thousands of years before Confucius yet gained special distinction through his teaching. In the Anyang excavations, the most astonishing discoveries aside from the oracle bones were found mainly from the royal tombs.

In the tomb area the field party discovered that in the Yin-Shang dynasty an enormous amount of human labor was spent on building gigantic tombs to bury the royal dead; royal fortunes were also buried; and, what is most amazing, a great number of human beings were sacrificed in each of these tombs. These elaborate burials were no doubt the results of a long historical evolution. Field archaeologists have found that as early as the early neolithic age a dead body was buried accompanied by useful articles which indicated both the dead man's rank and his fortune.

As has been mentioned in the preceding chapter, when the oracle bones first became known to the learned world and long before field archaeology had started, Lo Chên-yü, one of the pioneers in the study of these ancient scripts, first called to the attention of Wang Kuo-wei that in these new, strange records, he had discovered a strange name, Wang Hai, that is, King Hai. This name, previously unknown to Chinese historians, seemed to appear in the oracle bone records very often and Wang Kuo-wei made a concentrated study of this problem.[1] Wang succeeded in identifying Wang Hai's name in a number of books which ordinary historians had usually considered occult, such as the *Shan Hai Ching*, the *Bamboo Annals* and Ch'ü Yuan's *T'ien Wen*. In regular histories like the *Shih Chi* and *Han Shu*, his name was usually miswritten. The *Shih Chi* gives his name as Cheng and the *Han Shu* gives still another name. Wang Kuo-wei succeeded in clarifying all these points and identifying these names as Wang Hai. Since Professor Wang's introductory work, Wang Hai has been recognized as the father of Shang Chia Wei, the earliest of the later ancestors of the house of Shang, whose name was also made clear from Wang Kuo-wei's research. From Shang Chia Wei to the founder of the royal Shang dynasty, Ch'êng Tang or T'ien I, there are five more names on the ancestral roll: Pao Ting, Pao I, Pao Ping, Chu Jen, and Chu Kuei. When the later kings performed their rituals and offered sacrifice to the ancestor on more important occasions, Shang Chia Wei was usually named as the first person on the roll, a custom which continued to the last king of the dynasty.

Tung Tso-pin devoted a large portion of his *Yin-li-p'u* to the records concerning the various rituals followed in performing sacrificial offerings to the ancestors. He divided them into at least five main types, as already discussed in Chapter 7. Before we go into these five types, there are some general characteristics shared in common by all the rituals.

Since each ancestor had a posthumous title which included a celestial stem, it was the custom of the Yin-Shang royal house to offer a special sacrifice to the ancestor with the posthumous title Chia on the Chia day, I on the I day, and so forth. As there are six Chia days in a sexagenarian cycle, offerings to six ancestors with the Chia posthumous titles can be made in the same cycle. Tung Tso-pin verified that this was true in Ti I's and Ti Hsin's period at least. Lo Chên-yü and Wang Kuo-wei had both noticed half a century ago that sacrificial offerings to ancestors were made on the day when the celestial stem corresponded with the king's name. Some scholars have found exceptions, but the exceptions are so few that they cannot disprove the rule.

Another general characteristic is that oracles had to be consulted before the ritual took place, sometimes even two or three days before the event. If the ritual included the sacrifice of livestock, sometimes the oracles were consulted regarding the requisite number. In the reign of the last two kings, the five main types of rituals known as Yung, I, Chi, Kuan, and Hsieh sacrifices were performed on regular dates and in a definite sequence. The Yung sacrifice was accompanied by the beating of drums, while in the I sacrifice, feather dancing was necessary. It is not definitely known what kind of feather was used, but some idea of the Yin-Shang drum was obtained from the ruins of Yin. In the Chi sacrifice, according to the interpretation of our paleographer, meats were regularly offered, and in the Kuan sacrifice, grains constituted the main offering while the Hsieh sacrifice combined various elements.

Tung Tso-pin, in his *Yin-li-p'u*, was able to compile the recorded rituals in the reigns of Kings Tsu Chia, Ti I, and Ti Hsin on a chronological basis and to tabulate these data in chronological order. He showed that in the reigns of the last two kings, for instance, it took about 360 days to complete the offerings to the individual ancestors. The rules which they had to obey seem to have been the following.

The Yung ritual and the I ritual as well as the other three could not be performed on the same day even for the same ancestor. There was, however, a definite difference among the five types in their sequence. The cycles of the first two rituals, Yung and I, had to be completed separately in two different seasons, even if the sacrifices were offered to different individual ancestors; in other words, it took 110 days to complete the Yung rituals for the ancestor and another 110 days to complete the cycle of the I ritual; while the other three rituals, Chi, Kuan, and Hsieh, which could be overlapped, might together take only 130 days. These five ritual systems would, then, altogether consume 350 days or nearly a calendar year. In addition, there was an introductory 10-day period during which the complete ancestral roll of individual ancestors to be worshipped was reviewed in the ancestral hall.

In the oracle bone inscriptions, the character *ssŭ* was used sometimes for *year* rather than *nien*, which according to Tung Tso-pin did not occur until the time of Ti I and Ti Hsin. It was during the reign of these two kings that the rituals of ancestor worship individually and collectively took nearly a calendar year to complete a cycle. If we trace back all the individual ritual systems step by step to the earlier period, we find a great deal of change. The greatest change according to Tung Tso-pin occurred in the reign of Tsu Chia. Before Tsu Chia's era, the ritualistic performance was much more irregular and a great many other spirits besides ancestors were also given sacrificial offerings. But before we go into these details, the reader should have some idea about the five main types of rituals.

Here we must pay due acknowledgment to the great contribution of Tung Tso-pin, who has done more in interpreting these than any other scholar. When Lo Chên-yü first deciphered the oracle bone inscriptions, he merely recognized that certain terms indicated ritualistic offerings without having the least idea what these rituals were. Tung was not only one of the first scholars who definitely differentiated the nature and contents of the various ritual performances; he took the further step of putting these originally confused records into the orderly sequence in which they took place. In the case of the three kings mentioned above, namely Tsu Chia, Ti I, and Ti Hsin, the records are comparatively well preserved. Tung was able to gather the related records together and to chronicle the various events which took place during their reigns.

Let us take one example for illustration. This occurred in the first year of Ti I's era. The Yung sacrifice, starting in the fourth month, was first offered to the earliest ancestor Shang Chia (namely, Shang Chia Wei, the son of Wang Hai), on the day Chia Hsü; it was then followed by a similar sacrifice to T'ai Chia on the day Chia Wu, which was, in turn, followed by a sacrifice to Hsiao Chia on the day Chia Chen. These latter two both occurred in the fifth month. Then, in the sixth month, Yung was offered to Ch'ien Chia (Ho T'an Chia) on the day Chia Tzǔ, Chiang Chia (Wo Chia) on the day Chia Hsü, Hu Chia (Yang Chia) on the day Chia Sheng. Then in the seventh month, there was one more Yung sacrifice offered to Tsu Chia. So, in this year, it took almost four months to complete the subcycle of the Yung sacrifice offered to the various ancestors whose posthumous titles bore the Chia name. To recapitulate, in Ti I's time, there were seven ancestors with Chia as posthumous titles who were offered the Yung sacrifice on the Chia days. The Yung sacrifice was followed in time by the I sacrifice. These same ancestors were given the I sacrifice in the eighth, ninth, tenth, and

eleventh months. Then in the twelfth month, the other three sacrifices—Chi, Kuan, and Hsieh—were given in the same period, although not on the same day. These lasted from the twelfth month
to the third month of the second year of the king's reign.

The instances cited above concern only the ancestors with the
posthumous name Chia. Other ancestors with different *kan-chih*
posthumous names would receive their respective sacrificial offerings on the intervening days whose celestial stem corresponded
with their posthumous titles. In fact there was almost always some
kind of sacrificial ritual that had to be performed every day of the
year. It brings to mind the old Chinese custom which still continued
in the early days of the Republic that every day a joss-stick had to
be burned before the ancestral tablet. In the case of Shang worship,
however, a sacrifice was offered to the individual ancestor, while in
the custom surviving among the people in modern times the burning of the joss-stick was offered to the ancestors collectively. Tung
Tso-pin has also definitely established a *ssŭ* as a year in the time of
Ti I for the simple reason that a complete cycle of the five fundamental sacrificial offerings at that time actually took a year to complete as described above.

The ritual performance of the various sacrificial offerings included some important details that must be mentioned. One of
these is music. The Yung sacrifice as the initial ceremony of the
annual ancestral worship was, according to the interpretation of
Tung Tso-pin, dominated by drum music regarding which, very
unfortunately we have, of course, no data to supplement our con-
ception of this important sacrificial event. But in the excavation of
HPKM 1217, the remains of a complete drum with the original
frame on which it was hung was discovered in one of the tomb
passages, accompanied by musical stones. It is possible that the
drum used in the Yung sacrifice may have resembled the one excavated at HPKM 1217 (Figs. 56–57). Tung Tso-pin also observed
that in all these five rituals, whatever the difference in the offering
of the actual sacrifice might be, wine was always used on every
occasion. In the case of the Yung sacrifice, we know that at least
two elements were definitely present, namely, music and wine. In
addition to the musical stones, other musical instruments such as
the ocarina, pan-pipes, or even some kind of stringed instrument
may have been used. But it is impossible to say whether the entire
ceremony of the Yung sacrifice was accompanied by music. It is,

Figure 56. Reconstruction of drum found in HPKM 1217: lateral view

however, important to note that this sacrifice initiated the annual cycle of rituals of worship to the whole series of individual ancestors.

Tung concluded that feather dancing was the essential feature of the I sacrifice, accompanied also by wine offering. Judging by what survived in the Chou dynasty, it may be inferred that the number of dancers varied according to the rank of the spirits—the higher the rank, the greater the number. As to what kind of feathers might have been used, nothing is known. But archaeologists have found the bones of the peacock at Anyang. Might it be possible that peacock feathers were used?

The third and fourth rituals, the Chi and Kuan sacrifices, definitely involved offerings of food. In the Chi ritual meat was offered. Although what meat is not certain, it may have included mutton, beef, pork, or even dog meat. The Kuan sacrifice was a sort of thanksgiving; the offering consisted of grains—millets or perhaps even wheat and rice. In the study of Shang bronze implements and ceramics, it has been noticed that most of the bronze vessels and some of the ceramics were made for sacrificial offerings. Meat

Figure 57. Reconstruction of drum found in HPKM 1217: top view

and grains would have been offered in such receptacles as the *ting* and *chia*-tripods, the *kuei*-vessels, etc. As for wine containers, these are numerous, such as the *ku, chüeh, chih,* and so forth. All these bronzes and some of the potteries may have been used in the Chi and Kuan sacrificial rituals.

The exact nature of the last of the five sacrificial rituals, the Hsieh sacrifice, is still difficult to determine. Possibly it was something like the celebration of the traditional New Year's Day before the Republic, that is, it combined the essential elements of the other four sacrificial rituals, namely, the offering of meat and grains accompanied by music and dance on a grand scale to all the ancestors on the ancestral roll.

As pointed out above, the schedule of sacrificial offerings to individual ancestors was first standardized in King Tsu Chia's time. The detailed procedure and the other details were strictly followed by Ti I and Ti Hsin. While this schedule included the essential rituals developed in the latter period of the Yin-Shang dynasty, there were other aspects to the spiritual lives of the people as well as of the royal house. For instance, the records include sacrifices to a number of other spirits such as those of the five directions—east, west, south, north, and central—and of some rivers and probably also some mountains, as well as a number of other spirits. What has attracted the particular attention of students of comparative religion in the use of the term *ti,* which has been taken by some to have meant a supreme spirit, but the interpretation of this term still remains debatable.

There were also certain refinements of the sacrificial ceremonies such as *liao,* to put the offerings in fire, *chen,* to put the offerings in water, and *mai,* to bury the offerings alive.

The oracle bone records, according to Kunio Shima, included one hundred items of sacrificial offerings to Wang Hai.[2] The rulers of the dynasty would pray to his spirit with sometimes as many as three hundred oxen. In this particular case, most sacrifices were done by the *liao* process. Only rarely were the Yung sacrifice and the I sacrifice offered to the founder of this house. It is remarkable to note that although Wang Hai was the father of Shang Chia Wei, he was not included in the list of the regular rituals, especially in the time of Ti I and Ti Hsin. The list was almost always headed by Shang Chia Wei.

Wine offering also deserves some mention. Wine offering was formerly interpreted as a special service to the ancestors, but now it is generally agreed that wine accompanied almost all the sacrifices, including the special ones.

Besides *liao, chen,* and *mai* sacrificial usages, there were a number of others that are mentioned in oracle bone records but not understood by paleographers. The case of human sacrifice, mentioned several times before, should not be omitted here. If we cannot give any details, it is because it is difficult to say whether such sacrifices were made regularly or only occasionally, for instance, in war time. But the number of human sacrifices uncovered in the royal tombs seems to indicate that it was a regular practice. However, whether the victims were captives or slaves, or just subordinates, or all three categories is impossible to say. The author is strongly inclined to believe that it was a custom introduced through contact with the early Sumerians from whom early China probably also learned the wheeled carriage, some aspects of the technology of casting bronze, and something of astrological sciences.

15 Notes on the Physical Anthropology

of the Yin-Shang Population

THE SKELETAL MATERIALS collected from fifteen seasons of Anyang excavations amount to several thousands, most of which are definitely from the Yin-Shang period. The Institute of History and Philology created a special section and invited a biometrician, Dr. Woo Ting-liang, trained in the biometric laboratory of Dr. Karl Pearson in London, to take charge of the scientific investigation of this valuable collection. But the Japanese invasion and the war not only interrupted the program, but actually so disheartened Dr. Woo that he gave up the job when the war terminated. At the same time, the materials were greatly depleted. In the institute's migration from Nanking to Yünnan, to Szechwan, and to Taiwan, it was only because of the determined efforts of a few individuals in charge of transportation during these long treks that certain portions of this collection were finally brought to Taiwan.

Professor Young Hsi-mei, a trained biologist who had helped Woo Ting-liang in the biometric work during wartime, and was one of the few who came to Taiwan, was persuaded to take up the study of this collection. Here the author wishes to summarize some of his main reports.[1]

The collection brought here consists mainly of skulls of which there are 398 from Hou-chia-chuang; practically all of these came from what are called sacrificial pits—pits where only skulls were buried and no skeletons. The Institute of History and Philology has a complete record of the history of these pits and of their excavation. Most of these sacrificial pits contain ten skulls each (Fig. 58); a few contain only seven or eight or even as few as six. There are, however, exceptions which contain more than ten, and in one pit more than thirty-three skulls were buried (Fig. 59). In addition to these skull pits, the archaeologists found headless skeletons also buried in groups of ten. Sometimes the head and skeleton were found together, but had already been cut apart.

Figure 58. Sacrificial pit with ten skulls found in Hou-chia-chuang

Figure 59. Sacrificial pit with the largest number of skulls found in Hou-chia-chuang

Professor Young has made cranial measurements of each of the 369 skulls in our collection. He compared the standard deviations of the various measurements, especially the cranial index, head length, and head breadth, with those of other peoples, namely, the Ainus, Bavarians, Parisians, Naqadas, and English. He found that the standard deviations of the various values of the Hou-chia-chuang skulls are greater than any of the five groups of people with whose skulls he compared. In other words, whether compared with Englishmen, or Frenchmen in Paris, or Germans in Bavaria or the Ainus in Japan or the Naqadas, the Anyang collection evidences a more heterogeneous group. This is true even if we limit the comparison to the 319 skulls of the male sex.

Young's study includes a very interesting morphological analysis. He has been able to divide the Hou-chia-chuang skulls into five subgroups. Subgroup 1 (Fig. 60) is the Classic Mongoloid type. This subgroup usually is mesocephalic with broad cheek bones, depressed nasal bones, sloping frontal head; the faces look almost flat in profile. The skull top is almost flat. The bizygomatic width is

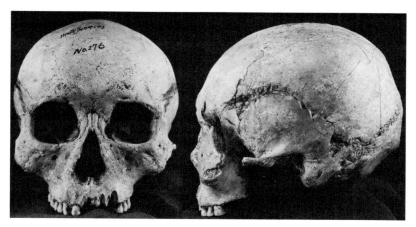

Figure 60. Classic Mongoloid type of human skull found in Hou-chia-chuang

probably wider than any other group. These Classic Mongoloids are found among typical representatives among Buriats and Chuckchis.

Subgroup 2 among these Hou-chia-chuang skulls (Fig. 61) is named by Young the Oceanic Negroid type. This group has a longer head with a cephalic index of 75. The nasal root is depressed, but at the lower end it rises up. The occipital bone looks like a gable roof. In this respect it closely resembles the Papuans or Melanesians.

Subgroup 3 (Fig. 62), which Young called Caucasoid, is a very small group. Young gives only two examples. A typical specimen of this group has a narrow head and a narrow face with a cephalic index of 73.58. The cheek bone is very small but with well-developed nasal bones. The skull has been compared with the skull of an Englishman born in America. They are so similar that it is difficult to differentiate them.

Subgroup 4 (Fig. 63) is known as the Eskimoid type. Like Subgroup 1, it possesses a broadly developed cheek bone and wide face. Unlike Subgroup 1, the Eskimoid type possesses a higher head. Its cephalic index is 76.35. The top of the skull from front to back has a keel-like ridge. The nasal bone is pinched angular and the lower jaw has an everted mandibular angle.

There is another group about whose morphological character Professor Young feels uncertain. The only thing that impresses him is that in every measurement these skulls are comparatively smaller

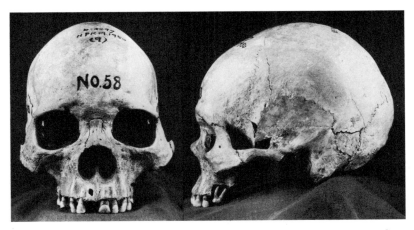

Figure 61. Oceanic Negroid type of human skull found in Hou-chia-chuang

than those of any other groups that he has been able to classify (Fig. 64).

In the above divisions, Young has been able to assign 30 to Subgroup 1, 34 to Subgroup 2, only 2 to Subgroup 3, 50 to Subgroup 4 and 38 to Subgroup 5.

Here we might make some interesting comparisons among the measurements of these five groups. The author would like to take

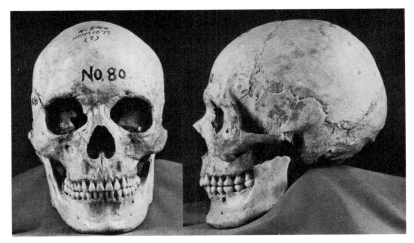

Figure 62. Caucasoid type of human skull found in Hou-chia-chuang

259

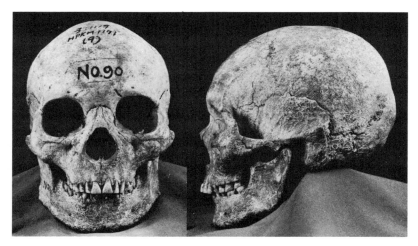

Figure 63. Eskimoid type of human skull found in Hou-chia-chuang

the bizygomatic breadth first, because this is the one characteristic that differentiates the Mongoloid people from other races. Let us see some of the comparisons:

Group 1 141.18mm.
Group 2 134.52mm.
Group 3 131.50mm.
Group 4 135.06mm.
Group 5 131.32mm.

So, it is quite clear that in both anthropometrical measurements and morphological characteristics, the Anyang crania, or should I say the Hou-chia-chuang crania, although limited in number, indicate a mixed character that is no doubt the result of a mixed race. There are, however, one or two points that we should clarify first. The primary question is, since this is a collection from the sacrificial pits, do any of the skulls or any of the subgroups represent the Yin-Shang people as a whole? This is probably one of the most difficult problems to answer because all the archaeologists are aware of the fact, attested both by the oracle bone records and by the archaeological diggings, that the victims whose heads were cut off and presented as sacrificial offerings either in the royal tombs or in other places were probably enemies who had either invaded the territory or offended the royal property. Tung Tso-pin devoted two

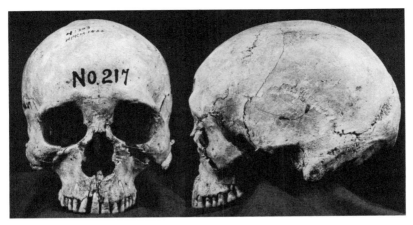

Figure 64. Representative of group of small skulls, unidentified

sections of his *Yin-li-p'u* to the war records of the Yin-Shang period. During the reign of Wu Ting, who conducted a series of military expeditions against the invasion of enemies in the Ordos region, chiefly from northern Shansi and Shensi, the names of the enemies were definitely given as Kung Fang, T'u Fang, and Hsia Chih (Fig. 65). Wu Ting spent three years in this northwestern war (from the twenty-ninth to the thirty-second year of his reign) near the end of the thirteenth century B.C. In those three years, he first conquered Hsia Chih, which took him ten months, and then T'u Fang, which took him a much longer time, more than two years. Kung Fang was the furthest to the northwest. The oracle bones record that in the seventh and eighth months of the thirtieth year of Wu Ting, he conscripted successively almost ten times in two months, each time as many as three thousand men. The maximum may reach five thousand. Tung Tso-pin later compared all the records relating to this war [2] and came to the conclusion that Kung Fang was another name for Kuei Fang, which was mentioned both in the *Book of Changes* and the *Book of Odes;* the *Bamboo Annals,* of course, also mentioned this important event. My colleague Tung was of the opinion that the exact location of Kung Fang was near the northwestern corner of the Ordos region, near where the earliest paleolithic finds were found. This location may also indicate that it was on the usual route of migration for central Asiatic nomads from the earliest times. So, it would not be surprising to find skulls of European type mixed with those of Buriats and

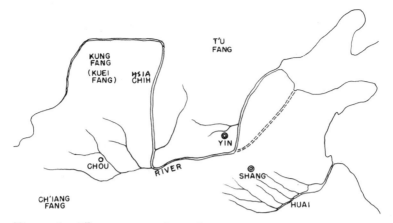

Figure 65. Three enemies from the Ordos region and eastern Mongolia

Eskimos in these hordes. There were, of course, battles on other fronts, such as King Ti Hsin's expedition to Tung I, which have also been abundantly recorded in the oracle bones. All these seem to serve as an adequate basis for an interpretation of the heterogeneous character of the various crania found in the sacrificial pits. They do not help us, however, to solve the question: What was the physical anthropology of the Yin-Shang people who ruled this territory for several hundred years? If we compare the various specimens in the subgroups that Mr. Young has studied, it seems definite that even among the Mongoloids there are three subgroups, namely, Subgroup 1 and Subgroups 4 and 5.

Years ago, Professor Davidson Black of the Peking Union Medical College, after a preliminary study of the prehistoric population whose remains were collected by Andersson and his associates, concluded that the neolithic people of north China were in no way essentially different from modern Chinese.[3] Black was a pioneer in this field and the number of specimens at his disposal were relatively few. His conclusion, though based on solid facts, was nevertheless only preliminary.

Now almost half a century after Black's time, although we have gathered a great deal of new data, none of them have been thoroughly studied by a competent authority like Davidson Black. The war of course was the main reason for this tragic fact, and at present, when the problem of the Yin-Shang population is studied, we are almost in a worse situation than Davidson Black. We can depend upon neither the skulls from the sacrificial pits nor the fragmentary skeletons for a reasonable deduction.

We are confronted with data that seem to be contradictory to what Davidson Black found, unless we dismiss these various subgroups such as the Classic Mongoloid, the Eskimoid, and the Oceanic Negroid as having nothing to do with the composition of the north China population.

As a matter of historic truth, we have, of course, a very good reason to consider these crania as invaders.

In 1932, *Biometrica* published a preliminary classification of Asiatic races based on cranial measurements, in which twenty-six series of anthropometric material were used for comparison.[4] No less than eighteen of these series are studies of skulls of the Oriental or Mongoloid people. The authors of this paper, T. L. Woo and Morant, divided these Orientals into three subgroups, namely, the Northern Mongolians; the Chinese and Japanese; and other Orientals including such people as Tibetans, Javanese, Dayaks, Tagals, and so on. This tripartite division was mainly based on what they called the "Coefficient of Racial Likness." According to Woo and Morant, the average value of bizygomatic breadth for the six series of Northern Mongols range from 139.8mm. to 144.0mm.; for the five series of Chinese and Japanese, the range is from 132–134.7mm.; and for the seven series of the other Orientals the range is from 131.0mm. to 134.7 mm. The average of the same measurements for the five Indian series, studied in the same paper, fall down to the maximum-minimum range of 127.8 to 124.3mm., respectively. The sharp contrast of the same measurement as shown above appears not only between the Orientals and the non-Orientals, but also among the three subgroups of Orientals which are even more striking. The excessively large value of the average facial width constituted without doubt a truly characteristic physical feature of the Mongoloid people. But, to quote Woo and Morant, "They are mainly located at present in outer Mongolia and southern Siberia with the center of distribution in the neighbourhood of Lake Baikal, Mount Altai and the city of Urga or north of the Gobi desert."

Morant's and Woo's paper clarified the status of Subgroup 1, which Young Hsi-mei called the Classical Mongoloid. The Eskimoid group, which has always been much more mixed than Subgroup 1, may be more related to the aborigines of northwestern Siberia.

Physical anthropologists have occasionally found traces of kinky hair in an anthropometric survey of the Chinese population, indicating the survival of some Papuans or Melanesians; but these are relatively very rare indeed. As for the fifth group and the so-called Caucasoid, it is still difficult to say how many of their genes could be definitely shown in the modern Chinese.

But on the whole, one is justified in saying the following. From the very beginning, the north China plain was a meeting place of many different ethnic stocks and it is partly from the mixture of these groups that the early Chinese population was formed, although we must not forget that the dominant group among these stocks was indubitably the Mongoloid group. The investigations and analyses by Professor Young are helpful to the extent that they definitely explain a certain percentage of the historical facts recorded both in archaeology and in the oracle bone records.

Notes

The following abbreviations are used in the Notes and the Bibliography:

PREA   *Anyang fa-chüeh pao-kao* (Preliminary Reports of Excavations at Anyang). Academia Sinica, Institute of History and Philology. Nos. 1, 2, Peking, 1929; no. 3, Peking, 1931; no. 4, Shanghai, 1933.

BIHP   *Kuo-li chung-yan yen-chiu-yüan li-shih yü-yen yen-chiu-so chi-k'an* (Bulletin of the Institute of History and Philology of Academia Sinica). 1928—

References to Academia Sinica publications in the Notes appear in English translation only. Chinese characters for these titles will be found in the Bibliography.

CHAPTER 1. *The Oracle Bone Inscriptions*

1. For a discussion of Sui and T'ang tombs excavated at Hsiao-t'un, see Chap. 4, note 8.

2. *Ch'ing-tai hsüeh-shu kai-lun* (General Discourse on the Learning of the Ch'ing Dynasty). This treatise is now included in *Yin-ping-shih*

ch'üan-chi, the complete works of Liang Ch'i-ch'ao; vol. 10 (1936) includes all works on special subjects, such as the discourse cited above.

3. See the Foreword to *Chin-shih-shu lu-mu* (Academia Sinica, Institute of History and Philology, series B, no. 2, 1930). This monograph, a catalogue of all books on bronzes and stones, mainly those with inscriptions, including a number of catalogues of books of this nature, was compiled by Yung Yüan under the guidance of her brother, Yung Keng, who wrote the Foreword for the work.

4. Berthold Laufer, *Jade: A Study in Chinese Archaeology and Religion* (Chicago: Field Museum of Natural History, 1912), p. 13. In this book the works of Wu Ta-ch'eng are constantly referred to and frequently quoted by this eminent American Sinologue.

5. The choice is between 1898 (according to Hsi Weng), and 1899 (according to Lo Chên-yü and Wang Kuo-wei), or even 1900.

6. Tung Tso-pin, *Chia-ku nien-piao* (Oracle Bone Chronicles), first published as an article in the *Bulletin of the Institute of History and Philology*, 2, no. 2 (1930): 241–60; revised, with assistance from Hu Hou-hsüan, and republished as a monograph in 1937. Hereafter cited as Chronicles (1937 edition referred to unless otherwise stated). A supplementary volume, continuing the narrative of Tung's work, edited by Huang Jan-wei, was published in 1967.

7. Liu Ngo (Liu T'ieh-yün), *T'ieh-yün ts'ang-kuei* (1903).

8. Lo Chên-yü, *Wu-shih-jih meng-hen-lu* (Diary of Fifty Days' Travel), published in *Hs'üeh-t'ang ts'ung-kê* (Collected Works) (1915).

9. *History of the Ch'ing Dynasty,* vol. 7, p. 5,967.

10. Liu T'ieh-yün's diary accounts concerning purchases and other dealings with the inscribed oracle bones were published in *K'ao-ku she-k'an,* no. 5, Shanghai, 1936.

11. Ch'en Meng-chia, *Yin-hsü pu-tz'ŭ tsung-shu* (Summary of Oracle Bone Inscriptions) (Peking: Science Press, 1956). From another entry for the same year in Liu T'ieh-yün's diary, Ch'en Meng-chia drew several other conclusions. The entry (dated the twenty-eighth day of the tenth month) reads: "This morning . . . the son of Wang I-yung came. . . . He told me that his father bought oracle bones twice; for the first lot, he paid 200 taels; for the second lot, 100 taels. The largest piece is not larger than two inches [Chinese] in dimension. . . ."

Ch'en Meng-chia drew the following conclusions from this entry: "Liu T'ieh-yün did not have the opportunity to see Wang's original collection of tortoise shells, because Wang obviously kept it secret as most collectors usually do. . . . Liu believed that in the year *Keng Tzu* [1900], Wang I-yung purchased two lots, without mentioning any complete shell in his collection. As Wang kept his treasured collection a secret, there were all sorts of rumors about these hidden treasures."

It is clear that of Ch'en Meng-chia's four conclusions only the one stated in the text above, which is based on the direct statement of Liu's diary, can be considered correct, if the diary itself is authentic. The other inferences sound fanciful, probably imaginary conclusions from Ch'en Meng-chia's productive mind. To say that Wang I-yung kept the discovery a secret is a charge without any substantial foundation. Liu

T'ieh-yün in his own Preface to the lithographic reproduction of ink-squeezes, *T'ieh-yün tsang-kuei*, published in 1903, had the following to say: "In the year *Keng Tzu* [1900], Dealer Fan brought to the capital over one hundred pieces [of the inscribed oracle bones], which caught the eye of Wang Wen Min Kung [post-mortem honorific title of Wang I-yung] who was excited with joy and paid the dealer a heavy price. . . ." In this statement, written by Liu himself, one certainly cannot find any evidence that Wang I-yung kept his purchase a secret.

12. Ch'en Meng-chia, *Pu-tz'ŭ tsung-shu*, p. 649.

13. Liu T'ieh yün, *T'ieh-yün ts'ang-kuei*.

14. The manuscripts of *Ch'i-wen chü-li* (Examples of Oracle Bone Inscriptions) by Sun I-jang, according to Lo Chên-yü's prefatory note of his essay on *Yin-shang chên-pu wen-tzŭ k'ao* (On the Oracle Bone Inscriptions of the Yin-Shang Period) (1910), seem to have been mailed to Lo by Sun I-jang himself. See further discussion on pp. 25–26.

CHAPTER 2. *Exploratory Period*

1. See the more detailed discussion at the end of this chapter.

2. Tung Tso-pin, *Chia-ku-hsüeh wu-shih-nien* (Taipei: Continental Magazine Company, 1955); English translation, *Fifty Years of Studies in Oracle Inscriptions*, trans. Paul Yang et al., ed. Kimpei Goto (Tokyo: Centre for East Asian Cultural Studies, 1964).

3. Menzies' lecture notes have never been published. A friend in Canada sent the author a copy, which is not definitely paged. The title of Section 3 is "The Buyers of *chia ku wen*." Menzies' notes are in Chinese.

4. Concerning early Japanese collections of oracle bones, see Tung's Chronicles, p. 20.

5. When the author visited Dr. Laufer in Chicago in 1928, he kindly showed the collection of oracle bones he had acquired for the Field Museum. In 1937 the author was invited to give a lecture in Edinburgh, where the museum authorities kindly exhibited for his benefit the museum's oracle bone collection.

6. Menzies later (1932–37) was professor of archaeology at Ch'i-lu (Chee-loo) University, and his lecture notes were apparently written during this period. Although, as stated above, these notes were never published, they were widely read and quoted.

7. See, for example, the early notes of Menzies.

8. Edouard Chavannes, "La divination par l'écaille de tortue dans la haute antiquité chinoise (d'après un livre de M. Lo Tchen-yu)," *Journal Asiatique*, vol. 17, 1911.

9. Frank H. Chalfant, "Early Chinese Writings," *Memoirs of the Carnegie Museum*, Pittsburgh, vol. 4, 1906–7.

10. Sun I-jang's *Ch'i-wen chü-li* (Examples of Oracle Bone Inscriptions), published in 1917, is divided into ten sections and two volumes. Vol. 1, covering the first eight sections, consists of 84 pages. Vol. 2 contains only two sections; section 9, on *wen-tzŭ*, consists of 92 pages,

while only a little over 3 pages are devoted to section 10 on miscellaneous examples.

11. According to Tung Tso-pin, *Ming yüan* was reprinted by the San Ch'ing T'ang Book Company, Shanghai.

12. Tung's source was Lo's Preface to his well-known publication, *Yin-hsü shu-ch'i ch'ien-pien* (Earlier Supplement to the Oracle Inscriptions of "Deserted Yin), which will be discussed below.

13. The first edition of *Yin-hsü shu-ch'i ch'ien-pien* contains a seal, which can be translated, "See, what Chang, Tu, Yang, Hsü did not see, characters."

14. Lo Chên-yü's debt to Sun I-jang thus seems to be an established fact, although Lo never made a public acknowledgment of this debt. In the early Republican era, some scholars were definitely of the opinion that Lo Chên-yü's main works, such as *Yin-hsü shu-ch'i k'ao-shih* (Interpretation of the Oracle Inscriptions at "Deserted" Yin), were actually authored by Wang Kuo-wei. The early history of the MSS of *Ch'i-wen chü-li* remains obscure up to the present time.

15. Lo's Preface lists his contributions to antiquarian studies, while Wang Kuo-wei in the Postscript concludes that the main contribution of the Ch'ing dynasty to Chinese learning is in the field of paleography. The founder of this important branch of learning is Ku Yen-wu, and Lo Chên-yü's *Yin-hsü shu-ch'i k'ao-shih* is the climax.

16. Actual count amounts to 571.

17. Lo prefaces section 6 of his work with these remarks: "In this section records are limited to those readable and complete entries; incomplete and unreadable entries are not included."

18. Wang Kuo-wei, "Yin-pu-tz'ŭ-chung, so-chien hsien-kung hsien-wang k'ao" (Notes on the Royal Ancestors of the Shang as Appear in Oracle Bone Records), *Hsüeh-shu ts'ung-shu* (Collected Historical Researches), 1917; reprinted in Wang's *Kuan-t'ang chi-lin* (Collected Essays), vol. 9. Wang compared his genealogical tree with the following three documents: "Annals of the Yin Dynasty" and "Generation Table of the Three Dynasties" in Ssŭ-ma Ch'ien's *Shih-chi* and "Tables of Men, Ancient and Modern" in Pan Ku's *Ch'ieh-han shu*.

19. See note 2, above.

20. Tung Tso-pin, *Fifty Years of Studies*, p. 63.

CHAPTER 3. *Field Method*

1. Mencius, *T'eng-wen-kung*, book 3, pt. 1, in James Legge, trans., *The Chinese Classics*, 2:249–50.

2. Boucher de Perthes, *De la création* (5 vols.; Paris, 1839–41). Compare *Manual d'archaeologie* (Paris, 1924), 1:6, 7, 18, 21.

3. David G. Hogarth, *Authority and Archaeology* (1899), p. vi.

4. The school system for modern education was officially adopted after the Boxer movement. The author attended the first primary school established in his native district Chung-hsiang, Hupei, at the age of just over ten, when the old examination system was already abolished.

5. For a complete biography of this remarkable man, see Hu Shih, *Ting-wen-chiang te chuan-chi* (Biography of Ting Wen-chiang). (The name should be translated as Ting Wen-chiang, but V. K. Ting is Ting's own spelling.) Hu's work was published by Academia Sinica in 1956. V. K. Ting died in 1936.

6. Thomas Huxley's essays on exposition on "Evolution," which in the late nineteenth and early twentieth centuries aroused so much academic controversy in Western Europe, especially in London, were first translated into old-style Chinese by Yen Fu in 1896 and printed in 1899, under the title *Tien Yen Lun*. The book proved to be an immediate success and was considered a masterpiece of Chinese literature.

7. It is regrettable that I have not been able to find a biography of A. W. Grabau, who played such an important rôle in introducing Western science to China. He was strongly against Weng Wen-hao's acceptance of an official appointment, first as chief secretary to the Administrative Yüan. He told everybody his frank opinion that there were many talented men who could render useful service as secretary to the Administrative Yüan, but nobody so well qualified to direct the Geological Survey after V. K. Ting. His words were almost prophetic.

8. J. G. Andersson's *Children of the Yellow Earth* was partly published in Swedish and was rendered into English in 1934 (London: K. Paul, Trench, Trubner and Co.).

9. J. G. Andersson, "An Early Chinese Culture," *Bulletin of the Geological Survey of China*, no. 5, 1923.

10. Andersson, *Children of the Yellow Earth*, pp. 164–65.

11. Raphael Pumpelly, *Explorations in Turkestan* (Washington, D.C.: Carnegie Institute, 1908).

12. T. J. Arne, *Painted Stone Age Pottery from the Province of Honan, China*, Palaeontologia Sinica, ser. D, vol. 1, fasc. 2 (1925).

13. About the origin and evolution of ceramics and the importance of this group of materials for historical study, consult, H. Frankfort, *Studies in Early Pottery of the Near East, I, Mesopotamia, Syria, and Egypt, and their Earliest Interrelations*. This monographic study was published as Occasional Paper no. 6, in 1921, by the Royal Anthropological Institute of Great Britain and Ireland.

14. Davidson Black, *The Ancient Human Skeletal Remains from the Fengtien Sha Kuo T'un Cave Deposit and from Honan Yangshao Ts'un in Comparison with Recent North China Skeletal Material*, Palaeontologia Sinica, ser. D, vol. 1, fasc. 3 (1925).

15. J. G. Andersson, *Children of the Yellow Earth*, pp. 95–96.

16. Ibid., p. 103.

17. Ibid., p. 108.

CHAPTER 4. *Early Period*

1. Cited here as *BIHP*. The first number was published in Canton in October 1928 and contained eight main articles, with a Foreword by Director Fu Ssŭ-nien, who eloquently expounded the reasons for the

creation of the institute. The bulletin was designed as a quarterly publication, with four issues each year constituting a volume. This publication has been continued uninterruptedly for forty-six years, the current numbers being vols. 46 and 47.

2. Tung and party arrived at Anyang on October 7; he started digging on the thirteenth of this month. The actual digging time, according to Tung's own account, was eighteen days, October 13–30.

3. Cited here as *PREA*. These reports were planned exclusively, as the title indicates, for the publication of the field work carried on in Anyang, including studies of the field materials. The first issue was published in 1929, in Peiping. Only four numbers were issued; no. 4 was given to the public in 1933 in Shanghai, when the headquarters of the Institute of History and Philology was on the move to the capital, Nanking. This report was later continued under different names: as *Field Reports in Archaeology* and finally as *Chinese Journal of Archaeology*.

4. Concerning the Hsin-cheng bronzes, there were a great many reports in Chinese newspapers at the time; a good summary of this important find is Carl Whiting Bishop, "The Hsin-cheng Bronzes," *China Journal of Science and Arts*, no. 3, 1925.

5. There is a complete file, I understand, of all the official correspondence between Mr. Bishop and me in the Freer Gallery of Art, Washington, D.C., which interested readers may examine by special request.

6. Li Chi, *Hsi-yin-ts'un shih-ch'ien ti i-ts'un* (Prehistorical Remains at Hsi-yin Ts'un) (Ts'inghua Research Institute, 1925); English translation, *New Stone Age Pottery from the Prehistoric Site at Hsi-yin Ts'un, Shansi, China* (Memoirs of the American Anthropological Association, no. 37, 1930). Liang Ssŭ-yung, who was studying in America at that time, returned to China and worked on the ceramic collection from this prehistoric site; Liang later wrote his master's thesis on these materials.

7. Li Chi, "An Analysis of the Underground Conditions below the Surface of the Hsiao-t'un Site," *PREA*, no. 1 (1929), pp. 37–48.

8. The total number of Sui (A.D. 581–617) and T'ang (618–906) tombs excavated at Hsiao-t'un is 148. Three of these tombs contained square tombstones or bricks with biographical notes of the buried person either inscribed or handwritten in red or black ink. All of these were dated in the Sui dynasty—one in the seventh year of K'ai Huang (A.D. 587); the second in the third year of Jen Shou (A.D. 603); and the third also dated in the K'ai Huang era (A.D. 581–600), but the numeral for the year was already smeared in the tomb and therefore unreadable. Altogether, the contents of these 148 tombs excavated at Hsiao-t'un in twelve seasons (1928–37)—namely, tomb figures, porcelainous wares and porcelains, occasional tombstones, and other finds in metal—serve to indicate that the burials took place in the Sui or, in some cases, the ensuing T'ang dynasty.

9. The official permit was given almost five years after the Antiquities Protection Law was passed by the Legislative Yüan, mainly because the curio dealers exporting Chinese antiquities exercised considerable political influence.

10. Li Chi, "First Analytic Study of the Soil Condition under the Surface of Hsiao-t'un," *PREA*, no. 2 (1929).

11. Tung Tso-pin, "Four Big Inscribed Tortoise Shells," *PREA*, no. 3 (1931).

12. Both archaeologists and historians participated in this discussion. Some of the papers were published in *PREA* and *BIHP*. The question, it may be said, still remains unanswered.

13. Shih Chang-ju, *K'ao-ku nien-piao* (Archaeological Chronology) (Taipei: Academia Sinica, Institute of History and Philology, 1952).

14. The earliest discovery of this important group of remains can be dated to the sixth season, in June 1932, when in subarea E a picture was taken of a number of field archaeologists standing in front of the foundation boulders to show the locations of the boulders.

CHAPTER 5. *The Royal Tombs*

1. Nils Palmgren, *Kansu Mortuary Urns and the Pan-shan and the Ma-ch'ang Groups*, Paleontologia Sinica, ser. D, vol. 3, fasc. 1, 1934.

2. Shih Hsing-pang et al., *The Neolithic Village at Pan p'o, Sian* (Peking: Wen Wu Press, 1963); An Chih-min, "Miao-ti-kou, San-li-ch'iao," *K'ao-ku Hsüeh-pao* (Journal of Archaeology), 1 (1965): 57–61.

3. Shih Chang-ju, "Yin Tombs Discovered at Hou-kang," *BIHP*, 13 (1948): 21–28.

4. See *Po-ku t'u-lu*, 1:25, on *T'ao-t'ieh Ting*, from Yeh-chün (Changte).

5. See, e.g., *Illustrated London News*, June 21, 1930, and August 8, 1931, each with full illustrations.

6. Seiichi Mizuno, ed., Seizanso Siesho (Illustrated Catalogue of the Nezu Collection), vol. 6, *Chinese Bronzes* (Tokyo: Nezu Art Museum, 1942), plates 1–8.

7. Kao Ch'ü-hsün, "The Royal Cemetery of the Yin Dynasty at Anyang," *Bulletin of the Department of Archaeology and Anthropology* (National Taiwan University), nos. 13–14 (Nov. 1959), pp. 1–9.

8. Li Chi, Preface, in Liang Ssǔ-yung, *HPKM 1001: Text*, ed. Kao Ch'ü-hsün, Archaeologia Sinica, no. 3 (Hou-chia-chuang), vol. 2, pt. 1 (Taipei: Academia Sinica, Institute of History and Philology, 1962).

9. Liang Ssǔ-yung, *HPKM 1004*, ed. Kao Ch'ü-hsün, Archaeologia Sinica, no. 3 (Hou-chia-chuang), vol. 5 (Taipei: Academia Sinica, Institute of History and Philology, 1970).

10. Kao Ch'ü-hsün, "The Royal Cemetery of the Yin Dynasty," p. 6.

11. See Kao Ch'ü-hsün, *HPKM 1001: Plates*, Archaeologia Sinica, no. 3 (Hou-chia-chuang), vol. 2, pt. 2 (Taipei: Academia Sinica, Institute of History and Philology, 1962), plate 16.

12. See Liang Ssǔ-yung, *HPKM 1004*, p. 41; the statue illustrated in this article was composed of several fragments, some of which were recovered from HPKM 1217 and others from HPKM 1004.

13. For the reconstructed figure of the drum, see Liang Ssǔ-yung, *HPKM 1217*, ed. Kao Ch'ü-hsün, Archaeologia Sinica, no. 3 (Hou-chia-

chuang), vol. 6 (Taipei: Academia Sinica, Institute of History and Philology, 1968), Fig. 9 (p. 26). Plates XIV–XVI of *HPKM 1217* show the different pieces of the drum *in situ* in the course of excavation.

CHAPTER 6. *Last Three Seasons of Field Work*

1. Shih Chang-ju, "Hong-t'u [Earth pounding], Pan-chu [Pisé], and Building in General of the Yin Dynasty," *BIHP*, 41, no. 1 (1969): 127–68.
2. Li Chi, "Important Discoveries at Yin-hsü in the Autumn Season of 1929," *PREA*, no. 2 (1929), p. 239.
3. Chang Ping-ch'uan, "Sacrificial Offerings Recorded in Oracle Bone Inscriptions," *BIHP*, 38 (1968): 181–232.
4. Pierre Teilhard de Chardin and C. C. Young, *On the Mammalian Remains from the Archaeological Site of Anyang*, Paleontologia Sinica, ser. C, vol. 12, fasc. 1, 1936.
5. Li Chi, *Pottery of the Yin and pre-Yin Period*, Archaeologia Sinica, no. 2 (Hsiao-t'un), vol. 3, fasc. 1, pt. 1 (Taipei: Academia Sinica, Institute of History and Philology, 1956).
6. Shih Chang-ju, *Burials of the Northern Section*, Archaeologia Sinica, no. 2 (Hsiao-t'un), vol. 1, fasc. 3 (Taipei: Academia Sinica, Institute of History and Philology, 1970).
7. Li Hsiao-ting, *Chia-ku wen-tzu chi-shih* (Annotated Dictionary of the Oracle Bone Characters), Institute of History and Philology, Special Publication no. 50, 1965, vol. 14, p. 4113.
8. Shih Chang-ju, "Recent and Most Important Discoveries from Yin Hsü," *Chinese Journal of Archaeology*, no. 2 (1947): pp. 1–81.
9. Hu Hou-hsüan, "Examples of Homologous Characters in the Oracle Bone Inscriptions," *BIHP*, 9 (1937): 135–220.
10. Chang Ping-ch'üan, who has been in charge of piecing together the tortoise shells from H127 in Taiwan, has published 349 restored tortoise shells in *Inksqueezes of the Restored Specimens*. . . . Archaeologia Sinica, no. 2 (Hsiao-t'un), vol. 2, fasc. 3. See more detailed discussion in Chap. 8.
11. Tung Tso-pin, *Inscriptions: Plates*, Archaeologia Sinica, no. 2 (Hsiao-t'un), vol. 2, fasc. 2, pt. 1 (Nanking: Academia Sinica, Institute of History and Philology, 1948).
12. The registered numbers of the inscribed bones from H127 are 13.0628—13.017756.

CHAPTER 7. *Wartime Efforts*

1. For a complete listing of these publications, see the entries under Liang's name in the Bibliography.
2. Aloys John Maerz and M. Real Paul, *Dictionary of Color* (New York: McGraw-Hill, 1930).
3. Wang Kuo-wei, "Yin-pu-tz'ŭ-chung so-chien hsien-kung hsien-wang

k'ao" (Notes on the Royal Ancestors of the Shang as Appear in Oracle Bone Records), *Hsüeh-shu ts'ung-shu* (Collected Historical Researches), 1917, reprinted in *Kuan-t'ang chi-lin* (Collected Essays), vol. 9; Tung Tso-pin, "Chia-ku-wen tuan-tai yen-chiu li" (Essay on Periodization of the Oracle Bone Inscriptions), *Ch'ing-chu Ts'ai yüan-p'ei hsien-shêng liu-shih-wu sui lun-wên chi* (Studies Presented to Ts'ai Yuan-p'ei on His Sixty-fifth Birthday) (Peking: Academia Sinica, Institute of History and Philology, 1933), pt. 1, pp. 323–424; Kuo Mo-jo, *Pu-tz'ŭ tung-ch'uan* (Annotations and General Discussions on Oracle Bone Inscriptions) (Toyko: Wen-Chiu-Tang, 1933); Tung Tso-pin, *Yin-li-p'u* (Tabulated Data of the Yin Dynasty according to Chronology of Recorded Events Found in the Oracle Bone Inscriptions) (lithograph ed., Li-Chuang, 1945).

4. Tung Tso-pin, "Some Important Problems of the Yin Calendar," *BIHP*, 4 (1934): 331–54.

5. See Chu Wen-hsin, *Tien-wen-k'ao-ku-lu* (Archaeological Records of Astronomy) (Shanghai: Commercial Press, 1933), pp. 100 ff.

6. Tung Tso-pin, "Chia-ku-wen tuan-tai yen-chiu li"; all the names after "heavenly stem" symbols are here capitalized to indicate post-mortem relationship with the king's birthday or death day.

7. Including the fourteen years of his reign before moving to Yin (Anyang).

8. Tung Tso-pin, *Yin-li-p'u*, vol. 2, leaf 16, p. 2.

9. Frankfort, *Mesopotamia, Syria, and Egypt, and Their Earliest Interrelations.*

10. See Chap. 6, note 5.

11. Li Chi, "Pre-Yin Cultural Deposits at Hsiao-t'un," *Hsüeh-shu hui-k'an* (Occasional Papers of Academia Sinica during Wartime), 1, no. 2 (1944): 1–12.

CHAPTER 8. *Postwar Academic Working Conditions*

1. Tung Tso-pin, *Inscriptions: Plates*, Archaeologia Sinica, no. 2 (Hsiao-t'un), vol. 2, fasc. 2, pt. 1 (Nanking: Academia Sinica, Institute of History and Philology, 1948).

2. Ibid.

3. Tung Tso-pin, *Inscriptions: Plates*, Archaeologia Sinica, no. 2 (Hsiao-t'un), vol. 2, fasc. 2, pt. 2 (Taipei: Academia Sinica, Institute of History and Philology, 1953).

4. Chü Wan-li, *Inscriptions: Annotations of Inscriptions of Part 1*, Archaeologia Sinica, no. 2 (Hsiao-t'un), vol. 2, fasc. 1, pt. 2 (Taipei: Academia Sinica, Institute of History and Philology, 1961).

5. Chang Ping-ch'üan, "Corpus Number Given to the Order Found on the Same Oracle Bone Plastron," *BIHP*, 28 (1956): 229–72. (This edition of *BIHP* was *festschrift* in honor of Dr. Hu Shih.)

6. Chang Ping-ch'üan, "Agriculture and Climate of the Yin-Shang Period," *BIHP*, 42 (1970): 267–336. (This edition of *BIHP* was a *festschrift: In Honor of Dr. Wang Shih-chieh on His Eightieth Birthday.*

Chang's paper was originally written at the request of the editorial board of the Ancient History of China series.)

7. For a complete listing of these publications, see entries under Liang's and Kao's names in the Bibliography.

8. Shih Chang-ju, *Architectural Remains*, Archaeologia Sinica, no. 2 (Hsiao-t'un), vol. 1, fasc. 2 (Taipei: Academia Sinica, Institute of History and Philology, 1959).

9. Shih Chang-ju, *Burials of the Northern Section*, Archaeologia Sinica, no. 2 (Hsiao-t'un), vol. 1, fasc. 3, pts. 1 and 2 (Taipei: Academia Sinica, Institute of History and Philology, 1972); *Burials of the Middle Section*, Archaeologia Sinica, no. 2 (Hsiao-t'un), vol. 1, fasc. 3 (Taipei: Academia Sinica, Institute of History and Philology, 1970).

10. For complete data on these publications, see entries under Li and Wan in the Bibliography.

CHAPTER 9. *Prehistoric Remains*

1. Li Chi, *Hsi-yin-ts'un* . . . (see chap. 4, note 6).

2. Wu Gin-ding (or Chin-ting), *Prehistoric Pottery in China* (London: Kegan Paul, Trench, Trubner & Co., 1938).

3. *The Works of Mencius,* Book 5, in James Legge, trans., *The Chinese Classics,* 2:358.

4. In his reconstruction Wang referred to the annotated *Bamboo Annals* (*Chu-shu chi-nien*), which he considered to be the older and more genuine version of the original account. See Wang Kuo-wei, *Kuan-t'ang chi-lin* (a selection of his works published in his lifetime), and *Hai-ning Wang-chung-chüeh-kung I-shu* (the more complete collection of his works edited by his friends and pupils and published after his death).

5. Wang Kuo-wei, "Yin-pu-tz'ǔ-chung . . ." (see chap. 7, note 3); *Shih-lin* (Historical Researches), vol. 1, pp. 1–15, in *Kuan-t'ang chi-lin* (Collected Essays).

6. *Shoo-king, The Books of Shang,* Book 7, pt. 1: "Pwan-Kang," in James Legge, trans., *The Chinese Classics,* 3:220–23.

7. Ibid., p. 221n.

8. Bernhard Karlgren, "Glosses in the Book of Documents," *Bulletin of the Museum of Far Eastern Antiquities,* 20 (1948): 39–315.

9. Liu Yüan-lin, "Development of the Technology of Making Oracle Bones," *BIHP,* 46, no. 1 (1974): 99–154.

10. Hsü Chung-shu, "A Second Discussion on the Relation between Hsiao-t'un and Yang-shao," *PREA,* no. 3 (1931), pp. 523–57.

CHAPTER 10. *Architecture*

1. Shih Chang-ju, "Architectural Remains of the Yin Period at Hsiao-t'un," *BIHP,* 26 (1955): 131–86.

2. Li Chi, "Pre-Yin Cultural Deposits at Hsiao-t'un."

3. Shih Chang-ju, "Further Examples of the Reconstruction of Archi-

tecture of the Shang Dynasty," *Bulletin of the Institute of Ethnology* (Academia Sinica), no. 29 (1970), pp. 321–41.

4. Ibid., p. 333.

5. Shih Chang-ju, *Architectural Remains*, Archaeologia Sinica, no. 2 (Hsiao-t'un), vol. 1, fasc. 2 (Taipei: Academia Sinica, Institute of History and Philology, 1959).

6. Shih Chang-ju, "One Example of Restored Yin Surface Building," *Annals of Academia Sinica*, no. 1 (1954), pp. 269–80.

7. Shih Chang-ju, "Hong-t'u [Earth pounding], Pan-chu [Pisé], and Building in General of the Yin Dynasty," *BIHP*, 41, no. 1 (1969): 127–68.

8. Section from the *Chou-li*.

9. See Shih Chang-ju, *Burials of the Northern Section*, Archaeologia Sinica, no. 2 (Hsiao-t'un), vol. 1, fasc. 3 (1970).

10. Kuo Pao-chün, "The Excavation of B Area," *PREA*, no. 4 (1933), pp. 607–8.

CHAPTER 11. *The Economy*

1. Woo Ch'i-ch'ang, "Chia-ku-chin-wen chung suo-chien-ti yin-tai nung-chia ching-kuang" (State of Yin Agriculture as Found in the Oracle Bone and Bronze Scripts), pp. 323–68 in a *festschrift* honoring Chang Chü-sheng (Shanghai: Commercial Press, 1937).

2. Hu Hou-hsüan, "Pu-tzŭ chung suo-chien shih yin-tai nung-yeh" (Agriculture of the Yin Period as Seen from the Oracle Bone Records), *Chia-ku hsüeh Shang-shih lun-ts'ung* (Collected Studies of Shang History Based on Oracle Bone Studies), vol. 2 (lithographed ed; Chee-loo University, Institute of Chinese Studies, 1945).

3. Chang Ping-ch'uan, "Agriculture and Climate" (see chap. 8, note 6).

4. Young Chung-chien, "Further Notes on the Mammals Excavated from Yin-hsü," *Chinese Journal of Archaeology*, no. 4 (1949), pp. 145–53.

5. Hu Wei, *Yü-kung chuei-chih* (Complete Geographical Commentary of Yü-kung in the Book of Documents), in *Huang-ch'ing ching-jei*, vols. 27–30.

6. Tung Tso-pin, *Yin-li-p'u*, part 2, vol. 9, p. 45.

7. Hu Hou-hsüan, "Ch'i-hou pien-ch'ien yu Yin-tai ch'i-hou chih chien-t'au" (The Changes of Weather and an Examination of the Weather during the Yin Dynasty), *Chia-ku-hsüeh* . . . , 2:20.

8. Young, "Further Notes on Mammals from Yin-hsü."

9. T'ang Lan, "Yin-hsü wen-tzu hsiao-chi" (Notes and Comments on Oracle Bone Inscriptions) (lithographed lecture notes, 1934), pp. 2–4.

10. Kunio Shima, *Yin-hsü pu-tz'ŭ ts'ung-lei* (Summary of Oracle Bone Characters) (Tokyo, 1967).

11. Chang Ping-ch'üan, "Agriculture and Climate," pp. 306–7.

12. Tung Tso-pin, "Report on the First Digging at Hsiao-t'un," *PREA*, no. 1, 1929.

13. Li Chi, "Illustrated Study of Edged Stone Tools from Yin-hsü," *BIHP*, 23 (1952): 523–615.

14. See Li Chi, *Pottery of the Yin and pre-Yin Period.*

15. For a complete listing of these publications, see entries in the Bibliography under Li Chi and Wan Chia-pao.

16. Li Chi and Wan Chia-pao, *Studies of the Bronze Ku-Beaker Excavated from Hsiao-t'un and Hou Chia Chuang: Its Casting Process and Decorative Patterns,* Archaeologia Sinica, n.s. no. 1 (Nankang, Taiwan: Academia Sinica, Institute of History and Philology, 1964).

CHAPTER 12. *Decorative Art*

1. Li Chi, "Diverse Backgrounds of the Decorative Art of the Yin Dynasty," *Proceedings of the Eighth Pacific Science Congress,* 1955, pp. 179–94; also published in *Annals of Academia Sinica,* no. 2, pt. 1 (1955), pp. 119–29.

2. Li Chi, *Pottery of the Yin and pre-Yin Period.*

3. Li Chi, "Evolution of the White Pottery of the Yin Dynasty," *BIHP*, 28 (1957): 853–82.

4. Li Chi, "Eight Types of Hairpins and the Evolution of Their Decorative Patterns," *BIHP*, 30, pt. 1 (1959): 611–70.

5. J. G. Andersson, *The Cave-Deposit at Sha Ko T'un in Fengtien,* Paleontologia Sinica, ser. D, vol. 1, fasc. 1, 1923.

6. This topic has recently been rediscussed by a number of scholars interested in this particular aspect of Chinese culture. Mrs. John Fairbank is highly skeptical of the view that the carved mark represents tattooing, but, as she has not had the opportunity to examine the original specimen, she is not definite. My colleague Wan Chia-pao, on the other hand, entertains a different opinion. He believes that these marks represent neither tattooing nor a dress, but were carved on the torso sheerly as a matter of ornamentation, just as the Yin artist had done on the stone tigers and elephant.

7. Li Chi and Wan Chia-pao, *Studies of the Bronze Ku-Beaker,* pp. 125–26.

CHAPTER 13. *Genealogy, Chên-Jên*

1. See Tung Tso-pin, *Fifty Years of Studies in Oracle Inscriptions,* p. 75.

2. Wang Kuo-wei, "Yin-chou chih tu luan" (Comparative Study of Yin-Chou Institutions), *Kuan-t'ang chi-lin,* vol. 10.

3. Ch'en Yin-k'o, conversation with the author.

4. Ting Shan, "Clan and Its Institution as Recorded in the Oracle Bone Inscriptions" (1948), and "A Gazetteer of Yin-Shang Clans" (incomplete MSS).

5. See Tung Tso-pin, *Fifty Years of Studies in Oracle Inscriptions,* p. 74.

6. Lo Chên-yü, *Yin-hsü shu-ch'i k'ao-shih*.

7. Ibid.

8. Wang Kuo-wei, "Yin-pu-tz'ŭ-chung so-chien hsien-kung hsien-wang k'ao."

9. Chang Ping-chuan, "Numerals in the Oracle Bone Inscriptions," *BIHP*, vol. 46, no. 3, 1975.

10. Kuo Mo-jo, *Chia-ku wen-tzŭ yen-chiu* (A Study of Oracle Bone Inscriptions), vol. 2 (Shanghai: Ta-tung Book Co., 1931).

11. Traditional Chinese accounts usually credit Ta Nao in the court of the Yellow Emperor with the invention of the celestial stems and earthly branches (*kan-chih*) system. From the archaeological viewpoint, however, field data thus far provide no record of the sexagenarian system of dating earlier than the Shang dynasty. In spite of half a century's labor in archaeological investigations, so far no one has been able to identify definitely the Hsia site, much less its written record.

CHAPTER 14. *Worship of Ancestors*

1. Wang Kuo-wei, "Yin-pu-tz'ŭ-chung so-chien hsien-kung hsien-wang k'ao."

2. Kunio Shima, *Yin-hsü pu-tz'ŭ ts'ung-lei*.

CHAPTER 15. *Notes on the Physical Anthropology*

1. For a listing of these reports, see the entries under Young Hsi-mei in the Bibliography.

2. Tung Tso-pin, *Yin-li-p'u*.

3. Davidson Black, *The Ancient Human Skeletal Remains from . . . Sha Kuo T'un;* see also Black, *A Study of Kansu and Honan Aeneolithic Skulls and Specimens from Later Kansu Prehistoric Sites in Comparison with North China and Other Recent Crania*, Palaeontologia Sinica, ser. D, vol. 6, fasc. 1 (1928).

4. T. L. Woo and G. M. Morant, "A Preliminary Classification of Asiatic Races Based on Cranial Measurements," *Biometrica*, vol. 24, 1934, pts. 1, 2.

Appendix

Chinese Characters for Proper Names and Other Terms

Anhui　安徽
Anyang　安陽
Ao　隞

Canton　廣州(廣東)
Chahar　察哈爾
Chang Ch'ang　張敞
Chang Chü-sheng　張菊生
Chang Hsüeh-hsien　張學獻
Chang Ping-ch'üan　張秉權
Chang T'ai-yen (Ping-lin)　章太炎 (炳麟)
Chang Wei-jan　張蔚然
Changte Fu　彰德府
Ch'ang Jo　昌若
Ch'angsha　長沙
Chao Chih-chai　趙執齋
chao ch'e　兆坼
Chao Ming　昭明
Chao Wan-li　趙萬里

Chao Yüan-ren　趙元任
Chekiang　浙江
Chen Chung-fan　陳鐘凡
chên　貞
chen　沈
chên-jên　貞人
Ch'en　辰
Ch'en Meng-chia　陳夢家
Ch'en P'an　陳槃
Ch'en Yin-k'o　陳寅恪
Cheng　振
Chêng-chou　鄭州
chêng ming　正名
chêng-tso　正坐
Ch'eng Tang　成湯
Ch'eng-tu　成都
Ch'êng-tzŭ-yai　城子崖
Chi　己
chi　稷
ch'i₁　棄

279

Hsüan T'ung　宣統

hsieh　穴

Hsün-p'u　旬譜

Hu Chia　虎甲

Hu Fu-lin　胡福林

Hu Hou-hsüan　胡厚宣

Hu Shih　胡適

Hu Wei　胡渭

Hua-yüan-chuang　花園莊

Huai　淮

Huan　洹

Huang Chi-kang　黃季剛

Huang Chün　黃濬

Huang-Ho-Pai-Ho (Museum)　黃河白
河博物館或北疆博物館

Huang Jan-wei　黃然偉

Huang-ti　黃帝

huang-t'u-t'ai　夯土臺

hui-k'eng　灰坑

Hun-chu　葷粥

Hupei　胡北

I　乙

I　伊

i　翌

I-chou-shu　逸周書

I-pin　宜賓

Jen　壬

Jen Shou　仁壽

jih-chih-p'u　日至譜

jih-p'u　日譜

ju　儒

ju-lüeh-chou-jih　儒畧週日

jun-p'u　閏譜

K'aifeng　開封

K'ai Huang　開皇

kan-chih　干支

Kansu　甘肅

kao　告

Kao Ch'ü-hsün　高去尋

kao-liang　高粱

Kao P'ing-tsǔ　高平子

k'ao chü hsüeh　考據學

K'ao-kung-chi　考工記

K'ao shih　考史

keng　庚

Keng Ting　庚丁

Kiangsu　江蘇

ko　戈

ku　觚

Ku Chieh-kang　顧頡剛

ku pu　骨卜

ku wen　古文

Ku Yen-wu　顧炎武

kuan　壹

Kuang Hsü　光緒

Kublai Khan　忽必烈汗

Kuei　癸

Kueichou　貴州

Kuei Fang　鬼方

k'uei　夔

Kung Fang　呂方

Kunming　昆明

Kuo Mo-jo　郭沫若

Kuo Pao-chün　郭寶鈞

Kwangsi　廣西

Lan Pao-kuang　藍葆光

Lei-chu　嫘祖

li　禮

Li Ch'eng　李成

Li Chi　李濟

Li Chin-tan　李景聃

Li-chuang　李莊

Li Hsiao-ting　李孝定

Li Kuang-yü　李光宇

Li Lien-ch'un　李連春

Li Tsung-t'ung　李宗侗

Liang Ch'i-ch'ao　梁啓超

Liang Ssǔ-yung　梁思永

liao　袤

Liao-tung　遼東

Lin-fên Hsien　臨汾縣

Lin Hsin　廩辛

Lintze　臨淄

Liu Ch'ung-hung　劉崇鋐

Liu Ngo (T'ieh-yün)　劉鶚(鐵雲)

Liu Yao　劉燿

Liu Yü-hsia　劉嶼霞

Liu Yüan-lin　劉淵臨

Lo　洛

Lo Chên-yü　羅振玉

Loyang　洛陽

Lu-chou　瀘州

Lung-ch'üen Cheng　龍泉鎮

Lunghai　隴海

lung ku　龍骨

Lungshan　龍山

ma　馬

Ma-ch'ang　馬廠

mai　薶

mai ts'ang　薶藏

Manchu　滿清(滿洲)

Mao　卯

Meiji　明治

Mencius　孟子

Miao　苗

Miao-ti-kou 廟底溝
Mien-ch'ih Hsien 澠池縣
Ming 明
Ming 冥
ming-ch'i 明器
Mizuno, Seiichi 水野清一
Mo-tzŭ 墨子

Naito, Torajiro 內藤虎次郎
Nan-ch'i 南溪
Nankai 南開
Nankang 南港
Nan Keng 南庚
Nanking 南京
nien-li-p'u 年曆譜
Ninghsia Fu 寧夏府
niu 牛
Nurhachi 努爾哈赤

pan 盆
pan-chu 版築
Pan-ch'üan 阪泉
Pan Ku 班固
Pan-p'o 半坡
Pan-shan 半山
P'an Ch'üeh 潘愨
P'an Keng 盤庚
P'an Tsu-yin 潘祖蔭
Pao I 報乙
Pao Ping 報丙
Pao Ting 報丁
Pao-ting 保定
Pei Wen-chung 裴文中
Peiping 北平
Peking 北京
Ping 丙
P'ing-yang Fu 平陽府
Po Chü-i 白居易
Pohai 渤海
pu fa 卜法
pu-tz'ŭ 卜辭

Ruey Yih-fu 芮逸夫

San Ch'ing T'ang 三傾堂
San-tai 三代
Sha-kuo-t'un 沙鍋屯
shan 山
Shan Hai Ching 山海經
Shang 商
Shang Ch'eng-tzu 商承祚
Shang Chia Wei 上甲微
Shanghai 上海
Shansi 山西
Shantung 山東

Shen 申
Shen Kang-po 沈剛伯
Shensi 陝西
Shih Chang-ju 石璋如
Shih Chi 史記
shih-ts'u 氏族
Shima, Kunio 島邦男
Shinjô, Shinzô 新城新造
shou-p'u 朔譜
shu 黍
Shu-ching 書經
Shui-tung-kou 水洞溝
Shun 舜
Shuo-wen 說文
Siang T'u 相土
Ssŭ 巳
ssŭ 祀
ssŭ 杻
Ssŭ-ma Ch'ien 司馬遷
Ssŭ-p'an-mo 四盤磨
ssŭ-p'u 祀譜
Sui 隋
Sun I-jang ((Chung-yung) 孫詒讓(仲容)
Sun Yat-sen 孫逸仙
Sung 宋
Szechwan 四川

Ta-jen-t'ang 達仁堂
Ta-ku 大沽
Ta-ku-chai 達古齋
Ta-li 大理
Ta-lien-k'eng 大連坑
Ta Nao 大橈
Ta-tai-li 大戴禮
Tai Chen 戴震
T'ai Chia 太甲
T'ai Keng 太庚
T'ai Ting 太丁
T'ai Wu 太戊
Taihang 太行
Taipei 臺北
Taita 臺(灣)大(學)
Taiwan 臺灣
Taiyüan 太原
Tan-t'u 丹徒
T'ang 唐
T'ang 湯
T'ang Lan 唐蘭
T'ang-yin 湯陰
tao 稻
tao chien yo 刀尖菥
Tao Kuang 道光
t'ao-t'ieh 饕餮
T'eng-wen-kung 滕文公

ti 帝
ti-chih 地支
Ti Hsin 帝辛
Ti I 帝乙
Ti Ku 帝嚳
T'ien I 天乙
t'ien-kan 天干
Tientsin 天津
T'ien Wen 天問
Ting 丁
Ting Shan 丁山
Ting Ven-kiang(Wen-chiang) 丁文江
tou 豆
tou 竇
Ts'ai-shih-k'ou 菜市口
Ts'ao Yü 曹圉
Tsinan 濟南
Ts'ing-lien-kang 青蓮崗
Ts'inghua 清華
Ts'ingtao 青島
Tsou 郰
Tsu Chi 祖己
Tsu Chia 祖甲
Tsu Hsin 祖辛
Tsu I 祖乙
Tsu Keng 祖庚
Tsu Ting 祖丁
tsung 琮
Tu Yeh 杜鄴
T'u Fang 土方
Tuan Fang 端方
Tuan Yü-ts'ai 段玉裁
Tung I 東夷
Tunhuang 敦煌
Tung Tso-pin 董作賓
Tungchi 同濟
T'ung-lo-chai 同樂寨
Tzŭ 子
tzu-ku-t'ou 字骨頭
Tz'ŭ-hsi 慈禧

Umehara, Sueji 梅原末治
Uturigawa, Menoza 移川子之藏

Wai Jen 外壬
Wai Ping 外丙
Wan Chang 萬章
Wan Chia-pao 萬家保
Wang 王
Wang Hai 王亥
Wang Hsiang 王湘
Wang Hsiang 王襄
Wang I-yung 王懿榮
Wang Kuo-wei 王國維
Wang Mang 王莽

Wang Nien-sun 王念孫
Wang Shih-chieh 王世杰
Wang Wen Min Kung 王文敏公
Wang Yin-chih 王引之
Wei 未
Wei Hsien 濰縣
Wei-tze 微子
wen-tzŭ 文字
Wen-wu Ting 文武丁
Weng T'ung-ho 翁同龢
Weng Wen-hao 翁文灝
Wo Chia 沃甲
Wo Ting 沃丁
Woo Ch'i-ch'ang 吳其昌
Woo Ting-liang 吳定良
Wu 戊
Wu 午
Wu Ch'ang-shou 吳昌綬
Wu Gin-ding 吳金鼎
Wu I 武乙
Wu Keng 武庚
Wu Ta-ch'eng 吳大澂
Wu Ting 武丁

yang 羊
Yang Chia 陽甲
Yang Hsung 揚雄
Yang-mei-cheng 楊梅鎮
Yangshao Ts'un 仰韶村
Yangtze 揚子
Yao Ts'ung-wu 姚從吾
Yeh-chün 鄴郡
Yeh Ming 葉銘
Yeh Yü-sheng 葉玉森
Yen Fu 嚴復
Yen Hsi-shan 閻錫山
Yen Jo-chü 閻若璩
Yen-shih 偃師
Yi 益
Yin 殷
Yin 寅
Yin-hsü 殷墟
Yin Huan-chang 尹煥章
Yin-Shang 殷商
Young Chung-chien 楊鍾建
Young Hsi-mei 楊希枚
Yu 酉
Yu-li 牖里
yu lun 餘論
Yü 禹
Yü-chien-chai 玉簡齋
Yü-kung 禹貢
Yüan 元
Yüan Fu-li 袁復禮
yüeh-p'u 月譜

283

yun-lei-wen 雲雷紋
yung 肜
Yung Chi 雍己

Yung Keng 容庚
Yung Yüan 容媛
Yünnan 雲南

Bibliography

The following abbreviations are used in the Notes and the Bibliography:

PREA   *Anyang fa-chüeh pao-kao* (Preliminary Reports of Excavations at An-
        yang). Academia Sinica, Institute of History and Philology. Nos. 1,
        2, Peiping, 1929; no. 3, Peiping, 1931; no. 4, Shanghai, 1933.
        安陽發掘報告. 一期, 二期, 1929; 三期 1931 北平; 四期 1933 上
        海.

BIHP   *Kuo-li chung-yang yen-chiu-yüan li-shih yü-yen yen-chiu-so chi-k'an* (Bulletin
        of the Institute of History and Philology of Academia Sinica). 1928—
        國立中央研究院歷史語言研究所集刊. 1928 至現在.

References to Academia Sinica publications in the Notes appear in English
translation only. Chinese characters for these titles will be found in the Bibliography.

An Chih-min et al. "Miao-ti-kou and San-li-ch'iao." *Archaeological Excavations
    at the Yellow River, Reservoirs Report No. 2*. Peking: Science Press, 1959.
安志敏等. 廟底溝與三里橋. 中國田野考古報告集考古專刊丁種第九號. 北
京：科學出版社.

Andersson, J. G. *The Cave-Deposit at Sha Ko T'un in Fengtien.* Palaeontologia Sinica, ser. D, vol. 1, fasc. 1. Peiping: Geological Survey of China, 1923.
奉天錦西縣沙鍋屯洞穴層．古生物誌，丁種，第一號第一冊．農商部地質調查所．北平．
——. *Children of the Yellow Earth.* London: K. Paul, Trench, Trubner and Co., 1934.
——. "An Early Chinese Culture," *Bulletin of the Geological Survey of China*, no. 5, 1923. (Paper in English and Chinese.)
中國遠古之文化．地質彙報，第五期．農商部地質調查所．北平．
——. "Researches into the Prehistory of the Chinese." *Bulletin of the Museum of Far Eastern Antiquities*, 15 (1943): 1–304.
Arne, T. G. *Painted Stone Age Pottery from the Province of Honan, China.* Palaeontologia Sinica, ser. D, vol. 1, fasc. 2. Peiping: Geological Survey of China, 1925.
阿爾納．河南石器時代之着色陶器．古生物誌，丁種，第一號，第二冊．農商部地質調查所，北平．
Bishop, Carl Whiting. "The Hsin-cheng Bronzes." *China Journal of Science and Arts*, no. 3, 1925.
Black, Davidson. *A Study of Kansu and Honan Aeneolithic Skulls and Specimens from Later Kansu Prehistoric Sites in Comparison with North China and Other Recent Crania.* Palaeontologia Sinica, ser. D, vol. VI, fasc. 1. Peiping: Geological Survey of China. 1928.
步達生．甘肅河南晚石器時代及甘肅史前後期之人類頭骨與現代華北及其他人種之比較．古生物誌，丁種，第六號，第一冊．國民政府農礦部直轄地質調查所．北平．
——. *The Ancient Human Skeletal Remains from the Fengtien Sha Kuo T'un Cave Deposit and from Honan Yangshao Ts'un in Comparison with Recent North China Skeletal Material.* Palaeontologia Sinica, ser. D, vol. 1, fasc. 3. Peiping: Geological Survey of China, 1925.
奉天沙鍋屯及河南仰韶村之古代人骨與近代華北人骨之比較．古生物誌，丁種，第一號，第三冊．農商部地質調查所，北平．
Chalfant, Frank H. "Early Chinese Writings." *Memoirs of the Carnegie Museum* (Pittsburgh), vol. 4, 1906–7.
Chang Ping-chüan. "Agriculture and Climate of the Yin-Shang Period." *BIHP*, 42, pt. 2 (1970): 267–336.
張秉權．殷代農業與氣象．史語所集刊，第四十二本，第二分．
——. "Corpus Number Given to the Order Found on the Same Oracle Bone Plastron." *BIHP*, 28, pt. 1 (1956): 229–72.
卜龜腹甲的序數．史語所集刊，第二十八本，上冊．
——. *Inksqueezes of the Restored Specimens of Inscribed Tortoise Shells, with Annotations.* Archaeologia Sinica, no. 2, Hsiao-t'un: The Yin-Shang Site at Anyang, Honan. Vol. 2, *Inscriptions.* Fasc. 3. Taipei: Academia Sinica, Institute of History and Philology. Pt. 1(i), 1957; pt. 1(ii), 1959; pt. 2(i), 1962; pt. 2(ii), 1963; pt. 3(i), 1967; pt. 3(ii), 1972.
殷虛文字丙編．中國考古報告集，之二，小屯．第二本 中央研究院歷史語言研究所，臺灣，臺北．
——. "Numerals in the Oracle Bone Inscriptions." *BIHP*, vol. 46, no. 3, 1975.
甲骨文中所見的『數』．史語所集刊．第四十六本，第三分．
——. "Sacrificial Offerings Recorded in Oracle Bone Inscriptions." *BIHP*, 38 (1968): 181–232.

祭祀卜辭中的犧牲. 史語所集刊, 第三十八本.

Chavannes, Edouard. "Divination de l'écaille de tortue dans la haute antiquité chinoise d'après un livre de M. Lo Tchen-yu." *Journal Asiatique*, vol. 17, 1911.

Ch'en Meng-chia. *Yin-hsü pu-tz'ŭ tsung-shu* (Summary of Oracle Bone Inscriptions). Peking: Science Press, 1956.

陳夢家. 殷虛卜辭綜述. 考古學專刊, 甲種. 第二號. 科學出版社.

Chu Wen-hsin. *Tien-wen k'ao-ku-lu* (Archaeological Records of Astronomy). Shanghai: Commercial Press, 1933.

朱文鑫. 天文考古錄. 上海：商務印書館.

Chü Wan-li. *Inscriptions: Annotations of Inscriptions of Part 1.* Archaeologia Sinica, no. 2, Hsiao-t'un: The Yin-Shang Site at Anyang, Honan. Vol. 2, fasc. 1, pt. 2. Taipei: Academia Sinica, Institute of History and Philology, 1961.

屈萬里. 殷虛文字甲編下冊. 中國考古報告集, 之二, 小屯. 第二本, 中央研究院歷史語言研究所, 臺灣, 臺北.

Frankfort, H. *Studies in Early Pottery of the Near East, I: Mesopotamia, Syria, and Egypt, and Their Earliest Interrelations.* Royal Anthropological Institute of Great Britain and Ireland, Occasional Paper no. 6, 1924.

Herrmann Atlas. Harvard-Yenching Institute, 1935.

Hsü Chung-shu. "A Second Discussion on the Relation between Hsiao-t'un and Yang-shao." *PREA*, no. 3 (1931), pp. 523–57.

徐中舒. 再論小屯與仰韶. 安陽發掘報告, 第三期. 史語所.

Hu Hou-hsüan. "Ch'i-hou pien-ch'ien yu yin-tai ch'i-hou chih chien-t'ao" (The Changes of Weather and an Examination of the Weather during the Yin Dynasty). *Chia-ku-hsüeh shang-shih lun-ts'ung* (Collected Studies of Shang History Based on Oracle Bone Studies), vol. 2. Part 2. Lithographed. Chi'-lu University, Institute of Chinese Studies, 1945.

胡厚宣. 氣候變遷與殷代氣候之檢討. 甲骨學商史論叢, 二集, 下冊. 齊魯大學國學研究所專刊之一.

———. "Examples of Homologous Characters in the Oracle Bone Inscriptions." *BIHP*, 9 (1937): 135–220.

卜辭同文例, 史語所集刊, 第九本.

———. "Pu-tzŭ chung suo-chien shih yin-tai nung-yeh" (Agriculture of the Yin Period as Seen from the Oracle Bone Records). In *Chia-ku-hsüeh shang-shih lun-ts'ung* (Collected Studies of Shang History Based on Oracle Bone Studies), vol. 2, pt. 1. Lithographed. Ch'i-lu University, Institute of Chinese Studies, 1945.

卜辭中所見之殷代農業. 甲骨學商史論叢, 二集, 上冊. 齊魯大學國學研究所專刊之一.

Hu Shih. *Ting-wen-chiang te chuan-chi* (Biography of Ting Wen-chiang). Taipei: Academia Sinica, 1956.

胡適. 丁文江的傳記. 中央研究院, 臺灣, 臺北.

Hu Wei. *Yu-kung chuei-chih* (Complete Geographical Commentary of Yu-kung in the Book of Documents). In *Huang-ch'ing ching-jei* (Studies of Ancient Classics of the Ch'ing Dynasty), vols. 27–30. Shanghai: Hung-wen, 1896.

胡渭. 禹貢錐指. 皇清經解. 上海鴻文書局. 光緒二十二年.

Kao Ch'ü-hsün. *HPKM 1001: Plates.* Archaeologia Sinica, no. 3, Hou-chia-chuang: The Yin-Shang Cemetery Site at Anyang, Honan. Vol. 2, pt. 2. Taipei: Academia Sinica, Institute of History and Philology, 1962.

高去尋. 第一〇〇一號大墓. 中國考古報告集, 之三, 侯家莊. 第二本下冊：圖版. 中央研究院歷史語言研究所, 臺灣, 臺北.

————. ed. *See* Liang Ssŭ-yung.

Karlgren, Bernard. "Glosses on the Book of Documents." *Bulletin of the Museum of Far Eastern Antiquities*, 20 (1948): 39–315.

Kuo Mo-jo. *Chia-ku wen-tzŭ yen-chiu* (A Study of Oracle Bone Inscriptions), vol. 2. Shanghai: Ta-tung Book Co., 1931.
郭沫若. 甲骨文字研究, 第二冊. 大東書局, 上海.

————. *Pu-tz'ŭ t'ung-ch'uan* (Annotations and General Discussions on Oracle Bone Inscriptions). Tokyo: Wen-Chiu-Tang, 1933.
卜辭通纂. 文求堂, 東京.

Kuo Pao-chün. "The Excavation of β Area." *PREA*, no. 4, 1933.
郭寶鈞. β 區發掘記. 安陽發掘報告, 第四期. 中央研究院歷史語言研究所.

Laufer, Berthold. *Jade: A Study in Chinese Archaeology and Religion.* Chicago: Field Museum of Natural History, 1912.

Legge, James, trans. *The Chinese Classics* (1861). 4 vols. Hong Kong: Hong Kong University Press, 1970.

Li Chi. "An Analysis of the Underground Conditions below the Surface of the Hsiao-t'un Site." *PREA*, no. 1 (1929), pp. 37–48.
李濟. 小屯地面下情形分析初步. 安陽發掘報告, 第一期. 史語所.

————. "Diverse Backgrounds of the Decorative Art of the Yin Dynasty." *Proceedings of the Eighth Pacific Science Congress*, 1955, pp. 179–94. Also published in *Annals of Academia Sinica*, no. 2, pt. 1 (1955), pp. 119–29.

————. "Eight Types of Hairpins and the Evolution of Their Decorative Patterns." *BIHP*, 30, pt. 1, (1959): 611–70.
笄形八類及其文飾之演變. 史語所集刊, 第三十本, 上冊.

————. "Evolution of the White Pottery of the Yin Dynasty." *BIHP*, 28, pt. 2, (1957): 853–82.
殷虛白陶發展之程序. 史語所集刊, 第二十八本, 下冊.

————. "The Formation of the Chinese People." Ph.D. dissertation, Harvard University, 1923.

————. *Hsi-yin-ts'un shih-ch'ien ti i-ts'un* (Prehistorical Remains at Hsi-yin Ts'un). Peiping: Ts'inghua Research Institute, 1925. Trans. as *New Stone Age Pottery from the Prehistoric Site at Hsi-yin Ts'un, Shansi, China*, Memoirs of the American Anthropological Association, no. 37, 1930.
西陰村史前的遺存. 北平清華學校研究院叢書, 第三種

————. "Important Discoveries at Yin-hsü in the Autumn Season of 1929." *PREA*, no. 2 (1929), pp. 219–52.
十八年秋工作之經過及其重要發現. 安陽發掘報告, 第二期. 史語所.

————. *Pottery of the Yin and pre-Yin Period: A Classified and Descriptive Account with a Corpus of All the Main Types.* Archaeologia Sinica, no. 2, Hsiao-t'un: The Yin-Shang Site at Anyang, Honan. Vol. 3, *Artifacts.* Fasc. 1, pt. 1. Taipei: Academia Sinica, Institute of History and Philology, 1956.
"殷虛器物" 甲編 "陶器" 上輯. 中國考古報告集, 之二, 小屯, 第三本, 中央研究院歷史語言研究所 台灣, 台北.

————. "Pre-Yin Cultural Deposits at Hsiao-t'un." *Hsüeh-shu hui-k'an* (Occasional Papers of Academia Sinica during Wartime), 1, no. 2 (1944): 1–12.
小屯地面下的先殷文化層. 國立中央研究院學術匯刊第一卷, 第二期.

————. "Illustrated Study of Edged Stone Tools from Yin-hsü." *BIHP*, 23, no. 2 (1952): 523–615.
殷虛有双石器圖說. 史語所集刊, 第二十三本, 下冊.

————, and Wan Chia-pao. *Studies of Fifty-three Ritual Bonzes Excavated from*

Hsiao-t'un and Hou-chia-chuang: Their Casting Process and Decorative Patterns. Archaeologia Sinica, n.s. no. 5. Nankang, Taiwan: Academia Sinica, Institute of History and Philology, 1972.

————, 萬家保. 殷虛出土五十三件青銅容器之研究. 中國考古報告集新編：古器物研究專刊第五本. 中央研究院歷史語言研究所, 台灣, 台北

————. *Studies of the Bronze Chia-Vessel Excavated from Hsiao-t'un and Hou-chia-chuang: Its Casting Process and Decorative Patterns.* Archaeologia Sinica, n.s. no. 3. Nankang, Taiwan: Academia Sinica, Institute of History and Philology, 1968.

殷虛出土青銅斝形器之研究. 中國考古報告集新編：古器物研究專刊, 第三本. 史語所.

————. *Studies of the Bronze Chüeh-Cup Excavated from Hsiao-t'un and Hou-chia-chuang: Its Casting Process and Decorative Patterns.* Archaeologia Sinica, n.s. no. 2. Nankang, Taiwan: Academia Sinica, Institute of History and Philology, 1966.

殷虛出土青銅爵形器之研究, 中國考古報告集新編：古器物研究專刊, 第二本, 史語所.

————. *Studies of the Bronze Ku-Beaker Excavated from Hsiao-t'un and Hou-chia-Chuang: Its Casting Process and Decorative Patterns.* Archaeologia Sinica, n.s. no. 1. Nankang, Taiwan: Academia Sinica, Institute of History and Philology, 1964.

殷虛出土青銅觚形器之研究. 中國考古報告集新編：古器物研究專刊, 第一本. 史語所.

————. *Studies of the Bronze Ting-Cauldron Excavated from Hsiao-t'un and Hou-chia-chung: Its Casting Process and Decorative Patterns.* Archaeologia Sinica, n.s. no. 4. Nankang, Taiwan: Academia Sinica, Institute of History and Philology, 1970.

殷虛出土青銅鼎形器之研究, 中國考古報告集新編：古器物研究專刊, 第四本. 史語所.

Li Hsiao-ting. *Chia-ku wen-tzŭ chi-shih* (Annotated Dictionary of the Oracle Bone Characters). Institute of History and Philology, Special Publication no. 50, 1965.

李孝定, 甲骨文字集釋, 中央研究院歷史語言研究所, 專刊之五十.

Liang Ch'i-ch'ao. *Ch'ing-tai hsueh-shu kai-lun* (General Discourse on the Learning of the Ch'ing Dynasty). Included in *Yin-ping-shih ch'uan-chi* (Collected Essays of the Ice Drinkers' Studio), vol. 10. Shanghai: China Book Co., 1936.

梁啓超. 清代學術概論, 飲冰室專集, 第十冊. 飲冰室合集, 上海中華書局, 民國二十五年.

Liang Ssŭ-yung. *HPKM 1001: Text.* Edited and supplemented by Kao Ch'ü-hsün. Archaeologia Sinica, no. 3, Hou-chia-chuang: The Yin-Shang Cemetery Site at Anyang, Honan. Vol. 2, pt. 1. Taipei: Academia Sinica, Institute of History and Philology, 1962.

梁思永未完稿, 高去尋輯補, 第一〇〇一號大墓. 中國考古報告集, 之三, 侯家莊. 第二本, 上册. 中央研究院歷史語言研究所, 台灣, 台北.

————. *HPKM 1002.* Edited and supplemented by Kao Ch'ü-hsün. Archaeologia Sinica, no. 3, Hou-chia-chuang: The Yin-Shang Cemetery Site at Anyang, Honan. Vol. 3. Taipei: Academia Sinica, Institute of History and Philology, 1965.

高去尋輯補. 第一〇〇二號大墓. 中國考古報告集, 之三, 侯家莊. 第三本. 史語所.

‎———. *HPKM 1003*. Edited and supplemented by Kao Ch'ü-hsün. Archaeologia Sinica, no. 3, Hou-chia-chuang: The Yin-Shang Cemetery Site at Anyang, Honan. Vol. 4, Taipei: Academia Sinica, Institute of History and Philology, 1967.

高去尋輯補. 第一〇〇三號大墓. 中國考古報告集，之三，侯家莊. 第四本. 史語所.

———. *HPKM 1004*. Edited and supplemented by Kao Ch'ü-hsün. Archaeologia Sinica, no. 3, Hou-chia-chuang: The Yin-Shang Cemetery Site at Anyang, Honan. Vol. 5. Taipei: Academia Sinica, Institute of History and Philology, 1970.

高去尋輯補. 第一〇〇四號大墓. 中國考古報告集，之三，侯家莊. 第五本. 史語所.

———. *HPKM 1217*. Edited and supplemented by Kao Ch'ü-hsün. Archaeologia Sinica, no. 3, Hou-chia-chuang: The Yin-Shang Cemetery Site at Anyang, Honan. Vol. 6. Taipei: Academia Sinica, Institute of History and Philology, 1968.

高去尋輯補. 第一二一七號大墓. 中國考古報告集，之三，侯家莊. 第六本. 史語所.

Liu Ngo (Liu T'ieh-yün). *Pao-ts'an-shou- ch'üeh-chai jih-chi. K'ao-ku hsuëh-she shê-k'an*, no. 5, Peiping, 1936.

劉鶚（劉鐵雲）抱殘守缺齋日記. 考古學社社刊，第五期. 北平燕京大學考古學社

———. *T'ieh-yün ts'ang-kuei*. Lithographed, 1931.

鐵雲藏龜，蟫隱廬影印本 民國二十年.

Liu Yuan-lin. "Development of the Technology of Making Oracle Bones." *BIHP*, 46, no. 1 (1974): 99–154.

劉淵臨，卜骨的攻治技術演進過程之探討，史語所集刊，第四十六本，第一分.

Lo Chên-yü. *Wu-shih-jih meng-hen-lu* (Diary of Fifty Days' Travel), published in *Hs'ueh-t'ang ts'ung-ke* (Collected Works), No. 20. 1915.

羅振玉. 五十日夢痕錄. 雪堂叢刻，第二十冊.

———. *Yin-shang chên-pu wen-tzŭ k'ao* (On the Oracle Bone Inscriptions of the Yin-Shang Period). Published by Yü-chien-chai in 1910.

殷商貞卜文字考. 玉簡齋印行.

———. *Yin-hsü shu-ch'i ch'ien-pien* (Earlier Supplement to the Oracle Inscriptions at "Deserted" Yin). 4 vols. Japan, 1913.

殷虛書契前編. 集古遺文第一.

———. *Yin-hsü shu-ch'i k'ao-shih* (Interpretation of the Oracle Inscriptions at "Deserted" Yin). Japan, 1914. Enlarged edition published by the Oriental Society in 1927.

殷虛書契考釋. 東方學會印.

———. *Yin-hsü shu-ch'i hou-pien* (Later Supplement to the Oracle Inscriptions at "Deserted" Yin). 2 vols. Lithographed, 1915.

殷虛書契後編. 藝術叢編第一集.

Mizuno, Seiichi. *Seizanso Siesho* (Illustrated Catalogue of the Nezu Collection), Vol. 6, *Chinese Bronzes*. Tokyo: Nezu Art Museum, 1942.

Palmgren, Nils. *Kansu Mortuary Urns and the Pan-shan and the Ma-ch'ang Groups*. Palaeontologia Sinica, ser. D, vol. 3, fasc. 1. Peking: Geological Survey of China, 1934.

Shang Ch'eng-tzu. *Yin-hsü wen-tzŭ lei-pien* (Classified List of Oracle Bone Characters). Privately published, 1923.

商承祚. 殷虛文字類編. 決定不移軒自刻本.

Shih Chang-ju. *Architectural Remains*. Archaeologia Sinica, no. 2, Hsiao-t'un: The Yin-Shang Site at Anyang, Honan. Vol. 1, *The Site: Its Discovery and Excavations*. Fasc. 2. Taipei: Academia Sinica, Institute of History and Philology, 1959.

石璋如 遺址的發現與發掘：乙編，建築遺存. 中國考古報告集，之二： 小屯 第一本 中央研究院歷史語言研究所，台灣，台北.

———. "Architectural Remains of the Yin Period at Hsiao-t'un." *BIHP,* 26 (1955): 131–86

小屯殷代的建築遺蹟. 史語所集刊，第二十六本.

———. *Burials of the Middle Section*. Archaeologia Sinica, no. 2, Hsiao-t'un: The Yin-Shang Site at Anyang, Honan. Vol. 1, *The Site: Its Discovery and Excavations*. Fasc. 3. Taipei: Academia Sinica, Institute of History and Philology, 1972.

遺址的發現與發掘：丙編，殷虛墓葬之二，中組墓葬. 中國考古報告集之二： 小屯，第一本. 史語所.

———. *Burials of the Northern Section*. Archaeologia Sinica, no. 2, Hsiao-t'un: The Yin-Shang Site at Anyang, Honan. Vol. 1, *The Site: Its Discovery and Excavations*. Fasc. 3, pts. 1 and 2. Taipei: Academia Sinica, Institute of History and Philology, 1970.

遺址的發現與發掘：丙編，殷虛墓葬之一，北組墓葬 （上下兩册） 中國考古報告集之二：小屯第一本. 史語所.

———. *Burials of the Southern Section and Supplement of the Northern Section*. Archaeologia Sinica, no. 2, Hsiao-t'un: The Yin-Shang Site at Anyang, Honan. Vol. 1, *The Site: Its Discovery and Excavations*. Fasc. 3. Taipei: Academia Sinica, Institute of History and Philology, 1973.

遺址的發現與發掘：丙編・殷虛墓葬之三，南組墓葬附北組補遺. 中國考古報告集之二：小屯第一本，史語所

———. "Further Examples of the Reconstruction of Architecture of the Shang Dynasty," *Bulletin of the Institute of Ethnology* (Academia Sinica), no. 29 (1970), pp. 321–41.

殷代地上建築復原的第二例. 中央研究院民族學研究所集刊，第二十九期. 臺灣，臺北.

———. "Hong-t'u (Earth pounding), Pan-chu (Pisé), and Building in General of the Yin Dynasty." *BIHP,* 41, no. 1 (1969): 127–68.

殷代的夯土・版築・與一般建築. 史語所集刊第四十一本第一分.

———. *K'ao-ku nien-piao* (Archaeological Chronology). Academia Sinica, Institute of History and Philology. Taipei, 1952.

考古年表. 中央研究院歷史語言研究所.

———. "One Example of Restored Yin Surface Building." *Annals of Academia Sinica*, no. 1 (1954), pp. 269–80.

殷代地上建築復原，之一例. 中央研究院院刊第一輯.

———. "Recent and Most Important Discoveries from Yin Hsü." *Chinese Journal of Archaeology,* no. 2 (1947): pp. 1–81.

殷虛最近之重要發現附論小屯地層. 中國考古學報，第二冊. 中央研究院歷史語言研究所.

———. "Yin Tombs Discovered at Hou-kang." *BIHP,* 13 (1948): 21–28.

河南安陽後岡的殷墓. 史語所集刊，第十三本.

Shih Hsing-pang et al. *The Neolithic Village at Pan P'o, Sian*. Peking: Wenwu Press, 1963.

石興邦等. 西安半坡. 中國田野考古報告集考古學專刊, 丁種, 第十四號, 文物出版社.

Shima, Kunio. *Yin-hsü pu-tz'ŭ ts'ung-lei* (Summary of Oracle Bone Characters). Tokyo: 1967;

島邦男. 殷虛卜辭綜類. 日本東京：大安株式會社.

Sun I-jang. *Ch'i-wen chü-li* (Examples of Oracle Bone Inscriptions). 1917.

孫詒讓. 契文舉例. 吉石盦叢書, 第三集, 第17–18冊, 民國六年.

————. *Ming yüan* (Origin, or Evolution, of Names). Published by the author in 1906; reprinted by San Ch'ing T'ang Book Co., Shanghai.

名原. 上海：三馬路三頃堂書局. 光緒三十一年.

T'ang Lan. "Yin-hsü wen-tzu chi" (Notes and Comments on Oracle Bone Inscriptions). Lithographed lecture notes, 1934.

唐蘭. 殷虛文字記. 考古學社社刊, 第一期. 北平：燕京大學考古學社.

Teilhard de Chardin, Pierre. *Early Man in China*. Peking: Institut de Géobiologie, 1941.

————, and C. C. Young. *On the Mammalian Remains from the Archaeological Site of Anyang*. Palaeontologia Sinica, ser. C, vol. 12, fasc. 1. Peking: Geological Survey of China, 1936.

Ting Shan. *Chia-ku-wen suo-chien chih-tsu chi ch'i chih-tu* (Clan Institutions as Shown in Oracle Bone Inscriptions). Peking: Science Press, 1956.

丁山. 甲骨文所見氏族及其制度. 科學出版社, 北平.

Tung Tso-pin. *Chia-ku-hsüeh liu-shih nien* (Sixty Years of Studies in Oracle Inscriptions). Taipei: I-Wen Publications, 1965.

董作賓. 甲骨學六十年. 臺北：藝文印書館.

————. *Chia-ku-hsüeh wu-shih-nien*. Taipei: Continental Magazine Company, 1955. English translation, *Fifty Years of Studies in Oracle Inscriptions*, trans. Paul Yang et al., ed. Kimpei Goto. Tokyo: Centre for East Asian Cultural Studies, 1964.

甲骨學五十年. 大陸雜誌社. 臺北.

————. "Chia-ku nien-piao" (Oracle Bone Chronicles), *BIHP*, 2, no. 2 (1930): 241–60. Revised, with assistance from Hu Hou-hsüan, and published as a monograph in 1937. Supplementary vol., ed. by Huang Jan-wei, published in 1967.

甲骨年表. 史語所集刊, 第二本, 第二分. 董作賓, 胡厚宣. 甲骨年表 史語所單刊乙種之四

————. "Chia-ku-wen tuan-tai yen-chiu li" (Essay on Periodization of the Oracle Bone Inscriptions). In *Ch'ing-chu Ts'ai-yüan-p'ei hsien-shêng liu-shih-wu sui lun-wên chi* (Studies Presented to Ts'ai Yüan-p'ei on His Sixty-fifth Birthday) (Nanking: Academia Sinica, Institute of History and Philology, 1933), pt. 1, pp. 323–424.

甲骨文斷代研究例. 慶祝蔡元培先生六十五歲論文集, 上冊. 中央研究院歷史語言研究所.

————. "Four Big Inscribed Tortoise Shells." *PREA*, no. 3, 1931.

大龜四版考釋. 安陽發掘報告, 第三期. 史語所.

————. *Inscriptions: Plates*. Archaeologia Sinica, no. 2, Hsiao-t'un: The Yin-Shang Site at Anyang, Honan. Vol. 2, fasc. 2. Academia Sinica, Institute of History and Philology. Pt. 1, 1948; pt. 2, 1949; pt. 3, 1953.

殷虛文字乙編. 中國考古報告集之二：小屯第二本. 中央研究院歷史語言研究所.

————. "Report on the First Digging at Hsiao-t'un." *PREA*, no. 1, 1929.

中華民國十七年十月試掘安陽小屯報告書. 安陽發掘報告, 第一期. 史語所.

―――. "Some Important Problems of the Yin Calendar." *BIHP*, 4 (1934): 331–54.

殷曆中幾個重要問題. 史語所集刊, 第四本.

―――. *Yin-li-p'u* (Tabulated Data of the Yin Dynasty according to Chronology of Recorded Events Found in the Oracle Bone Inscriptions). Lithographed by Li-chuang: Academia Sinica, Institute of History and Philology, 1945.

殷曆譜. 中央研究院歷史語言研究所.

Wang Hsiang. *Fu-shih yin-ch'i lei-ts'uan.* 1921.

王襄. 簠室殷契類纂.

Wang Kuo-wei. *Hai-ning Wang-chung-chueh-kung I-shu* (Collected Essays of Wang Kuo-wei).

王國維. 海寧王忠慤公遺書.

―――. *Shih-lin* (Historical Researches). In *Kuan-t'ang chi-lin* (Collected Essays), vols. 9–22.

史林. 觀堂集林. 卷九至卷二十二.

―――. "Yin-chou chih tu-lun" (Comparative Study of Yin-Chou Institutions). In *Kuan-t'ang chi-lin* (Collected Essays), vol. 10.

殷周制度論, 觀堂集林. 卷十.

―――. "Yin-pu tz'ŭ-chung so-chien hsien-kung hsien-wang k'ao" (Notes on the Royal Ancestors of the Shang as Appear in Oracle Bone Records), *Hsüeh-shu ts'ung shu* (Collected Historical Researches), 1917. Reprinted in *Kuan-t'ang chi-lin* (Collected Essays), vol. 9.

殷卜辭中所見先公先王考. 觀堂集林, 卷九.

Woo Ch'i-ch'ang. "Chia-ku chin-wen chung suo-chien-ti yin-tai nung-chia ching-kuang" (State of Yin Agriculture as Found in the Oracle Bone Scripts). Pp. 323–68 in a *festschrift* honoring Chang Chu-sheng. Shanghai: Commercial Press, 1937.

吳其昌. 甲骨金文中所見的殷代農稼情況. 張菊生紀念論文集. 上海: 商務印書館.

Woo Ting-liang, and G. M. Morant. "A Preliminary Classification of Asiatic Races Based on Cranial Measurements." *Biometrica*, vol. 24, 1934, pts. 1, 2.

Wu Gin-ding. *Prehistoric Pottery in China.* London: Kegan Paul, Trench, Trubner & Co., 1938.

Wu Ta-ch'eng. *Ku-yü t'u-k'ao* (Studies of Ancient Jade). Shanghai: T'ung-wen Publishing Co., 1889.

吳大澂. 古玉圖考. 上海, 同文書局石印本, 清光緒十五年.

―――. *Shuo-wen ku-chou pu* (Supplements to the Ancient Seal Characters of the Shuo-wen Dictionary). 1883.

說文古籀補. 蘇州振新書社石印本, 清光緒九年.

Young Chung-chien. "Further Notes on the Mammals Excavated from Yin-hsu," *Chinese Journal of Archaeology*, no. 4 (1949), pp. 145–53.

楊鍾健. 安陽殷墟之哺乳動物群補遺. 中國考古學報, 第四期. 中央研究院歷史語言研究所. 南京.

Yung Yuan. *Chin-shih-shu lu-mu* (Bibliographical Notes on Studies of Bronzes and Jades). Foreword by Yung Keng. Academia Sinica, Institute of History and Philology, series B, no. 2, 1930.

容媛. 金石書錄目. 中央研究院歷史語言研究所單刊, 乙種, 之二.

Index

Arne, T. G., 42
Arrowhead, 113, 204
Axe, 40, 66, 200, 201, 205–7

Bamboo Annals, 163, 169, 245, 248, 261
Bell, 113, 187
Bergen, Paul, 18
Biology, 37
Birds, 201, 214, 217, 219, 233
Bishop, Carl Whiting, 56, 57, 58
Black, Davidson, 36, 42–45, 48, 262, 263
Black Pottery Culture. See Lungshan Culture
Bohlin, Birger, 44, 45
Bone, carved, 78, 209, 210, 214, 218, 219–21
Book of Changes, 261
Book of Documents (Shu-ching), 4, 162, 164–66, 169, 170
Book of Odes, 261
Boulders: as supports for pillars, 73, 177, 182–86, 188, 201
Bowls, 201
Breuil, Henri, 48
Bronze Age, 67, 75, 77, 105, 200
Bronze inscriptions, 5, 6, 8, 12, 22, 23, 25, 26
Bronzes: fragments of, discovered at Anyang, 54; Hsin-cheng, 55–56; plundering of, 77; excavations of, at Hou-chia-chuang, 78, 80; weapons, 92, 94, 205, 206, 207, 240; as used for chariots, 111, 113, 114, 205, 208; research on, 125, 140, 156; publications on, 156; technology for producing, 156, 231, 240, 254; molds discovered, 178, 205–6; ceremonial, 205–7 passim, 228, 231–33, 253; objects to accompany dead, 205; tools, 205–7 passim; origin and evolution of, 206–7; decorative devices, 210, 231–34; mentioned, 42, 76, 110, 127, 203, 204, 209
Brush, 171–73
Buffalo, 108, 109, 192, 194, 195
Burials, 65, 71, 97, 98, 104, 137, 150, 155, 175, 186, 188, 205. See also Cemetery; Hou-chia-chuang

Cache-pits. See Pits
Calendar system, 22, 123, 129–35

passim, 144, 183, 236, 243, 249, 250. See also Sexagenary cycle
Canton, 49, 51, 59
Caste, 75, 205, 240, 254
Cattle, 159
Caucasoid skulls, 258, 259, 264
Celestial stem, 236, 239, 243, 245, 248, 251. See also Calendar system; Sexagenary cycle
Cemetery, 78, 79, 82–85, 90, 92, 124; royal, 76, 77, 96, 145, 149. See also Burials; Hou-chia-chuang
Cenozoic Laboratory, 36, 44, 45, 47, 108
Central University, 19
Ceramics. See Pottery
Ceremony. See Sacrifice
Chalcedony, 201
Chalfant, Frank H., 16, 18, 21
Chang Ch'ang, 23
Chang Chü-sheng, 191
Chang Hsüeh-hsien, 16, 17
Chang Ping-ch'üan, 106, 145–47, 191, 198, 244
Chang T'ai-yen (Ping-lin), 31
Chang Wei-jan, 61, 68
Ch'ang-te Fu, 9, 17–19, 24, 51
Chao Yüan-ren, 56, 143
Charcoal, 109, 156
Chariot, 104, 111–15, 156, 205, 208, 228
Chavannes, Edouard, 21
Chen Chung-fan, 19
Ch'en Meng-chia, 12, 195
Ch'en P'an, 143
Ch'en Yin-k'o, 56, 143, 238
Chêng-chou, 168, 169, 174, 190, 196
Ch'êng Tang, 248
Ch'êng-tu, 135, 191
Ch'êng-tzŭ-yai, 67–69, 137, 160, 167, 168
Ch'i, 161, 164
Ch'i-lu (Chee-loo) University, 191
Ch'i Yen-p'ei, 77, 97
Chia (vessel), 207, 230, 253
Chia Ch'ing, 6
Chia ku. See Oracle bones
Chia-ku-wen. See Oracle bone inscriptions
Chia-yu, 193
Chiang Chia. See Wo Chia
Chiao (cellar), 99, 101
Ch'ien Chia. See Ho T'an Chia
Ch'ien Lung, 5, 6
Ch'ien-shan-yang, 198

Honan, 8, 9, 19, 24, 51, 53, 63, 75, 168, 174, 192, 194, 195, 240
Hong Kong, 59, 142–44
Hopei, 161, 168, 194, 195, 240
Hopkins, L. C., 16, 18, 19, 21
Horn-shaped vessel, 231
Horse, 23, 26, 108, 109, 111–14, 159, 208
Ho T'an Chia, 135, 250
Hou-chia-chuang: inscribed oracle bones discovered, 72, 117; plundering of tombs, 77, 81, 85, 88; cemetery site discovered, 77–78; excavations, 78–84; artifacts, 92–94, 110, 111, 140, 207, 214, 222, 227–28, 231; research on collection, 122–24, 137, 145, 148, 149, 156; skulls discovered, 256–60; mentioned, 96, 115, 136, 174, 209, 210, 231. *See also* Tombs
Hou-kang, 71, 76
Hsi-pei-kang. *See* Hou-chia-chuang
Hsi Weng, 8
Hsi-yin Ts'un, 58, 159, 170
Hsia Chih, 261
Hsia dynasty, 161–63, 170, 245
Hsia Hsien, 58, 169, 170
Hsia Nai, 79, 140
Hsiao, 168, 190
Hsiao Chia, 135, 250
Hsiao Hsin, 133
Hsiao I, 133
Hsiao Tsung, 193
Hsiao-t'un: early oracle bone discoveries, 7–9, 15–17, 20, 24; Tung Tso-pin makes preliminary investigation of site, 52; excavations, 53–54, 59–73, 96–104, 115–18; artifacts, 53–54, 65–67, 70–71, 113, 169, 207, 214, 220–28 *passim*, 231; research on findings, 104–15, 122, 145–46, 149–50; architectural reconstruction, 150–55, 179–89; mentioned, 76, 168, 171, 203, 210
Hsieh, 245
Hsien (steamer), 207, 231
Hsin-cheng, 55
Hsiung-nu, 161
Hsü Chung-shu, 169–71
Hsü Fang, 16, 18
Hsü Shen, 5, 6, 20, 22, 23, 29, 244
Hsü Shen-yü, 141
Hsüan T'ung, 16
Hsüeh (pits), 99, 102, 103

Hu (pot), 182, 207, 231
Hu Chia. *See* Yang Chia
Hu Fu-lin, 77
Hu Hou-hsüan, 117, 122, 123, 191, 194
Hu Shih, 55, 143, 144, 163
Hu Wei, 193
Hua-yüan-chuang, 62
Huan River, 8, 16, 17, 52, 53, 62, 64, 65, 71, 72, 77, 105, 151, 153, 155, 159, 185
Huang Chi-kang, 31
Huang Chün, 16, 18
Huang-ho-pai-ho (Museum), 46
Huang-ti, 161
Huang-t'u-t'ai, 186, 188, 189
Human figures: in art, 92, 93, 213, 215, 220, 226, 228, 229
Human sacrifice. *See* Sacrifice
Hun-chu, 161
Hupei, 195

I River, 169
I-chou-shu, 169
Ink-squeezes: of inscribed oracle bones, 12–14, 16, 21, 23, 24, 26, 27, 30, 123, 133, 140, 145, 146
Institut de Géobiologie, 47
Institute of Ethnology, 143
Institute of Geology, 126
Institute of History and Philology: Fu Ssŭ-nien as director of, 49, 95, 141; formation of, 51; headquarters moved to Peking, 61; foundations supporting research of, 67–68, 144, 155, 206; headquarters moved to Kunming, 118, 121, 122; collections of, transported during war, 121–22, 255; headquarters moved to Li-chuang, 121, 123, 136; wartime research of, 122–23, 129; headquarters return to Nanking, 139; postwar research of, 139–57 *passim*; headquarters moved to Taiwan, 141; Tung Tso-pin as director of, 142; Li Chi as director of, 143, 144; and research on skeletal materials, 255–56; mentioned, 3, 7, 117, 207, 239
—Archaeological Section: formation, of, 59; Li Chi as head of, 59, 116, 135; excavates site of Ch'êng-tzŭ-yai, 67; begins Hsiao-t'un excavation, 69; members of, 69, 79, 122–

Miao-ti-kou, 171, 184, 185
Mien-ch'ih Hsien, 40
Millet, 159, 192, 195, 196, 198, 253
Ming dynasty, 5, 193
Ming-ch'i (bronzes), 228
Miocene period, 37
Mizuno, Seiichi, 77
Moist, 75
Mo-tzŭ, 75
Molds, 66, 67, 71, 156, 178, 180, 182,
  205, 206, 231
Mongolia, 37, 38, 47, 262, 263
Mongoloid skulls, 158, 159, 257, 258,
  260, 262–64
Mortar, 201
Mulberry, 198
Music, 252
Musical stone, 94, 252

Naito, Torajiro, 21
Nan-ch'i, 128
Nankai University, 54, 56
Nankang, 143, 144, 148–51, 156, 167
Nanking, 50, 53, 95, 116, 117, 120,
  121, 126, 139–41, 145, 255
National Academy. *See* Academia
  Sinica
National Central Museum, 79, 122,
  128, 135, 139, 140
National Government, 95, 121
National Taiwan University, 141–44,
  156
Needham, Joseph, 128
Nelson, N. C., 48
Neolithic, 38, 43, 67, 74, 75, 159,
  161, 167, 184, 192, 247, 262
Net-sinker, 204
Nezu Art Museum, 77
Nien (year), 134, 249
Ninghsia Fu, 47
Niu-ting (cauldron), 233
Nomenclature, 245
Nurhachi, 120, 239

Ocarina, 219, 220, 252
Oceanic Negroid skulls, 259, 263
Oracle bone inscriptions: intellectual
  background to study of, 4–7; and
  studies of stone and bronze inscriptions, 5, 6, 26; early scholarship on,
  12–15, 21–31; and calendar system,
  22, 123, 129–34 *passim,* 243–45;
  and divination, 22, 24, 25, 28, 117,
  167, 240–43; and evolution of Chinese characters, 22–26 *passim,* 29,

171–73, 244; and reconstruction of
  Shang dynasty and ancestors, 24,
  25, 30, 129–33 *passim,* 163–64, 167,
  235–36, 241, 243–45, 247–48; and
  sacrificial offerings, 28, 29, 106,
  107, 134–35, 188, 242, 245, 248–
  54 *passim,* 260; dictionaries of
  characters, 30–31, 147; wartime research on, 122, 123, 129–30; postwar research on, 145–47; and agriculture and climate, 147, 191, 194–
  99 *passim;* and kinship terms, 245–
  46; and war records, 261, 262; mentioned, 3, 40, 49, 122, 136, 144,
  170, 182, 190, 193, 264
Oracle bones: discovered in Sui dynasty, 3–4; early discoveries of, at
  Anyang, 7–9, 15–18; early collections of, 11, 16, 17, 18–20; forgeries
  of, 19–20, 51; discovery of provenance of, 24; Tung Tso-pin
  searches for, at Anyang, 51–52;
  official excavations of, 53, 54, 61,
  63, 65, 66, 70, 71, 72, 104, 115–18
  passim; artifacts contemporaneous
  with, 66–67, 78; problems of excavating and transporting, 116–17;
  technology of, 117, 167–68, 241;
  H127 findings, 117–18; reconstruction of, 146–47; discovered at
  Ch'êng-tzŭ-yai, 168; mentioned, 11,
  59, 67, 96, 177, 179, 200, 204
Oriental Society, 27
Ordos, 47, 261, 262
Owl, 201, 228
Ox, 23, 26, 106–9, 194, 199, 204,
  214, 215, 219, 241, 245, 254

Painted Pottery Culture. *See* Yangshao
  Culture
Palace, 103
Palace Museum, 141
Paleography, 3, 5, 12, 14, 15, 22, 25,
  34, 142, 166, 240
Paleolithic, 47, 159
Paleontology, 33–37, 46
Palmgren, Nils, 75
Pan-ch'üan, 161
Pan (pot), 182
Pan-p'o, 171, 184, 233
P'an (plate), 231
P'an Ch'üeh, 97, 136, 137, 150
P'an Keng, 98, 103, 104, 117, 133,
  134, 164–69 *passim,* 173, 179, 190,
  196, 241

P'an Tsu-yin, 12
Pao I, 248
Pao Ping, 248
Pao Ting, 248
Pao-ting, 161
Peacock, 109, 253
Pei Wen-chung, 45
Peking (Peiping), 19, 21, 34, 36, 37, 40, 41, 43, 45, 47, 54, 56, 59, 61, 140, 161, 220
Peking Government University, 19, 36, 43
Peking Man, 37, 43, 45, 158, 204
Peking Union Medical College (P.U.M.C.), 42, 44, 45, 262
Pelliot, Paul, 80
Petroglyph, 22
Philosophy, 32
Pi (disc), 113, 201
Pictography, 26
Pien (jug), 207
Pig, 26, 106, 107, 108, 159, 192, 201
P'ing-yang Fu. See Lin-fên Hsien
Pisé. See Pounded earth
Pits: major excavation of, 98; dating of, 98, 103, 104, 179, 182; dwellings, 99, 101–3, 175–79; storage, 99, 115–16, 118, 179–82; sacrificial, 103, 106, 111–13, 256, 260, 262, 263; chariot burial, 111–13; mentioned, 96, 137, 149, 150, 204, 240
Plastron. See Oracle bones
Pleistocene, 47, 109, 194, 195
Po Chü-i, 50
Pohai, 193
Pot-sherds, 41, 61, 65, 66, 71, 109, 126, 140, 171, 177, 180, 182, 195, 202, 203
Pottery: at Yangshao Ts'un, 41, 42, 136, 137; Mesopotamian, 41; painted, 41, 42, 57, 58, 67, 71, 75, 110, 160, 169–73 passim, 188, 202, 233, 234; red, 41, 202, 212; gray, 42, 202, 203, 210, 211; at Anau, 42; ting and li, 42, 136, 137, 182; excavation of, at Anyang, 54, 67, 78; research on Anyang collection, 61,122, 125–26, 135–38; at Ch'êng-tzǔ-yai, 67, 137; black, 71, 110, 137, 202, 233, 234, 241; summary of Anyang collection, 109–10, 202–4; white, 110, 202, 203, 210, 211, 212, 219; glazed, 125, 126, 196, 198, 203, 212, 213; incised, 160, 210; at Hsi-yin Ts'un, 170; at

Pan-p'o, 171; at Miao-ti-kou, 171; hard, 202, 203; decoration of, 210–13; ritual use of, 253; mentioned, 105, 107, 127, 150, 200, 206, 207
Pounded earth (pisé): discovery of, at Ch'êng-tzǔ-yai, 68; excavation of, at Anyang, 69–73, 96, 98; use of, in tombs, 76; technology of, 96, 98; and underground structures, 99, 102–4 passim, 175–80 passim; dating of, 104, 174; studies on Anyang finds, 151–55; and reconstruction of surface buildings, 182–88 passim; mentioned, 84, 86, 87, 111, 168
Primogeniture, 237, 238
Pumpelly, R., 41

Renaissance (China), 5, 49
Revolution of 1911, 34
Rhinoceros, 106, 107, 192
Rice, 159, 192, 195, 196, 198, 253
Royal Asiatic Society, 18
Royal House. See Ancestors, Shang
Ruey Yih-fu, 143

Sacrifice: as recorded in oracle bone inscriptions, 28, 29, 106, 107, 131, 134–35, 188, 242, 245, 248–54 passim, 260; human, 84, 88, 91, 97, 105, 106, 254, 256, 260, 262, 263; funeral, 87, 91, 105; in connection with building activities, 105, 127, 188; to spirits, 105, 106, 188; of animals, 106, 107, 127, 249, 254; main types of, to ancestors, 134, 188, 248–54; buildings associated with, 188, 189; of grain, 249; dancing as part of ritual, 249, 253; of meat, 249, 253; use of wine at, 252, 253, 254; music as part of ritual, 252, 253; vessels used in, 253; mentioned, 198, 239
San-tai (three dynasties), 169
Sexagenary cycle, 131, 236, 243, 244, 245. See also Calendar system
Scapula, 16, 17, 53, 71, 168, 193, 204, 241, 242
Scapulimancy, 25, 68, 69, 160, 167, 240, 241, 243
Seal characters, 8
Sericulture, 161, 196, 198
Sha-kuo-t'un, 39, 220
Shang Ch'êng-tzu, 19, 30
Shang Chia Wei, 236, 248, 250, 254

Shang dynasty: reconstruction of list of, 236–40 *passim. See also* Ancestors, Shang
Shanghai, 17–19, 59, 121, 128, 145
Shan Hai Ching, 248
Shansi, 57, 58, 75, 169, 199, 240, 261
Shantung, 15, 19, 67, 69, 160, 168, 194, 195, 199, 222, 240
Sheep, 23, 26, 106, 107, 159, 199, 241
Shell, 24, 54, 66, 109, 173, 199, 200, 240, 241; cowry, 54, 65
Shen Kang-po, 143
Shensi, 162, 199, 261
Shih Chang-ju: as member of Anyang expedition, 69, 72, 77, 97; reports excavation, 69, 115, 118, 145, 149, 150; on subterranean structures, 98–103 *passim*, 106, 175–80 *passim*; on sacrificial burials, 106, 111, 188; reconstruction of chariot, 113; on architectural remains, 151–55 *passim*, 182–88; mentioned, 127, 140, 156, 207
Shih-t'su (clan organization), 240
Shima, Kunio, 195, 254
Shinjô, Shinzô, 244
Shovel-shaped incisor, 158
Shu (millet), 192, 195
Shu-ching. See Book of Documents
Shun, 161
Shuo-wen (Hsü Shen), 5, 6, 20, 25, 29, 244
Siberia, 263
Silk, 196, 198, 208; cocoon, 58
Sinanthropus lantienensis, 158
Sinanthropus pekinensis. See Peking Man
Sinology, 5, 21, 27, 110
Sjara-Osso-Gol, 47
Skeleton, 54, 66, 90, 256, 263
Skulls, 45, 65, 66, 90, 183, 256–61, 263
Slaves, 254
Smith, Elliot, 45
Society for the Study of Chinese Architecture, 128
Spearheads, 71, 89, 91, 156, 200, 206
Spindle-whorls, 204
Ssŭ (spatula), 204, 214, 215, 217, 219
Ssŭ (year), 134, 249
Ssŭ-ma Ch'ien, 30, 134, 161–63, 169, 188, 220, 235, 238, 239, 245
Ssŭ-p'an-mo, 71

Stone: inscriptions, 5, 6, 12; implements, 40, 41, 47, 48, 61, 66, 75, 200, 201, 204; sculpture, 84, 92, 125, 201, 209, 220–28; mentioned, 54, 67, 170, 171, 173, 205
Sui dynasty, 3, 4, 65
Sui-Tang dynasty, 61, 71, 188
Sun I-jang (Sun Chung-yung), 12, 14, 22–26
Sun Yat-sen, 120
Sung dynasty, 33, 193; Northern, 4, 5, 76
Sword, 113
Szechwan, 121, 123, 127, 128, 138, 139, 145, 183, 255

Ta-li, 135
Ta-lien pit (Ta-lien-k'eng), 64–66, 70, 117, 123, 188, 240
Tai Chen, 4
T'ai Chia, 135, 250
T'ai Ting, 238, 241
Taihang Mountains, 194, 199
Taipei, 141, 142, 144
Taita. *See* National Taiwan University
Taiwan: move of Institute of History and Philology to, 141–48 *passim,* 255, 256
Taiyüan, 57
T'ang, 163, 164
T'ang Lan, 195
T'ang-yin, 8, 9
Tao Kuang, 5
T'ao-t'ieh (zoomorphic mask), 209, 219, 222, 227
Taoist, 75
Tattoo, 209, 220, 222
Technology, 73
Teilhard de Chardin, Pierre, 36, 46–48, 108, 109
Temple, 103, 188
T'eng-wen-kung (Mencius), 33
Tetrapod, 88, 89, 110, 138, 204, 207, 231
Textiles, 200, 208
Ti-chih. See Earthly branch
Ti Hsin, 131, 133–135, 238, 241, 248–50, 253, 254, 262
Ti I, 131–34, 238, 241, 248–51, 253, 254
Tibetan Plateau, 37
T'ien I, 235, 236, 248
T'ien-kan. See Celestial stem
Tientsin, 19, 46, 47, 54–56, 140
T'ien Wen (Ch'ü Yuan), 248